GLIMPSES INTO THE REVELATION

By

Rayford Bullard

Franklin Springs, Georgia 30639

Printed in U.S.A.

DEDICATION

To the memory of two great men: Rev. G. F. Taylor, whose writings sparked my interest in prophecy as a child, and later in adult years, caused me to begin a lifelong study of the subject. And Rev. M. L. Dryden, whose lectures in my early Christian life, influenced so much of my thinking while preparing this study.

CONTENTS

JESUS IS COMING

Jesus is coming with angels descending;
Saints of all ages will make up His train.
Secret the first time of His appearing,
Then all the world shall His glory behold.

Tell to the nations that Jesus is coming;
Herald the glad tidings throughout all lands.
Tell to the lost ones, tell to the weary,
That soon that glad day will burst in full bloom.

Then fear all ye sinners; spurning His mercy;
Trouble and sorrow will soon be your lot.
Shout ye redeemed ones; sing aloud His praises,
Glory and honor give to His name.

So hasten the day, Lord, of Your glad coming;
Come quickly and take us to our new home.
Rough is the road, Lord, which we must travel
But the end of the way is now in our sight.

Our journey will end at the gates of that City;
And Jesus will be there to welcome us in;
Forever, we'll bask in His glad presence
And know no sorrows nor unhappy days.

—R.B.

FOREWORD

"Glimpses into the Revelation" is just that—glimpses. It is not a verse by verse exposition of the Apocalypse. Rather it is as a searchlight seeking to probe into the depths of its mysteries, symbols, signs and wonders, bringing to light certain salient facts which will make its message more clear. Also, the parts enacted by its characters and the scenes they portray are examined in an effort to throw light on events which must shortly come to pass.

It will be noticed that extraneous material has been introduced. This subject matter only indirectly furthers the progress of the divine drama, but it does give significant background to its chief actors. For instance, a short sketch is given of Christ from creation to the eternal ages under the heading "The Person of Christ." This shows Him enfolded in the Old Testament and unfolded in the New. Likewise, one knows more about the church universal and its place in the eternal plan of God after reading what is said about "The Body of Christ." The identity of Satan is somewhat clarified by the particulars rehearsed in the "Trail of the Serpent." In an effort to show the significance of the rainbow "round about the throne," "God's Wonderful Bow of Promise" is offered. A fictionalized character of the Antichrist is given under the head "Abdulah." An imaginary description of the New Babylon seeks to show something of what this capital city of the Beast will be like. It is admitted that the entire study is fragmentary. Much has been left out; much more has been very inadequately shown.

This study takes the position that there is to be a pre-Tribulation rapture. Only a select company of "Ready Ones" called the Bride, will make up this first company. Other groups will be raptured during the Tribulation. A mighty conflict, called the Battle of Armageddon, will bring an end to this period of divine judgment. Then Christ will establish His earthly kingdom which will last a thousand years. At its close Satan will be loosed from the Bottomless Pit into which he was cast at the beginning of the Millennium. He will seek to overthrow the kingdom of Christ. He will be unsuccessful; instead, fire from heaven will destroy his army and he himself will be consigned to the Lake of Fire.

Then will come the Great White Throne Judgment, at which time the wicked will be judged and consigned to the Lake of Fire. The righteous will receive rewards. Thus, eternity, which has been interrupted by the period we call time, will begin again—nevermore to be interrupted.

To the above outline there is a widespread agreement, although many of the details are subjects of disagreement. May God help us in our study of this wonderful Book of Revelation!

No effort has been made to be sensational. Some have done so in their interpretation, only to have the actual events prove them wrong to the point of complete repudiation. The trap into which some have fallen has been to survey the world situation at a given date and endeavour to fit all the events into a prophetic pattern. This simply cannot be done successfully. Some events are of prophetic import; some are not.

The test of the value of any interpretative writing on prophetic subjects is how well it wears. Read what was written ten, twenty, thirty or even a hundred years ago. How much of it is relevant today? There are a few authors whose writings on these subjects are just as current now as when written ten, twenty, fifty or a hundred years ago. These writers have stayed with the Scripture Text itself and have not gone off on tangents, however tempting such excursions may be.

It is the hope that this work will prove of such a nature, and is offered with the prayer that it may aid in the clarification of God's program for the end time.

INTRODUCTION

As the Book of Revelation opens, we find the beloved Apostle John on the lonely Isle of Patmos, in banishment by the Roman government "For the word of God, and for the testimony of Jesus Christ." One has described this inhospitable place as "A mere mass of barren rocks, dark in color and cheerless in form. It lies out in the open sea, near the coast of Asia Minor (Modern Turkey). It has neither trees nor rivers. It is about ten miles long and at its northern end about six mile wide."

Imagine, if you will, the venerable apostle gazing out across the great expanse of the Aegean Sea toward the distant mainland. About the only sounds he hears are the cries of birds whirling overhead, and the slap-slap of the waves as they break on the dismal shore.

Suddenly, he hears a powerful voice behind him. He describes it as the "voice as of a great trumpet." Turning, he sees the glorified Christ, and recognizes the sound as the voice of his risen Lord. He describes Him as with head and hair like snowy white wool, eyes as flaming fire, feet like burnished brass. He is clothed with a garment down to the feet, encircled with a golden girdle. He holds in His right hand seven stars, and is flanked by seven golden candlesticks as a back-drop.

John does not know it at this time, but he is to see in panoramic view the entire church age; the Tribulation Judgment Court sitting in heavenly splendor; the four Apocalyptic horsemen riding through the earth heralding war, famine and death. He is to get a glimpse of God's people as they appear in different glorious companies. He is to view hail, fire, blood and the burning of trees and green grass, the destruction of ships, and the wholesale death of men as the sea becomes bloody. He is going to watch as fresh water becomes bitter as wormwood and more men die. He is going to gaze in awe as the darkened sun and the bloody moon are revealed. As these frightful woes are visited upon mankind, he is going to shudder at the awful spectacles. He is going to behold infernal creatures as they appear on earth to torment men. He will observe the convulsions of the universe in gigantic upheaval as earthquakes shake nations, fifty pound hailstones hurtle out of angry skies, and men pray to be destroyed by rocks and mountains rather than face an offended God.

He is to take notice of the rise, reign and fall of the Antichrist; vision millions of men enticed to the slaughter at the Battle of Armageddon; see the Dragon, the Beast and the False Prophet as they reach their final abode in the Lake of Fire to be tormented eternally.

He is to witness the reign of Christ in Millennial bliss; watch as the New Jerusalem is seen coming down from God out of heaven, orbiting the earth, and giving light to the nations as they live forever in pristine perfection.

* * * * * * *

But before John ever had the least inkling that he would be writing his letters to these seven churches, so representative of the church ages, Jesus had already given the outline. This is recorded in the seven parables of the kingdom found in the thirteenth chapter of Matthew. Here they are. Study them and you will see how perfectly they describe the seven church ages pictured by the seven churches of Asia.

PARABLE ONE—The Sower: "... Behold a sower went forth to sow.... And when he sowed some fell by the wayside.... Some fell on stony places.... And some fell among thorns.... But others fell into good ground" (Matthew 13:3b, 4a, 7a, 8).

This is the Ephesian Church—sowing the seed of the kingdom; watching some of it being devoured by birds; seeing some spring up, but wilt and die for lack of depth and roots; some trying vainly to grow among thorns; but watching as some seed fall into good ground and bring forth varying amounts of fruits. This is the Apostolic Age.

PARABLE TWO—The Wheat and Tares: "... The kingdom of heaven is likened unto a man which sowed good seed in his field.... But ... his enemy came and sowed tares among the wheat.... He said unto them (his servants), An enemy hath done this. The servants said unto him, Wilt thou then that we go and gather them up? But he said, Nay, lest while ye gather up the tares, ye root up also the wheat with them. Let both grow together until the harvest" (Matthew 13:24, 25, 28b, 29, 30).

This is Smyrna—fighting against great odds; opposing false Jews who are blaspheming and sowing tares among the good wheat; suffering severe persecution and tribulation; but heartened by the admonition to be faithful unto death, so a crown of life could be given. This is the Age of Persecution.

PARABLE THREE—The Grain of Mustard Seed: "The kingdom of heaven is likened to a grain of mustard seed, which a man took and sowed in his field.... It is the least of all seed: but when it is grown, it is the greatest among herbs" (Matthew 13:31b, 32a).

This is Pergamos, the church settled in the world—growing rapidly, but at the expense of sound doctrine and becoming aligned with the secular empire. This is the Imperial Age.

PARABLE FOUR—The Woman with the Leaven: "The kingdom of heaven is likened unto leaven, which a woman took and hid in three measures of meal, till the whole was leavened" (Matthew 13:33b).

This is Thyatira, with her Jezebel; adding corruption to the three measures of meal furnished by the three previous church epochs. This church is about to become completely corrupted with her nauseating fornication. This is the Medieval Age.

PARABLE FIVE—The Hidden Treasure: "... The kingdom is likened unto a treasure hid in a field; the which when a man hath found, he hideth, and for joy thereof goeth and selleth all that he hath, and buyeth that field" (Matthew 13:44).

This is Sardis with its large but barren field, containing a peculiar treasure, worth selling all a person has to possess. This is the picture of the remnant.

PARABLE SIX—The Pearl of Great Price: "Again the kingdom of heaven is likened unto a merchant man, seeking goodly pearls: who, when he hath found one pearl of great price, went and sold all that he had, and bought it" (Matthew 13:44).

This is Philadelphia with her pearl of great price—love. In this parable the field of the hidden treasure has been expanded to include the whole world. The Reformers came out from Rome, but their imperfect works made necessary a further coming out even from them as a group. This is the Age of Brotherly Love.

PARABLE SEVEN—The Drag Net: "... The kingdom of heaven is like unto a net, that was cast into the sea, and gathered of every kind" (Matthew 13:47).

This is Laodicea with every kind of fish in the net—wretched fish, miserable fish, poor fish, blind fish, naked fish—all lukewarm. Outside the door of this church Christ stands and knocks—dealing with individuals. This is the Modern Church.

* * * * * * *

As to the tribulation itself, Israel as God's instrument of judgment upon the wicked inhabitants of Canaan offers a striking parallel to the part the Bride of Christ will play in calling forth judgments upon the sin-cursed world of the last days.

Canaan, at the beginning of the conquest, was ripe for judgment. Her sins cried out for punishment. Even though without the knowledge of the true God, nevertheless there was no excuse for her utter degradation. God has used many instruments of chastisements. He sent the flood. He sent the confusion of tongues. He will use many methods in bringing to a halt man's exceeding sinfulness in the end-time. When God determined to punish the inhabitants and drive them out of the land of Canaan, He used the Children of Israel as His instrument.

Let the crossing of Jordan illustrate the rapture and Israel as the Bride of Christ. Israel was to clear the land of its evil natives. This can be likened unto the activities of the Bride under the figure of the Four Living Creatures, using the four horsemen and other characters in other scourging activities.

Christ promised the overcomers of Thyatira "Power over the nations (to) rule them with a rod of iron, and break them in shivers as the vessel of a potter." Those who compose the Bride will be the "Overcomers." Since the Bride is shown as the four Living Creatures and these creatures play an important role as God's avengers in the Tribulation, it follows that a partial fulfillment of the promise to the Overcomer is shown here.

Israel never did drive out all the inhabitants of Canaan, so were never really permitted to enjoy the land to its fullest. God's people will do for the world what Israel failed to do for Canaan—completely subjugate the earth. The final battle will put down all opposition to Christ and His rule. Then, Christ and His retinue of white horse riders will come down and take possession of the earth, inaugurating a reign of righteousness which will last for a thousand years.

Some may object to this line of thinking. Some may say, that the Lamb and the angels will do most of the work of clearing the earth of the undesirables. This is true; but what about Israel? How much were their victories won by their own strength and ingenuity? Very little. More victories were won because they simply "stood still and saw the salvation of the Lord" than when they did their own fighting.

* * * * * * *

Thus the stage is set for the beginning of the divine drama. John saw the entire script. Christ gave a foreview of the church ages with his seven parables. And Israel typified the clearing out of the usurpers in their conquest of their promised land.

CHAPTER ONE

THE REVELATION OF JESUS CHRIST

"The Revelation of Jesus Christ, which God gave unto him, to show unto his servants things which must shortly come to pass; and he sent and signified it by his angel unto his servant John: Who bare record of the word of God, and of the testimony of Jesus Christ, and of all things that he saw.... I was in the spirit on the Lord's day, and heard behind me a great voice, as of a trumpet.... And I turned to see the voice that spake with me. And being turned, I saw seven golden candlesticks; And in the midst of the seven candlesticks one like unto the Son of man, clothed with a garment down to the foot, and girt about the paps with a golden girdle. His head and hairs were white like wool, as white as snow; and his eyes were as a flame of fire; And his feet like unto fine brass, as if they had burned in a furnace; and his voice as the sound of many waters, And he had in his right hand seven stars: and out of his mouth went a sharp twoedged sword: and his countenance was as the sun shineth in his strength (Revelation 1:1, 2, 10, 12-16).

THE REVELATION OF JESUS CHRIST! Not the revelation of Saint John the divine; not the revelation of the Antichrist; nor of the mark of the Beast; nor the fall of Babylon; nor the battle of Armageddon; nor the Millennium; nor the New Jerusalem; nor the eternal ages. But—THE REVELATION OF JESUS CHRIST! Although all these other things are in the picture, the major message of the book is Christ in all His completeness.

In the Scriptures He is seen in the crimson stream beginning in Eden and ending at Calvary, but the efficacy of this flow only becomes apparent in Revelation. He is seen in the "Fountain that shall be opened in the house of David . . . for sin and uncleanness," but only in Revelation does it find a final fulfillment. Only in Revelation can be found how Christ can be the Root and Offspring (Father and Son) of David. The eternal purposes of His role as the "Lamb slain from the foundation of the world," are only explained in Revelation. The Lion of the Tribe of Judah comes to a full disclosure only in John's prophecy. In order to trace our Lord through the pages of Scripture, a few words about the PERSON OF CHRIST is given here.

THE PERSON OF CHRIST

To understand the Revelation one needs to know something about its Chief Character. So we find that Jesus Christ is the Son of God, the Second Person of the Holy Trinity, of God the Father, God the Son and God the Holy Ghost. He is the incarnation of God the Son in human flesh. Jesus is His human name; Christ is His divine title. Taken together, they identify Him as "Very God and Perfect Man."

In Genesis God the Son is revealed as LORD GOD (Jehovah Elohim). The word Jehovah is the redemptive name of Deity. This dual name is used in the Bible only after the creation of man. Therefore, Jehovah's special activity has to do with man's redemption.

JEHOVAH reveals Himself as the Redeemer in Exodus 6:3 where He speaks to Moses and says, "I am the LORD (Jehovah); and I appeared unto Abraham, and unto Isaac and Jacob by the name of God Almighty, but by my name JEHOVAH was I not known unto them." Man did not know God in His redemptive character until He here revealed Himself.

The Bible is the story of Man's Redeemer and man's redemption. Take these out and you have nothing to hold the sacred writings together; left in, they have meaning and purpose. Christ is the center of this story.

The progressive revelation of the Person of Jesus Christ as completed in the Book of Revelation runs the entire scale of His physical appearance, essential divinity, complete humanity, relation to His people and relation to His enemies. This is set forth in the Holy Scriptures in types, shadows, symbols, pictures, sacrifices and many other ways. As the Redeemer of Mankind, He reveals Himself as best suits the understanding of the age to which a particular message is sent.

The Gospels, the Revelation and all prophetic scripture should be studied together in order to get firmly established in the mind the two-fold nature of Christ's ministry earthward. For a full picture of Christ we need to see Him in His eternal being as portrayed in all Scripture. So, we find that:

JESUS CHRIST IS—The same yesterday, today and forever; veiled in type and shadow in the Old Testament Scriptures; the Seed of the woman who bruises Satan's head as told in Genesis; typified by Abel's more excellent sacrifice in the morning of human history; the anti-type of Isaac who was offered (in spirit) by Abraham on Mount Moriah; prefigured in Joseph as the sustainer of life for the family of Jacob; typified by the slain Lamb whose blood was placed on the lintels and posts of the doors, and whose body was roasted with fire and consumed by the Israelites the night they left Egypt; the brazen serpent in the wilderness, to look upon which, was to escape death from the serpent's bite.

JESUS CHRIST IS—The Lamb slain from the foundation of the world to those who accept Him; the Lion of the Tribe of Judah to those who reject Him. The breaking Stone to those who come to Him; the crushing Stone to those who turn away from Him. Manifested in the flesh in the Gospels; working in His body, the church, through the Holy Spirit as recorded in the Book of Acts. But SET FORTH IN ALL HIS GLORY IN THE BOOK OF REVELATION!

In the New Testament when He came in the flesh to dwell among men, we learn that:

JESUS CHRIST—Was born of the Virgin Mary; grew up in Nazareth; was baptized and began His ministry at the age of thirty.

IN THIS MINISTRY HE—Preached and taught; healed the sick; raised the dead; cleansed the leper; cast out devils; opened blinded eyes; loosed the tongue of the dumb; caused the lame to walk.

IN ADDITION TO THIS HE—Bound up the broken-hearted; liberated the captives; loosed the prisoners; multiplied the loaves and fishes; calmed the boisterous waves; walked the stormy sea.

FOR THIS HE WAS—Despised and rejected of men; cursed and spit upon; mocked and scourged; thorn-crowned and crucified.

BUT HE MANIFESTED HIS POWER BY — Rising from the dead; returning to heaven; sending back the Holy Spirit; operating in the lives of His people through the Holy Spirit in the Gospel dispensation.

There is the greatest contrast between the picture of Christ as shown in the Gospels and in the Revelation. In the Gospels He is shown as the "Suffering Messiah," and the "Lamb slain from the foundation of the world." In the Revelation He is shown as the triumphant "Lion of the tribe of Judah." In the Gospels He is overcome by His enemies; in the Revelation He overcomes His enemies. In the Gospels He is the "Servant." In the Revelation He is "King of kings and Lord of lords."

According to the Book of Revelation, in addition to the foregoing, it is found that:

JESUS CHRIST IS THE—Root of David; Lamb with seven horns; Faithful Witness; First Begotten of the dead; Bright and Morning Star; Prince of the kings of the earth; Alpha and Omega; Word of God.

ALSO, HE IS DESCRIBED AS—Like the Son of Man; having a countenance and face as the sun shining in its strength; clothed with a garment down to the foot; being girt about with a golden girdle; having head and hairs like wool, white as snow; having eyes as a flame of fire; having feet like furnace-burned brass, and pillars of fire; being clothed with a cloud; having a rainbow upon His head; being crowned with a golden crown; being called Faithful and True; having an unknown name; being clothed with a blood-dipped vesture.

HIS ACTIVITIES ARE DESCRIBED AS—Walking in the midst of the seven golden candlesticks; holding in His right hand the seven stars; holding in His hand a sharp sickle; riding a white horse.

Also, Jesus Christ has a special relationship with each individual and church. This is brought out beautifully in the study of the Seven Churches of Revelation. For instance:

JESUS CHRIST IS REVEALED—To Ephesus as the One who holds the seven stars in His right hand, and who walks in the midst of the Seven Golden Candlesticks; to Smyrna as the First and Last, which was dead and is alive; to Pergamos as the One who has the sharp sword with two edges; to Thyatira as the One whose eyes are like a flame of fire, and whose feet are like fine brass; to Sardis as the One who has the Seven Spirits of God; to Philadelphia as He that is Holy, He that is true, He that hath the key of David, He that openeth and no man shutteth, and shutteth and no man openeth; to Laodicea as the Amen, the Faithful and True Witness, the beginning of the creation of God.

Some may see this description of Jesus Christ and His ministry as only applying to Him in some past or future time. This is not the case; this is His description NOW! Scripture bears out that He would reveal Himself in the historic church ages according to the particular need of the time. Now He reveals Himself to present day churches just as truly as He did in the past. Also, He reveals Himself to individuals in the capacity necessary to their need. To present day Ephesian Christians He reveals Himself as "The One who holds the seven stars in His right hand, and walks in the midst of the Seven Golden Candlesticks." To the present day Smyrnan Christian He is the "First and the Last, which was dead, and is alive." To all other present day Christians He reveals himself according to their need and capacity to understand His message and ministry.

* * * * * * *

I John, who also am your brother, and companion in tribulation, and in the kingdom and patience of Jesus Christ, was in the isle that is called Patmos, for the word of God, and for the testimony of Jesus Christ.... I... heard behind me a great voice, as a trumpet.... Saying, I am Alpha and Omega, the first and the last. What thou seest write in a book" (Revelation 1:9, 10b, 11a).

With the foregoing Introduction to the leading Character, the study of the Book of Revelation begins. The word "Revelation" is defined as "The act of making known that which before was secret or private." So the purpose of this Book is to "Make known that which before was secret or unrevealed" as to Jesus Christ. This was John's burden, and its weight rests heavily on this writer.

Many people contend this is a sealed book and not meant to be understood. Therefore, they ignore it as far as its prophetic message is concerned. This is wrong; it takes this book to complete the story of man and his redemption. Without it we would be left in the dark as to many things of the future. For instance, Genesis gives the beginning of everything; Revelation the final consumation of everything. Genesis begins man's story with the creation; Revelation completes it with the New Jerusalem and the eternal ages. Not only does Revelation throw light on the future, but many things of the past are also made plain. In between the eternity of the past and the eternity of the future is a parenthesis which is called time.

Revelation is an extraordinary book. It differs in many respects from other portions of predictive prophecy. Peter and Jude addressed their epistles to a general audience of Christians and dealt with specific phases of the subject. And Paul, in writing to the Thessalonians and to Timothy, did the same. Christ couched much of His teachings of the end time in parables, and dealt with broad details of the Great Tribulation in His Olivet discourse. But John communicated his message to the church universal, as represented by the Seven Churches of Asia, and covered the entire spectrum of end-time prophecy.

Paul told us (2 Tim. 3:16), "All scripture is given by inspiration of God." Peter says (2 Pet. 1:21), "The Old Testament prophets spake as they were moved on by the Holy Ghost." And of course, the words of Jesus had all the authority of deity. When one comes to Revelation it is found that all these methods were used—"Inspired of God"—"Moved on by the Holy Ghost"—Spoken words of Jesus.

In order that there be no misunderstanding, John was careful to trace the Revelation to its source—God the Father. Thus the message comes direct from the mind and heart of God. It is meant for the Church. It is given to Jesus Christ who passes it on to His angel. The angel communicates it to John, who in turn sends it on to the Church.

Why all the elaborate details of the channel the message followed to get to its destination? When it is realized that the Church is the Body of God's Son, then it becomes more clear. Since a great portion of the Body of Jesus Chirst is still here on earth, the great interest of God is in seeing that the words of the Revelation reach it. The great sacrifice the Father made in sending His only Son to earth, and the equally great sacrifice Jesus made in coming here, is an eternal investment which God will preserve.

While the message of Revelation is primarily to the Church as the Body of Christ, it does not ignore God's ancient people, Israel. In this respect, it is a continuation of Daniel's prophecies. "Go thy way, Daniel; for the words are closed up and sealed till the time of the end," the man "Clothed in linen" tells the prophet. Now the "Time of the end" has come, and John is granted the privilege of giving the finishing touches to these ancient predictions.

In the Revelation John is the divinely appointed recorder. He fills this office in a threefold manner: He bears record of the Word of God, the testimony of Jesus and what he sees. This is the same John who wrote the Gospel of John and the three epistles which bear his name. In all his writings is found a clear testimony to the divinity of Jesus Christ. Matthew shows Jesus as the King of the Jews; Mark shows Him as the Servant and Luke as the Son of Man, but to John was left the task of showing Him as the Son of God.

The Revelation is not a book to be taken lightly. Blessings and curses are pronounced upon those who come in contact with it. Blessings are to those who read and hear the words and keep those things written therein; curses in the form of the plagues found in the book will be visited upon those who add to the record. The curse to those who take away from the record, will also be to have taken away their part of the Book of Life, the Holy City and the blessings promised. The blessings will be to enjoy everything promised the overcomer.

Seeing this, how careful one should be to give only the exact message—no more, no less. Yet how many treat this book so lightly! Modern scholarship usually writes it off completely as far as its predictive message is concerned. Many others write and speak in connection with the book with only a superficial knowledge of its purposes and contents. One should approach the study of this book humbly and reverently, and realize the limitations of the human mind to unravel its signs, symbols and mysteries. However, this should not discourage its study. Study it to receive its blessings, always praying that any error in interpretation will arise only because of limited human knowledge, and not from a desire to be sensational.

Study the text itself. So many know only what someone else has said or written about it. Study it word by word, verse by verse, chapter by chapter. Study it subject by subject, sign by sign, symbol by symbol. Get a good Bible dictionary or a Bible encyclopedia and a complete concordance. The Bible is its own best commentary. So, study Revelation in connection with the whole Bible, study Revelation in the light of Old Testament prophecies. Study it in connection with the teachings of Jesus in the Gospels. Study it as it is related to other writings of the New Testament. Add to all this a study of recognized authorities, who accept the Bible as the fully inspired Word of God.

In the main, Revelation is to be understood in chronological order. There are some over-lappings and flash-backs, but these are exceptions. For instance, the account of the killing of the two witnesses by the Beast is given in the eleventh chapter, and the Beast himself is not revealed until the thirteenth chapter. But since these witnesses are introduced in this eleventh chapter and have had a three and one-half year ministry, when they are killed, this presents no problem. The picture in the thirteenth chapter shows the Beast only as he comes into absolute control. His beginning was three and one-half years previous—perhaps at the sounding of the seventh trumpet. The killing of the two witnesses is part of the culmination of his rise to supreme power as will be shown later.

Revelation is a continuation of the Book of Acts. In the earlier book Luke leaves off abruptly with Paul in his own hired house in Rome, preaching and teaching concerning the kingdom of God and Jesus Christ—"No man forbidding him." Fragments of the history of the primitive Church are found in other New Testament writings, but it is left to John in Revelation to tell the results of the work of these early beginnings. He does this in these inspired messages to the Seven Churches of Asia. In them is seen all the strong points as well as all the weaknesses of the primitive church. Not only this, but a prophecy and a foreview are found of what the Church is to be down through the centuries until her Lord shall come at the end of the Gospel dispensation.

In John's salutation to the Seven Churches, grace and peace are pronounced as a benediction. This benediction is not limited to the Seven Churches of Asia; it is for the Church of all ages. These churches and individuals all through the centuries, even down to the twentieth, are as much in the mind and heart of God as those of the early Christian era.

The complete Holy Trinity is involved in this salutation and benediction. Jesus Christ, the same yesterday, today and forever, is shown in all His majesty and power. He is the Alpha and Omega, the beginning and the ending. He is the Faithful Witness, the first begotten of the dead, and the Prince of the kings of the earth. He loved (loves) us, and washed (washes) us from our sins in His own blood. He made (makes) us kings and priests unto His Father. Besides Father and Son, the Holy Spirit is revealed in His seven-fold sphere of operation.

It is recorded in this very first chapter of the return of the Lord and how it will affect mankind. All shall see Him, even those who "pierced him," and "all kindreds of the earth shall bewail because of him."

The Seven Stars are the angels of the Seven Churches. These are not heavenly beings, as some may suppose. They are symbols of the messengers (or pastors) of these Churches. This is in keeping with the use of the word in Scripture. To make them members of the heavenly order would take away their significance here.

John sees the glorified Christ as holding these Seven Stars or pastors in His right hand. This scene should be expanded to include those of every age and clime. For this is just what Jesus Christ does—holds His earthly ministers in His right hand. Seeing this, how careful one should be not to hinder them in their work or lay hands on them except in direst necessity. The writer of Psalm 105 bears this out when, in the fifteenth verse, he says, "Touch not mine anointed and do my prophets no harm."

The anointed of God are a special people, and bear a close relationship to their heavenly Master. Jesus is in their midst whether they be of Ephesus or Laodecia or a church of this modern age. In His walk He is observing, weighing, impelling, influencing, guiding and directing. In spite of their many imperfections, He is in their midst. They are part of the divine plan. They are of His body, and from this body will come His Bride. So, do not think of a local church as just another earthly organization. Think of it as a part of the Body of Christ.

Since the Church has been introduced in this first chapter, a further view of it as the Body of Christ will be given here.

THE BODY OF CHRIST

The first chapter of Revelation deals with the Person of Jesus Christ; the second and third with the Body of Christ, or the Church. The Apostle Paul tells us in his writings that Christ is the head and the Church is His Body (1 Cor. 12:27; Eph. 1:23; Col. 1:18). He says that Christ is the Last Adam, and explains, *"The first Adam was made a living soul; the last Adam was made a quickening spirit"* (1 Cor. 15:45).

The body of the first Adam was created out of the dust of the earth. It was complete before God breathed into its nostrils the breath of life and it became a living soul. But it was like the lifeless carcasses of dry bones in the thirty-seventh chapter of Ezekiel before God breathed upon them. When God blew breath into man's body it began to grow warm; it began to draw air into its lungs; its heart began to beat; blood began racing through its veins; it felt the surge of life and strength come into it.

Likewise, the Body of the Last Adam (the Church) was complete before Pentecost, but, like the first Adam before God breathed into his lungs, it had never breathed. What happened at Pentecost could be likened to the birth of a child. The Church drew God's spiritual oxygen into its spiritual lungs for the first time in that upper room in Jerusalem.

A word of explanation is in order. From a casual reading of the foregoing one could draw the conclusion that the contention here is that there was no spiritual life in the disciples before Pentecost. This IS the teaching of a great portion of present day Christianity. Many say the disciples were converted at Pentecost. However, this does not agree with the General teaching of Jesus and New Testament writers. You remember, once when the disciples returned from a particularly successful effort and exclaimed, "Even the devils are subject unto us through thy name," Jesus rebuked them and told them not to rejoice because of this, but rather rejoice because their names were written in heaven. If this does not include conversion, then language has no meaning.

Also, in speaking of the Holy Spirit, Jesus said to His disciples, "Ye know Him; for he dwelleth with you and shall be (at Pentecost) in you." Remember, the subject is the Body of Christ and not the individuals who make it up. True, the church came into being at Pentecost, but it was made up of ingredients already in existence.

What happened on the Day of Pentecost was that God the Holy Spirit blew His breath into the almost inert mass of the Church. It came with such a force that it started a fire and created a power which have not subsided to this day. Also, there was a fusing and melting of the Spirit of God and the Church to such an extent that Christ's Body—the Church—partook of deity to a degree never before experienced by any except by Jesus Christ Himself.

With all reverence, it could be said that God did for the disciples what He did for the Virgin Mary about which He prophesied when He said, "The Holy Ghost shall come upon thee, and the power of the highest shall overshadow thee; therefore also that holy thing which shall be born of thee. . . ." Stop here in this thirty-fifth verse of the first chapter of Luke and finish with the words, "Shall be called the Church." Thus the conception was the work of the ministry of Jesus, and the birth was realized at Pentecost.

In the first four chapters of Acts we find the Body of Christ in one accord; Spirit-filled; doctrinally sound; stedfast in fellowship and love. It was a praying group. It had a good outside influence. It was a Church where miracles were witnessed, and a Church to which the Lord added members daily.

But the Church—the body of the Last Adam—was to be tried and tested just as the first Adam was. No sooner had the infant Church began to function than Satan began his attacks. In the fifth chapter of Acts we find weaknesses developing. Ananias and Sapphira, in their greed and hypocrisy, lied to the Church and the Holy Ghost concerning their gift to the Church. For their sin they were struck dead. In the sixth chapter there were murmurings and complaining. Some widows felt they were being neglected while provisions were made for others.

By the time of John's visions on the Isle of Patmos, serious defects had become apparent. The once glorious Church was being torn apart by Satan. In Ephesus it was loss of first love; in Pergamos the doctrines of Balaam and the Nicolaitanes; in Thyatira seduction by Jezebel; in Sardis deadness; in Philadelphia weakness and in Laodicea lukewarmness.

The assaults made by Satan upon the Church from the Day of Pentecost to the end of the Church age is a recording of the continuing warfare which started in Eden. Looked at from a natural standpoint, one might be tempted to say the Church has been a failure. It started out with such wonderful prospects at Pentecost, but too many of the local churches succumbed to loss of love, false doctrines, deadness, weakness and lukewarmness. However, from God's standpoint the Church was not—and is not—a failure. The harvest of these early years was counted in multiplied thousands of redeemed souls from many lands. Added millions were to be gathered into its fold as the centuries were to come and go. In the end the Church will emerge as triumphant. The battle which has raged around it since its infancy is only that—a battle. The war itself has to be looked upon from a larger perspective; and from that view, it is a foregone conclusion that the Body of Christ is to be the ultimate victor.

THE SEVEN CHURCHES OF ASIA

"John to the seven churches which are in Asia: Grace be unto you, and peace from him which is, and which was, and which is to come; and from the seven spirits which are before his throne; and from Jesus Christ, who is the faithful witness, and the prince of the kings of the earth. Unto him that loved us, and washed us from our sins in his own blood, and hath made us kings and priests unto God and his Father. I was in the Spirit on the Lord's day, and heard behind me a great voice, as of a trumpet, saying. . . . What thou seest write in a book, and send it unto the seven churches which are in Asia. . . . And I turned to see the voice that spake with me. And being turned, I saw seven golden candlesticks, and in the midst of the seven golden candlesticks, one like unto the Son of Man. . . . And in his right hand seven stars. . . . The mystery of the seven stars

which thou sawest in my right hand and the seven golden candlsticks. The seven stars are the angels of the seven churches: and the seven candlesticks which thou sawest are the seven churches" (Rev. 1:4-6, 10, 11b, 12, 16a, 20).

The seven churches singled out by Jesus Christ to receive John's letters were representative of the congregations of that day. Not only so, but they were characteristic of the seven church ages from Pentecost to the Rapture. In addition to this, they are typical of every church of every age. Also, every Christian of every age can be catalogued into one or the other of these seven churches.

While the seven church ages blend into one another and it is hard to state categorically that a certain definite date marks a distinct line between some of them, yet certain dates stand out with such clarity as to indicate almost certain divisions.

With this in mind, here is a suggested list of these ages with the dates corresponding nearest to those lines. The Apostolic Age (30-100 A.D.)), represented by Ephesus. The Age of Persecution (100-313 A.D.), pictured by Smyrna. The Imperial Age (313-476 A.D.), symbolized by Pergamos. The Medieval Age (475-1517), paralleled by Thyatira. The Age of the Reformation (1517-1729), as seen in Sardis. The Age of Brotherly Love (1729-????) likened to Philadelphia. The Modern Age (19??-????), typified by Laodicea.

These local churches were situated in the western part of the ancient Roman province of Asia (now Modern Turkey). The first one mentioned was Ephesus. Paul spent much time here. The Apostle John evidently made this his headquarters during his latter years, and spent a great amount of time, not only with Ephesus, but with all these others. No two of them were much more than one hundred miles apart. So it would be natural for him to be familiar with the entire group. And since they furnished such a cross-section of local churches of that age, it is not strange that Christ should use them as examples, and give John these messages to deliver to each according to its need.

There is an unusual geographical arrangement in the location of these churches and their position in relation to the Isle of Patmos. This barren patch of earth out in the Aegean Sea was some fifty miles southwest of Ephesus. An interesting pattern can be formed if one will get a map of the area and draw a solid line from Patmos to Ephesus. Then from Ephesus draw a line to Smyrna, Pergamos, Thyatira, Philadelphia and Laodicea, then back to Ephesus. Now start again at Ephesus and draw a broken line to Pergamos, another line to Thyatira, Sardis, and Philadelphia. This will give a striking picture of a ribbed fan. Leave the handle off (the line from Patmos to Ephesus) and this diagram will look surprisingly like a bird in flight. Another interesting thing is that these churches are named in perfect clockwise order. Start with Ephesus, follow with Smyrna, and bear always to the right until Laodicea is reached. Or to carry the thought a little further, a line can be drawn from Ephesus to any of the other churches without crossing any other line. This may not have any special significance, but it is an interesting sidelight.

Chapter Two

THE CHURCHES

EPHESUS: The Church of the Apostolic Age (30-100 A.D.)

"Unto the angel of the church of Ephesus write: These things saith he that holdeth the seven stars in his right hand, and who walketh in the midst of the seven golden candlesticks; I know thy works, and thy labor, and thy patience, and how thou canst not bear them which say they are apostles, and are not, and hast found them liars; And hast borne, and hast patience, and for my name's sake hast labored, and hast not fainted. Nevertheless I have somewhat against thee, because thou hast left thy first love. Remember therefore from whence thou art fallen, and do the first works; or else I will come unto thee quickly, and will remove thy candlestick out of his place, except thou repent. But this thou hast, that thou hatest the deeds of the Nicolaitanes, which I also hate. He that hath an ear, let him hear what the Spirit saith unto the churches: To him that overcometh will I give to eat of the tree of life, which is in the midst of the paradise of God" (Revelation 2:1-7).

John's first letter was to Ephesus. This church was located in one of the most important cities of the ancient Roman province of Asia. Situated on the coast of the Aegean Sea, its location was conducive to its development as a religious, political and commercial center.

According to an ancient myth, this was the birthplace of the mother goddess of the earth. This city of antiquity began as an Oriental civilization, but its capture by the Greeks resulted in a blending of the two cultures.

It was the home of the native Goddess Diana, and the location of the temple erected for her worship. Through Greek influence, however, her worship and identity merged with that of the Greek goddess Artemis, and the temple which was originally named for Diana became known as the temple of Artemis—one of the seven wonders of the ancient world.

This magnificent temple was the seat of great wealth and prominence. Pilgrims from all over the Oriental world generously supported it. Besides the many priests and priestesses, it employed a great host of other people. Among them were to be found artesans in great numbers who made images or shrines to this goddess.

It was into this city of Ephesus that the fiery Apostle Paul came, preaching Jesus Christ and Him crucified. In the eighteenth chapter of Acts we find him entering the Jewish synagogue, and for a short time, reasoning there with his brethren "according to the flesh." After this brief visit he leaves, but later returns and finds disciples. These know only the baptism of John. He instructs them in the Gospel, baptizes them, lays hands on them and they receive the Holy Spirit. Returning to the synagogue he preaches Christ again to the Jews for three months. They reject his message, so he leaves and goes to the school of Tyrannus. Here he spends two full years. This is the early beginning of the church at Ephesus.

Sometime later the beloved Apostle John came to Ephesus and made it his home. How long he stayed here is not known. But evidently this was where he lived at the time he was banished to the Isle of Patmos. From this pivotal point we find Christianity spreading out and establishing new communions.

Now for the church as representative of the Apostolic Age:

The great success of Christianity at Ephesus gives us a wonderful insight into its success in the entire Roman Empire during the Apostolic Age. Indeed, the city of Ephesus is a picture in capsule form of the Empire. It was like the Empire in that it was filled with idolatry; great emphasis was placed on politics and commerce; it had great wealth; religion was an overshadowing element; it had been under many different governments; its population was a mixture of Orientals, Greeks, Romans and natives of the district.

We find this Apostolic Church was doctrinally sound; noted for its good works; laboring untiringly to cultivate its field. It was strong in its morality and stern in its abhorrence of the evil about it. It investigated and denounced every false apostle and exposed every unsound doctrine.

One of the many points in its favor was its hatred of the deeds of the Nicolaitanes. There is a diversity of opinions as to who these were. The Scofield Bible note infers that the term "Nicolaitanes" means to "Conquer the laity, and divide an equal brotherhood into Priests and Laity." Dr. Seiss in his Apocylypse seems to bear this thought out, also. However, the International Standard Bible Encyclopedia quotes several of the early church fathers in support of the theory that it was a sect founded by Nicolas, one of the seven deacons of the church at Jerusalem. Whoever is right, it is still true that they were of evil influence; therefore their deeds were hated by these Ephesians.

With all the good things said about the Apostolic Age, there was something sad which had to be reported as it ended. It had left its first love. For it the magic had gone out of its espousel to Christ; the honeymoon love had cooled. At one time the church of this age was on fire with holy zeal; signs followed its ministry; great revivals crowned its efforts; fervent love flowed from heart to heart. Now it was motivated more by a sense of loyalty, orthodoxy and duty than from its supreme love for Christ. So it was in danger of being removed out of its place among the heavenly candlesticks because of this defect. Jesus tells it to remember from whence it had fallen and do the first works—works motivated by its love for Christ.

To the Apostolic Age represented by Ephesus, as well as to the other six there was the admonition to hear what the Spirit "saith unto the churches," and a promise to the overcomer. The Spirit here gives a message and a promise for this age that "to him that overcometh will I give to eat of the tree of life which is in the paradise of God." It was this tree of life which was denied Adam when he sinned. God in mercy drove him from the Garden of Eden lest he eat of it and live forever in his sinful state. In Genesis God took the tree of life away from man; in Revelation He promises to restore it to him.

The condition attached to this promise is that one must overcome. This was the condition originally. Had Adam overcome the temptations of Satan, man would have been permitted to eat of this tree of life millenniums earlier. Notice, too, that this promise is not given wholesale, but to "him," the individual who overcomes, will the privilege be given to eat of this tree—whether he live in the time of Ephesus or Laodicea.

SMYRNA: The Church of the Age of Persecution
(100-313 A.D.)

"And unto the angel of the church in Smyrna write: These things saith the first and the last, which was dead and is alive: I know thy works, and tribulation, and thy poverty, (but thou art rich) and I know the blasphemy of them which say they are Jews, and are not, but are the synagogue of Satan. Fear none of these things which thou shalt suffer: behold, the devil shall cast some of you into prison, that ye may be tried; and ye shall have tribulation ten days: be thou faithful unto death, and I will give thee a crown of life. He that hath an ear, let him hear what the Spirit saith unto the churches; He that overcometh shall not be hurt of the second death" (Revelation 2:8-11).

Smyrna was a church at which no criticism was levelled by her Lord. It was a group in which work was the order of the day. Although nothing but commendation was offered, at the same time tribulation and poverty were to be its lot. This was a stronghold of heathen religions and bigoted Jews. There were at least four things which caused it trouble and kept it poor:

(1) In 23 A.D. a grand temple was erected here to honor Emperor Tiberias and his mother Julia. The Christians drew the wrath of the Emperor-worshippers because they refused to recognize him as a god and pay him divine homage.

(2) Zeus, the supreme god of the Greeks, was represented in Smyrna by a magnificent temple. Christians offended his devotees by ignoring this heathen worship.

(3) Cybele, the native goddess of nature, came in for her place with majestic temple and sensual worship, but Christians insisted on worshipping the one true God, thereby incurring the enmity of her followers.

(4) Perhaps the greatest opposition of all came from the Jews. To preach Jesus Christ as the Son of God and Savior of the world, was to them the rankest blasphemy. Their antagonism reached its height when they assisted in burning Polycarp, the sainted bishop of Smyrna, at the stake. The evidence indicates that the Roman government was neutral in this case; it did not sanction this shameful action,

but, sad to say, neither did it seek to prevent it. On the other hand, the insane rage of these "False Jews," as they are called in the Revelation, ignored one of their most sacred traditions—keeping the Sabbath day holy. It is said they carried wood on this day for the fire to burn the beloved bishop.

The elements that made life so miserable for the church at Smyrna were the same elements Christians faced in this period of grievous persecution—from the death of the last apostle to the rise of Emperor Constantine early in the fourth century.

In this era the Christian church challenged the Pagan world to do battle. It asked no quarter nor gave any. Had it been content to be just another religion among many, it probably would not have been seriously molested. But it said there was "... none other name under heaven given among men whereby we must be saved"—meaning the name of Jesus Christ. It told other religions, "You are false and have to be forsaken." Thus, the lines of battle were drawn. Christianity would grow just to the extent Paganism and other false religious systems were pushed back. So the church brought tribulation upon itself, and for over 200 years severe persecution was its lot.

Jesus told the persecuted church of this age in His message to Smyrna that "Ye shall have tribulation ten days." According to church history, there were ten severe persecutions during the reign of ten Roman Emperors in this time. Also according to church history, these emperors were Nerva, Trajan, Antonous Pius, Marcus Aurelius, Septimis, Servis, Decium, Valreian, Diocletian and (jointly) Calenious and Constantius (father of Constantine). Imprisonment and death were the order of the day. A number of these persecutions were instituted by ambitious emperors themselves; others were brought about by weak rulers who were goaded by the populace into trying to exterminate Christianity, although really desiring to favor them. When charges were brought they felt they had no choice but to follow the law. This law said a believer must renounce Christianity or be put to death.

In spite of the opposition of Satan through Apostate Jew, Pagan World and Roman Emperors, much was done to establish the church as a permanent force in the Empire.

We note three things which were outstanding in the period which helped to bring this about: Completion of the New Testament Canon, Formation of a strong ecclesiastical organization, and the development of systemic doctrine.

PERGAMOS: The Church of the Imperial Age
(313-476 A.D.).

"And to the angel of the church in Pergamos write: These things saith he which hath the sharp sword with two edges: I know thy works, and where thou dwellest, even where Satan's seat is; and thou holdest fast my name, and hast not denied my faith, even in those days wherein Antipas, my faithful martyr, who was slain among you, where Satan dwelleth. But I have a few things against thee, because thou hast there them that hold the doctrine of Balaam who taught Balak to cast a stumbling block before the children of Israel, to eat things sacrificed unto idols, and to commit fornication. So has thou also them that hold the doctrine of the Nicolaitanes, which thing I hate. Repent; or else I will come unto thee quickly, and will fight against thee with the sword of my mouth. He that overcometh will I give to eat of the hidden manna, and will give him a white stone, and in the stone a new name written, which no man knoweth saving he that receiveth it" (Revelation 2:12-17).

The third letter from John was to Pergamos. This church was in a city of Mysia in the Roman province of Asia. It contained an important acropolis (military fortress), several elegant theaters and many beautiful buildings. In addition, there were four great temples—one each to Dionysus, Athena, Asklepios and Zeus. An altar to the latter is said to have been forty feet high. Three majestic temple were also built in honor of three mighty Roman Emperors.

Just which shrine or temple was meant as the "Seat of Satan," in Revelation 2:3, we do not know. Any one of several could fit the picture. Possibly the city was so given over to false religions that the whole place was so considered. However, there was one temple and its voluptuous worship which stand out—Asklepios. We are told that Asklepios was the ancient god of medicine, and was worshipped under the form of a serpent. Immediately, we think of Satan in the form of a serpent in the Garden of Eden. To the temple of Asklepios, we are told, "invalids from all parts of Asia flocked, and there, while they were sleeping in the court, the god revealed to the priests and physicians by means of dreams the remedies which were necessary to heal their maladies."

Into this hotbed of Pagan idolatry and heathen practices, came Christianity. The church here became a working church. It was a church which held fast the name of Jesus. Although persecution was not generally practiced, at least one person—Antipas—experienced martyrdom. Possibly this act was instigated by the adherents of Asklepios, or those who accorded Emperors divine honors. The shortcomings of this church give a picture of the shortcomings of the period it represented.

The most important person and the one who brought the great change in Rome's official attitude toward Christianity was Emperor Constantine. When the seat of the Emperor became vacant in 305 A.D., there were several aspirants to the position. However, only two really powerful rivals had a chance for the crown—Maxentius and Constantine. "Maxentius represented the old heathen persecuting element; Constantine was friendly toward the Christians," although at that time a worshipper of the sun god. These two met on the field of battle to settle the issue. History tells us that before the battle Constantine prayed to this sun god. He saw a vision of the setting sun—the emblem of the sun god—but above it was a cross over which were these words: "In *this* sign conquer." He at once forsook his Pagan god, embraced Christianity, made the cross his banner, and did, indeed, win the battle and become the Emperor.

Christianity came into the world as a religion of peace and good will, and the use of military power had never been used to strengthen its position. Now the cross was made the battle standard, and the martial spirit of the Empire infused the church.

Shortly after taking the throne the new Emperor signed the Edict of Toleration (313 A.D.), which officially put an end to the persecutions, giving equal rights and freedom of worship to heathen as well as Christian. In 324 A.D. Christianity became the official religion of the state and the darling of the Roman Empire.

This was a period of work for the church. Constantine labored vigoriously to make the Empire Christian. Building church edifices became the order of the day. "Government endowments were bestowed upon church and clergy. Through gifts, legacies ... money and land grants, the church began to amass great riches."

Two things can be noted which parallel the words of the message to Pergamos: the martyrdom of Antipas and the holding fast the name and faith of Jesus. In the message to Pergamos, only one martyr was mentioned. This would indicate that there was some persecution in the Imperial Age, but not on a large scale. And this is just what happened. Although Christianity had become the official religion of the Empire, there was a short period in which an effort was made to restore Pagan worship and abandon Christianity. This was under the reign of Julian the Apostate (361-363 A.D.). No doubt there were some martyrs in this period, but the effort failed and never again were these false religions so serious a threat to the church.

It is significant that mention is made in the Pergamos message of holding fast the name and faith of Jesus. During this period two great controversies arose respecting the nature of Christ. In the first, certain elements held that He was not equal with the Father; other elements held He was equal. This argument brought into being the formula of Christian faith, known as the Nicean Creed (325 A.D.), which affirmed the equality of Father and Son. This is one of the basic tenets of present day fundamental Christianity. In the second controversy over the nature of Christ, one side argued that He was God in human form, but not a man. The majority of the leaders of the church of that day taught that He was "Very God and Perfect Man." The position of the majority prevailed and the Council of Constantinople (381 A.D.) established another important doctrine as to the nature of Jesus Christ. This is also a basic belief of present day evangelical Christianity.

But all was not well with this church. The message to this age was that a sword was dangling over its head, ready to fall at any time. The main complaints were about the throne of Satan, the doctrines of Balaam and the Nicolaitanes. In writing of Pergamos, Dr. Seiss in his Apocalypse says the word Pergamos carries with it the thought of a tower, meaning pretense to loftiness and power, and also of marriage. A. C. Gaebelein considers an unholy alliance was made with the world when Constantine made the church a world institution. Broomfield says a secular ruler sitting on an ecclesiastical throne would make it the throne of Satan.

There is a trite saying that "If you cannot defeat them, join them." This is what happened here. Paganism could not defeat the church, so it joined and corrupted it. Regardless of whether or not Constantine was sincere when he embraced the Christian faith, the result was the mixing of old ideas borrowed from Pagan worship with Christianity. This brought the threat of divine judgment. Balaam could not curse the Children of Israel in the wilderness, so he taught Balak how to seduce them to commit fornication with the Moabites. This accomplished the same purpose and brought God's curse upon them. Likewise, all the power of Pagan Rome was not able to weaken the church, but the church allowed itself to be weakened by adopting Pagan forms and ceremonies as part of its worship.

Hurlbut tells us: "During this period images of saints and martyrs began to appear in the churches. The Virgin Mary was substituted for the worship of Venus and Diana; the Lord's Supper became a sacrifice in place of a memorial; and the elder evolved from a preacher into a priest."

This is also the period in which the rise of the Papacy began. The church of that day was divided into five districts, with a bishop over each. These bishops were located at Jerusalem, Antioch, Alexandria, Constantinople and Rome. The ecclesiastical districts took their names from these cities. These Bishops were supposed to be equal in authority, but the one at Rome felt he had the right to assume authority over the others. Rome insisted that Saint Peter established the church there, and Saint Paul ministered there. Also, that Peter was head of the church and was given the "Keys to the Kingdom" by Christ. Thus the Roman Bishop was authorized to be the successor of Saint Peter—the claim the Pope makes today.

But even this period of church and state union, dilution with Paganism, and overlordship by the priests, there was a promise of hidden manna, a white stone and a new name —for those who were overcomers.

THYATIRA: The Church of the Dark Ages (476-1517 A.D.)

"And unto the angel of the church in Thyatira write;

These things saith the Son of God, who hath his eyes like unto a flame of fire, and his feet like fine brass; I know thy works, and thy charity, and service, and faith, and thy patience, and thy works; and the last to be more than the first. Notwithstanding, I have a few things against thee, because thou sufferest that woman Jezebel which calleth herself a prophetess, to teach and to seduce my servants to commit fornication, and to eat things sacrificed to idols, And I gave her space to repent, and she repented not. Behold I will cast her into a bed and them that commit adultery with her into great tribulation, except they repent of their deeds. And I will kill her children with death; and all the churches shall know that I am he which searcheth the reins and hearts, and I will give unto every one of you according to your works. But unto you I say, and unto the rest in Thyatira, as many as have not this doctrine, and which have not known the depths of Satan, as they speak; I will put upon you none other burden, but that which ye have already, hold fast till I come. And he that overcometh, and keepeth my works unto the end, to him will I give power over the nations: and he shall rule them with a rod of iron; as the vessels of a potter shall they be broken in shivers: even as I received of my Father. And I will give him the morning star. He that hath an ear, let him hear what the Spirit saith unto the churches" (Revelation 2:18-29).

Thyatira was a church which received severe condemnation in John's letter to it. This church allowed at least three things to influence and hinder it from fulfilling the will of its Lord and Master.

First: It was located in a wealthy city. And great wealth usually is not conducive to the promulgation of pure Christianity. It tends to corrupt and cause the church to depend more upon material than spiritual things for its progress.

Second: It was a city given over to rank idolatry. Gods and goddesses were worshipped in ornate temples. In one of these was to be found a certain infamous prophetess who uttered messages which the local god Sambethe was supposed to interpret to the deluded worshippers. This vile practice was so corrupt that this evil character was likened to the ancient wicked Jezebel, wife of King Ahab of Israel.

Third: Thyatira was noted for its trade guilds. Hurlbert

says, "These were closely connected with the Asiatic religion of the place, with which immoral practices were associated. Therefore the nature of these guilds was such that they were opposed to Christianity."

With this sketchy background we come to its application to that long period of history known as the "Dark Ages." This lasted from the break-up of the Roman Empire of the west, to the beginning of the Protestant Reformation. At the opening of this epoch, we see the corrupted church riding on the back of the crumbling empire—guiding, controlling and many times over-shadowing it. The central government was in fatal decline. Hordes from the German tribes of the north, and the followers of Attila the Hun from the steppes of Asia had been making inroads into its territory for many years. Finally, it became so weak and helpless that in 476 A.D. the "Roman senate sent to Constantinople an embassy ... (expressing its willingness) to give up its claim to an emperor of its own, and to request that the German chief, with the title of Patrician, might rule Italy as its viceroy. This was granted; and Italy now became in effect a province of the empire of the east."

All this time while the empire in the west was growing weaker, the church was becoming stronger and more centralized at Rome. With the fall of Antioch, Jerusalem, and Alexandria into the hands of the Mohammedans, only Rome and Constantinople were left of the original five church districts. Thus, the Roman bishop soon held unquestioned sway over all Christendom. At the time the fickle populace was losing faith in the strength of the civil government, it was giving more and more allegiance to the church.

Hurlbut further tells us: "The development of the Papal power is the great outstanding fact in the ten centuries of the middle ages.... The Pope of Rome claimed to be 'Universal Bishop' and head of the church ... claiming to be ruler over nations above kings and emperors."

Fraudulent documents were said to have been produced to back up such claims. One was to the effect that Constantine, the first Christian Emperor, had given the Roman Bishop supreme authority over the church and the emperors themselves. Another claim, said to be false, set forth the "Absolute supremacy of the Pope of Rome over the Universal Church; the independence of the church from the state: (absolving) the clergy ... from accountability to the state.... No secular court could judge in matters pertaining to the clergy or the church."

Like the wicked Jezebel of old she was debasing everything with her spiritual fornication. She spoke and kings trembled. She decreed and all men bowed to her will. She placed men on thrones and removed them at will. If there was ever an absolute despot in the long history of mankind, then the Papal Church of the middle ages was one. Hers was the last voice to be heard; what she said was final.

Spiritual fornication as defined in Scripture includes the combining of spiritual with secular power. This is what had developed in the Medieval Church. The Church was first persecuted, then tolerated, then subsidized by the government. Finally, it gained the ascendency over the dying empire and, in effect, ruled it.

As an example of this we are told that Innocent III (1198-1216 A.D.) declared upon his elevation to the position of Pope, "The successor of Saint Peter stands midway between God and man; above man; below God; Judge of all, judged by none." He claimed that not only the church, but the whole world had been committed to him.

It took a long time for the church to be completely transformed from the persecuted to the persecutor, but with the help of Satan and power-hungry men, she eventually reached that place.

CHAPTER THREE

THE CHURCHES
(Continued)

SARDIUS: The church of the Reformation (1517-1729 A.D.)

"And unto the angel of the church in Sardis write: These things saith he that hath the seven Spirits of God, and the seven stars; I know thy works, that thou hast a name that thou livest, and art dead. Be watchful, and strengthen the things which remain, that are ready to die: for I have not found thy works perfect before God. Remember therefore how thou hast received and heard, and hold fast, and repent. If therefore thou shalt not watch, I will come on thee as a thief, and thou shalt not know what hour I will come upon thee. Thou hast a few names in Sardis which have not defiled their garments; and they shall walk with me in white: for they are worthy. He that overcometh, the same shall be clothed in white raiment; and I will not blot out his name out of the book of life, but will confess his name before my Father, and before his angels. He that hath an ear, let him hear what the Spirit saith unto the churches" (Revelation 3:1-6).

Very little of special significance affecting this church is known about the city of Sardis. But the church there had a reputation of being a live, active church. Its works gave it this image. The One that "Hath the seven Spirits of God, and the seven stars" knew this was just the outward appearance. He saw it was mostly a dead church, knowing it took more than this superficial show to make it a really live one.

Although this was a dying church, there were some in it who were not dying. What little life was left needed watching and strengthening. Imperfect works were about to snuff out the feeble flame. A complete about-face was the only thing which would save it; otherwise swift judgment would come as a thief in the night.

The message to this dying church speaks of defilement, but not all in Sardis were defiled. A few select names were still among Christ's worthies. They would walk with Him in white; wear pure white raiment; keep their names in the book of life and stand uncondemned before the heavenly Father and His holy angels.

This is a remarkable view of the time of the Protestant Reformation, which began in earnest with the indomitable Martin Luther, and was drawing to a close during the rise of the holy Methodists under the leadership of the saintly John and Charles Wesley.

Many activities of the church of this age were being brought into serious question. Besides various doctrines which could not be substantiated by the Bible, it used many methods in its operations which were positively contrary to practices sanctioned by Scripture. One of these was called "Simony." This deep-rooted custom derived its name from Simon the Sorcerer who offered Peter and John money for the power to impart the Holy Spirit to others. Important positions in the church were being bought and sold outright. The sale of indulgences was another great evil which had developed over the years. This was entirely without Scriptural warrant, but was an important source of revenue for the money-hungry church. According to this system, one would be promised divine forgiveness of a sin if he contributed a certain amount to the church. Complete assurance of forgiveness even before a sin was committed was promised. This shows just how this base practice had gotten out of hand.

When the famous Saint Peter's Cathedral was being built in Rome, this nefarious scheme was exploited to such an extent that it was one of the more important reasons why the rising Protestant revolt was able to grow with such great force and rapidity. A man by the name of John Tetzel was said to have been the chief promoter of this obnoxious practice. He is said to have stated: "As soon as your coin clinks in the chest, the souls of your friends will rise out of purgatory to heaven."

The meaning of the word Sardis, itself is significant in the two connotations attached to it. One was "a precious stone used as an amulet (charm) to drive away fear, give boldness, inspire confidence, sharpen wit and protect against witchcraft and sorceries."

This first definition gives an impressive insight into a very important part of the ritual of worship of that day. There was (and still is) what is known as the "Rosary." We are told this was a "Series of prayers ... consisting of fifteen decades, each containing ten Aves, preceded by a Patra Nostra, and followed by the Gloria Patra, and each related to an event in the life of Christ or the Virgin Mary that is contemplated during its recitation." Another definition for "Rosary" is "A string of beads for keeping account of these prayers so recited." So the amulet of Sardis was replaced by the Rosary of the Roman Church.

But another and quite different definition than that of the amulet is also given. This definition speaks of a remnant or an escaped few. These two definitions would complete the picture—the Roman Church with her images, her prayer-rote and other unscriptural practices on the one hand, and the Reformers who opposed such on the other.

We have seen in the Introduction to the Seven Churches, the fifth parable of the series on the Mysteries of the Kingdom in Matthew thirteen, bearing out the thought of a large field and a very small (comparatively) treasure. The church of this age can be likened to the large field, and the Reform Movement to the hidden treasure.

PHILADELPHIA: The Church of Brotherly Love
(1729-19?? A.D.)

"And to the angel of the church in Philadelphia write: These things saith he that is holy, he that is true, he that hath the key of David, and he that openeth, and no man shutteth; and shutteth and no man openeth; I know thy works; Behold, I have set before thee an open door, and no man can shut it: for thou hast a little strength, and hast kept my words, and hast not denied my name. Behold, I will make them of the synagogue of Satan, which say they are Jews, and are not, but do lie; behold, I will make them to come and worship before thy feet, and to know that I have loved thee. Because thou hast kept the words of my patience, I also will keep thee from the hour of temptation, which shall come upon the earth. Behold, I come quickly: Hold fast that which thou hast, that no man take thy crown. Him that overcometh will I make a pillar in the temple of my God, and he shall go no more out; and I will write upon him the name of my God, and the name of the city of my

God, which is New Jerusalem, which cometh down out of heaven from my God: and I will write upon him my new name. He that hath an ear, let him hear what the Spirit saith unto the churches" (Revelation 3:7-13).

This church is quite properly named Philadelphia, because it was, indeed, a church of brotherly love. It was a church of the open door. The city in which this church was located was founded in 189 B.C., making it one of the newer cities of the province of Asia. It was named in honor of Attulua II because of his loyalty to his elder brother, Eumenes II, king of Lydia. Hence the meaning—brotherly love. It contained a large colony of Jews and a synagogue. Also, it was later the seat of a Christian bishop.

While its Lord had only words of praise and commendation, at the same time this group was reminded of some things which greatly hindered its progress. Its little strength, the members of the Jewish "Synagogue of Satan," and the hour of great temptation all combined to keep it from being the successful church it should have been.

The period pictured by the church at Philadelphia began about the time of John Wesley and the rise of Methodism, and was drawing to a close sometime in the twentieth century. The era preceding this was one marked by two very important things. The first was the revolt from the Roman Catholic Church, bringing about the Reformation. The second was the theological warfare carried on among the Protestants themselves. These latter agreed that the Bible should be the only safe rule of conduct and the final authority for everything spiritual, but they disagreed as to the interpretation of specific points of doctrines. While their faith and practice were far above Rome's, yet they were in danger of succumbing to cold, dead orthodoxy.

However, here and there could be seen signs of true spirituality. Groups like the Moravians were seeking and experiencing a spiritual life deeper than was found in the established churches of the day. It was to one such groups that John Wesley once went for a prayer meeting. He was much impressed with their fervor in worship. From this meeting he says he went away "with his heart strangely warmed." As an outcome of this and his subsequent association with them he began to preach "Perfect Love," as a definite spiritual experience to be sought. Sometimes this experience was called the "Second Blessing," "Holiness," "Heart Purity," "Sanctification," "Christian Perfection," etc. So, from a humble prayer meeting, the great Methodist church was born, with John Wesley and his brother Charles as leaders. Thus began the great "Holiness" revival which was to last many years.

During the latter years of this Philadelphia era there was a cooling off of love and fervor and a lapse into cold formality even among the Methodists. At the same time a movement seeking to go back to the originals of brotherly love was taking shape. As a majority of those who advocated the doctrine of Christian Perfection allowed it to become only a theological concept, there was emerging those who firmly preached a renewal of the spirit of this doctrine. When the lines became firmly drawn and the battle completely joined, the small remnant advocating this renewal found themselves outside the organized denominations. Consequently, the latter half of the nineteenth century saw the rise of many "Holiness" groups. The Wesleyan Methodist, Free Methodist, Pilgrim Holiness, Nazarenes, etc., had their beginnings in this period.

Hard on the heels of this revival of the doctrine and practice of Holiness came another great wave of spiritual life, which was to influence the church world out of all proportion to its numerical strength. This was the Pentecostal revival of the early twentieth century. Starting as it did among the holiness denominations, it was to spread until by the middle of the century it would make a great impact even upon the old established churches.

For some fifty-odd years historical Christianity chose to ignore or oppose these so-called radical groups of Pentecostals. They were especially opposed for their unyielding stand on "Speaking in tongues as a necessary evidence of the Baptism of the Holy Spirit." Although most early leaders of the Pentecostal people came from the holiness denominations, many times these very holiness groups were more critical of this spiritual movement than were the large denominations.

In its early days the basic tenets of this new order differed very little from the Twenty-five Articles of Faith of Historic Methodism, and the Thirty-nine Articles of the Church of England (Episcopalian), but the emphasis upon the same manifestations of the Holy Spirit as was seen in the primitive church, and the doctrine of divine healing, caused it to be widely rejected.

Not until about the middle of this twentieth century did main stream Protestantism choose to take a second look at the rapidly growing Pentecostals. They were attracting too much world-wide attention to be ignored any longer. For instance, in South America they had become the leading voice of Protestantism. People by the thousands had left their own communions and cast their lot with these groups. Once the church world chose to seriously investigate this movement it became apparent that many were really impressed with what was being done. As a result multitudes accepted the doctrines of the Pentecostal people relative to the Holy Spirit, divine healing and many other beliefs and practices the older established churches fail to emphasize. Some of these people withdrew from their churches, but many more remained.

LAODICEA: The Modern Church (19??-????)

"And unto the angel of the church of the Laodiceans write; These things saith the Amen, the faithful and true Witness, the beginning of the creation of God: I know thy works, that thou art neither cold nor hot: I would thou wert cold or hot. So then because thou art lukewarm, and neither cold nor hot, I will spew thee out of my mouth. Because thou saith, I am rich, and increased with goods, and have need of nothing: and knowest not that thou art wretched, and miserable, and poor, and blind, and naked: I counsel thee to buy of me gold tried in the fire, that thou mayest be rich; and white raiment, that thou mayest be clothed, and that the shame of thy nakedness do not appear; and anoint thine eyes with eyesalve, that thou mayest see: As many as I love, I rebuke and chasten; be zealous therefore, and repent. Behold, I stand at the door and knock: if any man hear my voice, and open the door I will come in to him, and sup with him, and he with me. To him that overcometh will I grant to sit with me in my throne, even as I also overcame, and am set down with my Father in his throne. He that hath an ear, let him hear what the Spirit saith unto the churches" (Revelation 3:14-22).

The last of the seven churches was Laodicea. About the city of Laodicea the *International Standard Bible Encyclo-*

pedia has this to say: "A city of Asia Minor situated in the Lycos Valley in the province of Phrygia.... It was founded by Antiochus II (261-246- B.C.), who named it for his wife Loadike, and and populated it with Jews who were transplanted from Babylon to the cities of Phrygia and Laodicea....

"It was a place of little consequence until the Roman province of Phrygia was founded in 190 B.C.... Then it suddenly became a great and wealthy center of industry, famous specially for the fine black wool of its sheep and for Phrygian powder for the eyes, which was manufactured there. In the vicinity was the temple of Men Karou and a renowned school of medicine...."

"It was a city of great wealth, with extensive banking operations. Little is known of the early history of Christianity there; Timothy, Mark and Epaphras (Col. 1:7) seem to have been the first to introduce it...."

From the foregoing can be seen some of the hurtful influences which were brought to bear on the church at Laodicea and to cause such condemnation from its Lord. It claimed to be rich and have need of nothing. From a material standpoint this was probably true. It was a rich city and possibly this church was made up mostly of rich people. But in speaking of the true riches, Christ says that it was poor. In spite of the great outward show of self-satisfaction Christ knew it was filled with wretched people. Christ knew of the misery it sought to hide behind a false facade of well-being.

As has been previously seen, Laodicea was noted for a certain Phrygian powder for the eyes, but Christ knew this did nothing for its spiritual blindness. He knew of the fine black wool for which the region was famous, but knew this could not hide its spiritual nakedness from Him.

So Christ counsels it to buy of Him the true riches—gold tried in the fire, and not trust in its own riches. He counsels it to buy of Him white raiment, and not depend upon the black wool of its material prosperity. Thus clothed, its nakedness would be hid. He counsels it to buy of Him spiritual eyesalve and not depend upon the eye powder of the merchants of the city.

Finally, He gives the reason for these stern rebukes and His threatened chastening—His love. He says, "Be zealous."

This word carries with it the thought of warmth and heat. So, He tells it to leave its lukewarmness and bring warmth and heat into its worship and service—or be spewed out of His mouth.

The letter to Laodicea gives us a true picture of the church of the latter days. In connection with this epistle we find in the transition of the church from the Philadelphian to the Laodicean state a gradual blending of the two spirits. The fusing starts with a small amount of the lukewarmness of Laodicea being brought into the great warmth of brotherly love of Philadelphia. Slowly this lukewarm spirit grows, and the brotherly love is forced into the background. Eventually the era of Laodicea bursts forth in full bloom.

What are some of the things which usher in this age? Some early causes can be noted, such as higher criticism, liberalism, modernism, and the teaching of the Post-millennial theory (that Christ will not come until the close of the millennium). Through education, training and legislation, man would be brought to the millennial state, says this doctrine. After this Christ would come back to earth to reign.

Next in order would be the modern social gospel. This gospel is more concerned with making this world a better place in which to live than in getting people ready to live in a better world. In more recent years there has been a subtile change of emphasis by those who hold to the post-millennial doctrine. The Millennium of peace of some future time, brought about by the efforts of man in evangelizing the world has been lost sight of and the great stress now is placed on bettering man's lot here and now, with very little thought of his eternal state.

The ecumenical movement is another very significant contributing factor in the development of the Laodicean mood. Until well into the twentieth century, denominational lines were quite sharply drawn. Groups that were somewhat different in their doctrine and practice mixed very little with each other. But through the great influence of the World Council and National Council of Churches, there has been a great change. Modern leaders have discovered the great similarities of the different denominations. Especially has this been true in America. Since a great number had already forsaken the historic orthodox position on many doctrines, they found they were preaching about the same message. Differences in organizational structures, cultural backgrounds and national origins were the main things keeping them apart.

In many instances serious efforts were made to resolve these differences. A number of groups with similar backgrounds began studying the problem. Many denominations have already merged. Many more mergers are in the offing.

Roman Catholics, who had stood aloof from Protestants for centuries, began a serious study of the ecumenical movement. They sent observers to world and national meetings. They began to see the possibilities of closer ties with Protestantism. For the first time they began to talk of possible re-unification of all Christendom. Maybe, after all, the Reformation would turn out to be just a bad dream. Maybe the "Separated Brethren" would return to the fold of the church universal. They are now making efforts to communicate with these "Separated Brethren."

There is also a revolutionary change in the Catholic-Protestant dialog. Varying degrees of cooperation are taking place. Protestant ministers and Catholic priests are working together in different areas. Joint services are being held. Priests are filling Protestant pulpits and Protestant ministers are participating in Catholic services.

On the surface this all sounds good. Why should Christianity be fractionated into scores of different organizations, each professing to be the true church? But it is not the sincere effort in itself that is at fault. It is the basis of cooperation which is called in question. Should Christianity truly seek to come together in a world church with Christ as its Lord and His teachings as its rules of faith and conduct, the effort would have real merit.

But under present conditions, it would be necessary to compromise almost every basic New Testament doctrine to bring all professing Christians into a common fold. For instance, such a church could not preach Jesus Christ and Him crucified for man's sins. It could not teach the Virgin Birth, the bodily resurrection, the second coming of Christ, heaven for the righteous and hell for the wicked. By the time it was reduced to its lowest common denominator the church would be hardly recognizable.

The only alternative to this would be to allow all local churches and all ministers the right to teach what they thought was right "in their own eyes." This would be union without unity, and be no improvement upon the multi-denominational complex we have today.

When you come to the problem of Protestant-Catholic union the situation is still more difficult. Major concessions would have to be made by both sides, which neither is now ready to allow. For example, would Protestants accept the Pope as infallible and head of the church, appointed by Peter? Would it accept the doctrine of Purgatory? Would it agree to the celibacy of the ministry? Need more be said? Need mention be made of Protestant practices which would be unacceptable to Catholics?

Higher criticism, modernism, liberalism, the social gospel and the ecumenical movement have done their work well. Surely we must be in the closing days of the Laodicean age! Surely Christ will come after His waiting saints soon! When He does, the church age will close and a new phase of God's dealing with mankind will be brought in.

THE RAPTURE

If the chronological interpretation of Revelation is the proper one, then the Rapture of the saints or the catching away of the Bride must be placed between the third and fourth chapters. The final message to the church came to Laodicea at the close of the third chapter, and nothing more is heard of the church as such in the predictive portion of the book.

If Revelation were the only writings of Scripture given to prophecy, it would be hard to establish at all the fact of a pre-Tribulation catching away of the Bride of Christ. But this is not the case. Books and portions of books containing prophecy concerning this event are to be found all through the Bible. Many of these help establish the fact of the Rapture.

One very familiar Bible passage teaching the Rapture is 1 Thess. 4:13 - 5:4: *"But I would not have you to be ignorant, brethren, concerning them which are asleep, that ye sorrow not, even as others which have no hope. For if we believe that Jesus rose again, even so them also which sleep in Jesus will God bring with him. For this we say unto you by the word of the Lord, that we which are alive and remain unto the coming of the Lord shall not prevent* (precede) *them which are asleep. For the Lord himself shall descend from heaven with a shout, and with the voice of the archangel, and with the trump of God: and the dead in Christ shall rise first: Then we which are alive and remain shall be caught up together with them in the clouds, to meet the Lord in the air: and so shall we ever be with the Lord. Wherefore comfort one another with these words. But of the times and seasons, brethren, ye have no need that I write unto you. For yourselves know perfectly that the day of the Lord so cometh as a thief in the night. For when they shall say, Peace and safety: then sudden destruction cometh upon them, as travail upon a woman with child; and they shall not escape. But ye brethren, are not in darkness, that that day should overtake you as a thief."*

In dealing with the Rapture and the Resurrection in his letter to the Thessalonians, Paul seeks to allay their fears that the Rapture would take place and the dead saints would have no part in it. In discussing this problem he also gives us valuable light on the Rapture itself. He said the Lord would come as a thief in the night, and would come suddenly. Now the day of the Lord is not the Rapture, but the Rapture ushers in this day. The day of the Lord is that period of unparalleled trouble which begins with the Rapture, and ends at Armageddon, and precedes the setting up of Jesus' thousand-year earthly reign.

Many people fail to see the Rapture and the Revelation of Christ as two separate events. Neither could the Jews see both the first and second coming of Christ to this world. They would read of Messiah's coming in humiliation and also in power. Having a pre-conceived idea that He was coming to set up an earthly kingdom when He FIRST appeared they were deceived by their own hardened hearts and crucified their King. Likewise, when some read in one place of Christ's coming as secret, suddenly, and *for* His saints; and read in another place that He is coming *with* His saints, and that every eye shall see Him, they still fail to see the two appearings.

If we will compare Scripture with Scripture we will see that Jesus will make two appearings—first *after* His saints; next *with* His saints. The first time is just preceding the

Tribulation; the next is at the battle of Armageddon and at the end of the Tribulation. The period in between has been called the Great Tribulation, the Day of the Lord, the Day of Vengeance of our God, the Time of Jacob's Trouble, to name a few designations of this awful hour.

There is a teaching that when Jesus comes back He will take the entire Church back with Him—all the living and dead saints. But the weight of Scripture is against this theory. Just as Eve was not the *entire* body of Adam, just so the Bride of Christ will not be His *Entire* Body (The Church). It will be a select company. *"Unto them that look for Him."* Hebrews tells us, *"Shall he appear the second time without sin unto salvation."* This implies that there will be those who, though in Christ, will not be looking for the second coming. These people will be diliatory in their Christian lives and activities. Yet their names are written in heaven.

Some will say, "How can the dead be looking for the coming of Christ?" Their cases will be judged on whether or not they were looking for the coming of Christ while alive here on earth.

Paul, in speaking of the Rapture and Resurrection, declared, *"We shall not all sleep* (be dead), *but we shall be changed, in a moment, in the twinkling of an eye at the last trump; for the trumpet shall sound, and the dead shall be raised incorruptible, and we shall be changed."* Here is a dilemma. If it is taught that there will be a pre-Tribulation rapture, but Paul speaks of it as occuring at the *Last Trump,* how can this be reconciled since the Last Trump is the seventh trumpet which sounds after much of the Tribulation is past?

If one teaches that the Rapture and Resurrection take place in their entirety at the close of the church age, and before the beginning of the Tribulation proper, then there is, indeed, a conflict. If, on the other hand, allowance is made for a series of catchings away—at the beginning and during the Tribulation—the problem is solved.

The "Last Trump" does not usher in the Rapture, but witnesses its completion. It would be improper to designate the catching away at the "First Trump," or any other but the last, because Paul speaks of it as an accomplished fact. Hence, the "Last Trump." Let the matter be simplified by saying that the Rapture begins at the close of the church age and winds up during the sounding of the seventh trumpet.

A close study of Revelation will disclose that there are a series of companies raptured out during this period. Of course, the first is the one occurring at the beginning. This company is composed of the Bride and Bridal Company. These are the firstfruits of the Rapture and are seen under the figure of the Four Living Creatures. In Revelation 5:9, they sing, "Thou . . . hast redeemed us . . . out of every kindred, and tongue, and people and nation." In Revelation 7:9, John beholds a great multitude "of all nations, and kindred, and people and tongues (standing) before the throne, and before the Lamb." In this fourteenth verse they are identified as "These are they which came out of (the) Great Tribulation." This is a company distinct from that symbolized by the Four Living Creatures, because nothing is said about the "Great Tribulation" in connection with the first group.

In the twelfth chapter there is a group under the figure of the Manchild. This company is the same company mentioned in the seventh chapter and fourteenth verse—the 144,000 Israelites. In the seventh chapter they are sealed for divine protection but are left on earth. In the fourteenth chapter they are portrayed as in heaven. In the fourth verse we find "These are without fault before the throne of God." A careful study of the figure of the Manchild will reveal a picture of their being raptured in the twelfth chapter under the figure of the Manchild.

Another company is introduced in the Fifteenth chapter. This company is composed of those who have "gotten the victory over the beast, and over his image, and over his mark and over the number of his name." Note carefully that nothing is said about the Tribulation in connection with that company under the figure of the Four Living Creatures, because the Tribulation has not started. But of the company of the redeemed ones in the seventh chapter it is said "They came up out of great Tribulation." Nothing is said about the beast in connection with this company because the beast does not appear until the thirteenth chapter. The company in the fifteenth chapter had to contend with the mark and worship of the beast.

From this it will be seen that there are at least four companies making up those who are raptured—perhaps other companies also. They are found under the figure of the four Living Creatures, the palm bearers, the manchild and the harpers. So it would be improper to place the completed Rapture anywhere but where Paul places it—at the Last (or seventh) Trump.

THE BRIDE OF CHRIST

In the beginning, God created Adam from the dust of the ground, breathed into his nostrils the breath of life and he became a living soul. He was given dominion over the fish of the sea, the fowls of the air, beasts of the earth and all creeping things. God placed him in a garden called Eden. He was to keep this garden and eat of every tree of the garden except the tree of knowledge of good and evil. After this was done, there was still something lacking. He needed a companion. So God caused a deep sleep to fall upon him, removed one of his ribs and from it made Eve.

In following through with the thought of Christ as the Last or Second Adam, we have a striking picture of the Bride of Christ. If you will accept the New Testament statement that the Church is the Body of Christ and follow through with the parallels of the first Adam, you will see plainly that the *entire* body of Christ is not the Bride of Christ, just as the *entire* body of Adam was not used to form Eve.

When Adam's bride was taken from his body you remember he was in a deep sleep. Likewise, when the Bride of Christ is made up you will notice the Church as a body will be in a deep sleep.

IT WILL—

Not be looking for the coming of Christ; be saying, "My Lord delayeth his coming," and will be taken up with the things of this world.

IT WILL BE ASLEEP IN ITS—

Lack of first love; Doctrine and practices of Balaam and the Nicolaitanes; Seduction by Jezebel; Imperfect and dead works of wood, hay and stubble; Lukewarmness in the midst of material riches.

But from this sleeping body will come that group of saints known as the Bride of Christ.

THEY WILL BE THOSE WHO—

Have the first honeymoon love for their heavenly Bridegroom; are the poor-rich people, who through many hard trials will be able to overcome every obstacle of Satan and stand approved before God; will have the martyr's faith; hold fast to patience, charity and good works; are worthy and undefiled; are kept from the hour of temptation which will try the whole world; will buy heavenly gold, white raiment and eyesalve and be prepared when their Lord shall appear.

The foregoing qualifications of the Bride and Bridal company are abundantly shown in John's letters to the seven churches. Those lined up on the negative side of these letters will not be in this company. Those on the positive side will make up this blessed company of Christ's choice ones.

For additional qualifications one has but to examine the description of the Four Living Creatures in the fourth chapter. Look at the description of these beings. The first was like a lion. The insignia of the kingly tribe of Judah is the Lion. Jesus is "The Lion of the Tribe of Judah." According to rabbinical literature the lion was the standard of that group of tribes which camped on the east side of the tabernacle in the wilderness. We know that Judah was leader of this group; Issachar and Zebulun being the others. One face of the Living Creatures of Ezekiel was that of a lion. Throughout history the lion has been known as the king of the forest.

The second one was like an ox or calf. This animal represented one face of the Living Creature of Ezekiel. In that day the ox was the most dependable of work animals.

The third Living Creature had the face of a man. Reuben, camping with his company on the south side of the tabernacle had a standard on which was the face of a man (so the rabbis say). One of the faces of Ezekiel's Living Creatures was that of a man. Man is king of God's creation.

The last Living Creature had the face of an eagle. The company of Dan on the north side of the tabernacle marched under the banner of the eagle. An eagle's face was on the Living Creatures seen by Ezekiel. The eagle denotes vision and speed, and is considered the greatest of God's flying creatures.

If the four Living Creatures represent the Bride and the Bridal company and if those four faces mean anything special, then it follows that to be in these groups we must have the attributes pictured by these four faces.

Add to all this the attribute of watchfulness. The Living Creatures John saw were "Full of eyes before and behind." "This," says Seiss, "is the symbol of intense intelligence, looking backward into the past, and forward into the future, and inward upon themselves and into the nature of things, and able to direct their ways and administrations with unlimited penetration and discretion."

These four Creatures had each six wings. This calls to mind Isaiah's vision of the Seraphim in the sixth chapter of his prophecy. These heavenly creatures used these wings to express their worship and service to God. Two wings covered their faces, denoting reverence. Two covered their feet, speaking of humility. The remaining two wings were used to fly in service to the heavenly throne.

Notice the similarity in the worship of the Seraphim of Isaiah and the Living Creatures of John. Both cry, "Holy, Holy, Holy." Holy to the Father, Holy to the Son, Holy to the Spirit. The Seraphims see the Almighty as the God of battle, whose glory filled the whole earth. The Living Creatures see Him as Jehovah of the Old Testament and Christ of the New. They see Him as the Omnipotent one of "Yesterday, today and forever."

"Holy, Holy, Holy, Lord God Almighty, which was, and is, and is to come," is their cry. They keep this up day and night. A constant meditation on this one phase should keep one prepared for Jesus' coming. It speaks of the Omniscience (all-knowing) God, the Omnipotent (all-powerful) God, and the Omnipresence (everywhere present) God.

A summary of all these qualifications shows that to be in this company will require watchfulness, love, sound doctrine, faith, good works, heavenly gold as the price of redemption, white raiment as personal purity, and eyesalve of spiritual endowment. In addition to this it will take the courage of a lion, the patience of the ox, the intelligence of a man and the watchfulness of an eagle.

CHAPTER FOUR

THE TRIBULATION JUDGMENT COURT

THE HEAVENLY THRONE

"After this I looked, and behold, a door was opened in heaven: and the first voice which I heard was as it were of a trumpet talking with me; which said, Come up hither, and I will show thee things which must be hereafter. And immediately I was in the Spirit; and behold, a throne was set in heaven, and one sat on the throne. And he that sat was to look upon like a jasper and a sardine stone: and there was a rainbow round about the throne, in sight like unto an emerald.... And out of the throne proceeded lightnings and thunderings and voices: and there were seven lamps of fire burning before the throne, which are the seven Spirits of God" (Revelation 4:1-3, 5).

The action moves swiftly from the first on to the fourth chapter. The first chapter introduces Christ and gives hints as to the purpose of the Book. The voice, the vision and the messages conveyed, all have the Isle of Patmos as their location. Chapters two and three are occupied with the messages to the Seven Churches, and only indirectly advance the forward progress of the divine drama. In this fourth chapter the scene is moved to heaven, as evidence by the "Open Door." The trumpet-like voice of the first chapter again sounds forth, but this time from heaven. From this chapter to verse nine of chapter ten the seer is beholding the happenings from the vantage point of the celestial regions. This voice invites John to "Come up hither" to see "Things which must be hereafter." While in the heavenly realm he is to witness much of the results of the opening of the Seven Seals attached to the Little Book which is introduced in the fifth chapter.

Almost seven hundred years before John was given the Revelation, God gave Ezekiel the prophet visions similar to the ones described here. John's visions opened with a description of a throne: Ezekiel's closed with the description of a throne. John sees four "Living Creatures"; so does Ezekiel. Ezekiel sees a sapphire-like throne; John sees the Occupant of the throne as like a jasper and sardine stone. Both Ezekiel and John see the encircling rainbow.

The throne of this fourth chapter has its counterpart in the tabernacle in the wilderness of Moses' day, as will be shown later. The lightning, thunder and voices proclaim it a throne of judgment. The Spirit of God in His seven-fold sphere of operation, as signified by the seven lamps of fire, reveals Divine Majesty at work. Soon the Lion of the Tribe of Judah will stand before the Occupant of this throne, and from Him will take the Little Book. For the present, though, interest will be mainly in the description of this throne and its surroundings as the Tribulation Judgment Court.

God's judgment upon Pharaoh gives a faint foreview of those to be visited upon mankind during the Tribulation. Frogs, lice, flies, sores, hail, thunder, fire and death came upon the stubborn Egyptians before they became willing to release God's ancient people. Similar plagues, though intensified many times over will be experienced by the wicked of the end-time, with death reaching its climax at the battle of Armageddon.

In spite of the awful judgments to issue forth from this tribunal, it is a court of mercy. The emerald-like rainbow encircling the throne proclaims it to be such. In judgment God remembers mercy. As will be seen later, this august assize will convene and do its work ere man destroys himself in a frightful nuclear holocaust.

The message of the rainbow encircling the throne could well be illustrated in the following words: "The late evening sun, shining through a retreating mass of raindrops throws on the dark clouds of the east, a semi-circular halo of beautiful colors. 'I herald the approaching night,' says the setting sun, 'But' says the beautiful rainbow, 'I promise another and better tomorrow' "

The appearance of the Occupant of this throne was to look upon "Like a jasper and sardone stone." The two stones mentioned here were found in the breastplate of Israel's high priest as the first and last of a series of twelve, set in four rows of three each. Since Moses followed instructions and made everything pertaining to the tabernacle and the worship connected with it according to the heavenly pattern, it is evident that rays from the other ten stones also will contribute to the dazzling appearance of this Occupant.

Perhaps the reason no more is said about this Person on the throne is that man cannot describe God. He can only take futile words and endeavour to show Him as through a glass darkly. All expressions are inadequate; all vocabularies break down and the human mind can but feebly conceive of His resplendent glory.

Here John sees every hue and shade of scintillating light, flashing forth from His person. His attributes are shown in the vari-colored lights of the rainbow. In order to understand more fully the significance of the rainbow appearing here, some details concerning this wonderful phenomena of nature will be given under the heading.

GOD'S WONDERFUL BOW OF PROMISE

In Genesis God said, *"I do set my bow in the cloud ... for a token of a covenant ... between me* (God) *and every living creature ... upon the earth"* (Genesis 9:13).

A little research will give some information to show the significance of the rainbow in its relation to God and man. It is found that the prime colors are divided into two groups—the achromatic and the chromatic. The achromatics are black and white, with varying shades of gray in between, completing the classification. The chromatics are red, yellow and blue. Blending of these latter in their proper combinations also produces orange, green, indigo and violet. These are the rainbow hues or prismatics.

Breaking forth after a storm, the sun shines through the rifts and throws against the background of the somber retreating clouds this multi-colored bow of the chromatics. Its arch reaches high into the heavens, and its base appears to rest upon earth's horizon. Truly, this is a marvel of God's creation, and one of the most beautiful phenomena in all nature. In it is entwined God's redemptive message to man.

This bow is intricately woven into the scheme of divine things. To properly understand the importance of this spectacle we must know something about light. God realized the importance of light so much that His first creative act was to provide it. This is recorded in Genesis where He said, "Let there be light." You remember Jesus said He was the light of the world, and His people were the light of the world. Light is essential to life. With every other element present there would be very little (if any) life without light. Light is such a common thing that it is taken for granted most of the time. It is only when it fails that man begins to realize its true worth.

It sounds like a contradiction, but pure, undivided light cannot be seen at all. It is revealed as the radiant energy that stimulates the organs of sight and allows objects to be seen. However, there is much more to light than this. Pure, undivided light has the potential of producing all the colors of the rainbow. It only takes the proper conditions to bring this about. When the rays of the sun strike mist from a waterfall or a stream of water from a common garden hose at the proper angle, this rainbow effect is produced. Sunlight, shining through a prism of glass onto a white surface, will lengthen and shorten the rays of light and produce red, orange, yellow, green, blue, indigo and violet and all the shades in between.

God is light. He is everywhere. It only takes the right environment for Him to shine through and reveal Himself in all the rainbow hues. Since God thus reveals Himself, it follows that each color has some special meaning.

In studying the significance of the different rainbow colors, let us begin with red. This is the first color. It is described as "Having the color of blood, and that part of the visible spectrum having the longest wave-length and farthest from violet." Red in the bow signifies a bridge from Mount Ararat (the mountain on which the ark finally rested) to Mount Calvary," says the Rev. G. F. Taylor. This color speaks of the crimson stream which started in Eden and ended at Calvary. This symbolized the blood of Jesus Christ.

Orange is the next color and is between red and yellow in the spectrum. Since red is the color of blood and yellow is the color of gold, there appears the spectacle of the red blood of Jesus Christ as typifying His humanity, combining with the yellow (gold) of His divinity to give the picture of Him as "Very God and Perfect Man."

Yellow is not only the color representing the divine side of Christ; it also represents all deity. "It signifies that part of the atonement that was performed strictly by deity," says Taylor.

Next in the spectrum is green. This color comes between yellow and blue. It reminds one of the green vegetation of earthly life. But in God's rainbow it speaks of mercy. The whole bow does this, but it is left to green to carry out the promise of mercy throughout Scripture. This is a temporary color. Witness the vegetation of spring. It comes out a beautiful green, but takes on other hues as the seasons change. Likewise, mercy is temporary, and is subject to certain conditions. There is a time when mercy has to step aside and let justice and judgment enter in. God said, "My Spirit shall not always strive with man." Green is a blend of yellow and blue. This is also freighted with meaning. The yellow of divinity and the blue of heaven combine to form the green of the earth.

Blue is the heavenly color. It is defined as "Having the color of the clear sky; color between green and violet. It points upward to the sky and heaven and downward to the see and earth and man."

Indigo is defined as a "Blue coloring substance; a deep violet blue." In giving the significance of the various colors of the rainbow, Taylor tells us, "The indigo of the rainbow indicates that the seasons and months and day and night will continue in their present order and that seed will be sown and harvests reaped year by year as long as the earth shall stand."

Violet is the last of the colors. It is that portion of the visible spectrum having the shortest wave length. "The significance of the color is love. It means that God is love and that all His covenants with man are made in love." (Taylor.) This color especially calls to mind John 3:16, "For God so loved the world that he gave his only begotten Son that whosoever believeth on him shall not perish, but have everlasting life."

Summing up, it is found that God reveals Himself to man in this seven-fold way. He appears to him in the red of Christ's sacrifice; in the orange of the spectrum as the coming together of God and man in Christ; in the yellow (gold) of His divinity; in the green of His mercy; in the blue of His heavenly attributes; in the indigo of the promise of seed time and harvest, and summer and winter; and, finally, in the violet of His love.

So, right in the midst of the awful judgments recorded in Revelation God has placed the rainbow around the throne as a guarantee of mercy extended. He is still reminding humanity of the sacrifice of Christ's cross, that His mercy endureth forever, and His love is extended to all who will avail themselves of it.

THE TWENTY-FOUR ELDERS

"And round about the throne were four and twenty seats: and upon the seats I saw four and twenty elders sitting, clothed in white raiment; and they had on their heads golden crowns" (Revelation 4:4).

After contemplating the wonderful throne and its Occupant, John's attention is focused on those things surrounding this celestial habitation. Around about this shining throne he sees twenty-four seats (or thrones), and on each of them sits an "Elder." They are clothed in white raiment. They are wearing golden crowns. There are three strong clues as to their identity—thrones, white raiment and golden crowns. The fact they are seated on thrones indicates they have taken their places as participants in the coming judgments. The white raiment speaks of purity and holiness. The golden crowns are their badges of authority. More will be said about this at the proper time.

Here they seem to be taking second place to the Living Creatures (q. v.). When this last mentioned company "give honor, and glory and thanks" to the Occupant of the central throne these white-robed, golden-crowned Elders join in. They fall down, cast their crowns before the throne Occupant and worship. The burden of their praise is that the Lord is worthy to receive honor and power as the Creator. All things, they say, are and were created for His pleasure. Here they ascribe praise to God. They make no mention of the Lamb. Therefore, it is evident that God the Father is here meant.

In the fifth chapter where John is weeping because no one is found worthy to take the Little Book, break the seals and reveal its contents, one of these Elders speaks. He informs the seer that One has been found to perform this task—the Lion of the Tribe of Judah. This title is peculiarly Israelitish. It speaks of Christ in His judicial role, as the Great Prosecutor attached to the Tribulation Judgment Court. Also, it distinguishes Him as an Israelite, of the Tribe of Judah. But more about this in the fifth chapter.

Following the lead of the four Living Creatures, these Elders again fall down in worship. This time it is the Lamb Who receives adoration. Harps, and incense-filled golden vials containing the prayers of saints, are in their possession. The combined companies—Living Creatures and Elders—then sing of the worthiness of the Lamb. They are present when a great multitude of white-robed, palm-bearing saints are shown as having "Come up out of great tribulation." All the angels are in worship here.

The Elders appear by themselves to John in the eleventh chapter at the sounding of the seventh trumpet. They fall on their faces and worship God, just as in other scenes. They are present in the fourteenth chapter with the Living Creatures when the one hundred and forty-four thousand Israelites sing the new song before the throne. As the announcement that God hath judged the "Great Whore" (Babylon), these Elders (with the Living Creatures) are seen in a final worship service in the nineteenth chapter.

A brief resume will reveal several things. The first is that everywhere these Elders appear, God and His throne hold the prominent place. In chapters four, five, seven, eleven, fourteen and nineteen these Elders appear. In four places they are shown in worship. In two they are merely spectators. Their presence speaks of God as Creator, Almighty God and Avenger.

The text gives hints as to who they are and what position they occupy. It is said they are "Elders." The word elder is of a comparative degree, meaning they are older than some other group. The only group to which they can be compared is that company represented by the Four Beasts (Living Creatures).

A further suggestion more completely identifying them is given in verse nine of the fifth chapter. The song they sing (with the Living Creatures) proclaim them (with the Living Creatures) to be "Redeemed . . . out of every kindred, and tongue, and people and nation." So the two companies include redeemed mankind from every nation and race and age.

In verse nine they are considered as one group; in verse ten there is a division. They again become two companies. One body is composed of "Kings"; another is made up of "Priests." Since the twenty-four Elders are introduced first, and the song mentions "Kings" first, it follows naturally that they are represented by the "Kings." The Living Creatures are symbolized as "Priests."

A study of the camp of Israel in the wilderness will serve as an important key to throw light on many things connected with this heavenly court. The arrangement John sees is in perfect keeping with the plan of the ancient camp of Israel. In this camp there were two distinct bodies. One was made up of the "Congregation"; the other of the "Priests" (with Moses). The congregation took care of the secular affairs; the priests were responsible for the spiritual. Moses was the overall leader, but Aaron as the High Priest, had direct charge of spiritual matters.

Christ is both King and Priest. He identifies with both companies. In Luke 1:32, in speaking of Christ, we are told the "Lord God shall give unto him (Christ) the throne of his father David." While in Hebrews 3:1 the writer admonishes us to "Consider the . . . high priest of our profession, Jesus Christ." Thus, our Lord fills both these offices.

Jesus will sit upon the throne of His father David—and it will be here on earth in Jerusalem. He will be King, and "His brethren according to the flesh" will occupy ruling places which have been planned for them from the foundation of the world. All through Scripture are intimations that the "House of Jacob" will play a prominent part in ruling the earth after everlasting righteousness has been brought in.

It is a generally accepted belief among those who accept the futuristic interpretation of Revelation that Jesus will sit upon the throne of His Father David, and rule from Jerusalem during the Millennium. However, if one will accept the plain teaching of Scripture he will find His rule is not to end at the end of the thousand years. His rule upon this earthly throne *will be forever!* Listen to this: "The Lord shall give unto him the throne of his father David; and he shall reign over the house of Jacob *forever;* and of his kingdom *there shall be no end.*"

THE SEA OF GLASS

"And before the throne there was a sea of glass like unto crystal" (Rev. 4:6a). Before this rainbow-encircled throne John sees a "Sea of Glass," like unto crystal. Nothing is said as to the part this Sea of Glass will play in the opening actions connected with the Tribulation Judgment Court. However, it appears again in the fifteenth chapter, where it is occupied by "Them that had gotten the victory over the beast, and over his image, and over his name, and over the number of his name." More will be said about this Sea of Glass at the proper time.

THE FOUR LIVING CREATURES

"... And in the midst of the throne, and round about the throne, were four beasts full of eyes before and behind. And the first beast was like a lion; and the second beast was like a calf, and the third beast had the face as a man, and the fourth beast was like a flying eagle. And the four beasts had each of them six wings about him; and they were full of eyes within: and they rest not day and night, saying, Holy, Holy, Holy, Lord God Almighty, which was, and is, and is to come. And those beasts give glory and honour and thanks to him that sat on the throne, who liveth for ever and ever" (Revelation 4:6b-9).

After viewing the Sea of Glass the apostle's attention is taken up with the second company. This group is "In the midst of the throne, and round about the throne." The Authorized Version of our Bible calls them "Four Beasts." The marginal rendering is "Four Living Creatures." With this latter most commentators and other versions agree.

According to Strong's Concordance this word "Beast" is translated from the Greek word "ZOON," which means "life, live, quick, a live thing, an animal-beast." This same word is used in Hebrews 13:11 in speaking of animals for blood sacrifice, whose bodies were burned outside the camp. The writer of Hebrews shows that Christ fulfilled the type when He "Suffered without (outside) the camp." So the Authorized Version is in a measure correct. Jesus offered Himself just as these animals were offered. And those who are pictured as the "Four Beasts" are those who have offered themselves as "Living sacrifices, holy, acceptable unto God."

An altogether different word is used by John when speaking of the Antichrist as the "Beast." This word is "THERION" and is translated as a "Dangerous animal; venomous, wild beast," and, figuratively, it means "Destruction." But since the word "Beast" is usually thought of in the bad sense in modern times, the use of "Living Creatures" is preferred, and will be used to identify these "Four Beasts" hereafter.

As far as the record tells us, the Twenty-Four Elders are all alike and equal in rank. Not so with these "Living Creatures"; each one has a separate identity. One is described as like a lion; another like a calf, and another with the face of a man, and the last like a flying eagle.

Referring to the Living Creatures of Ezekiel's vision, we see a great similarity between them and those John saw. Ezekiel's creatures each had four faces and four wings; John's creatures had six wings and just one face each. The lion, man, ox and eagle are used to describe the faces of Ezekiel's creatures. John's creatures are said to resemble a lion, an ox (calf), and an eagle. The faces of only one—the third—was described as like the face of a man.

Both of these prophets—one from the Old Testament and one from the New—see these Living Creatures as attendants upon God's throne. Ezekiel's creatures are angelic beings; John's are redeemed man. Ezekiel's message is to the rebellious house of Israel; John's is to Christianity—real and apostate—wicked men, ripe for judgment as well as to Israel. Both prophesy of impending doom. Ezekiel sees a "Roll of a Book," containing lamentations and mournings and woes; John sees a "Little Book" and visions of the entire end-time.

Going back to the analogy of the camp in the wilderness as showing a reflection of the heavenly scene, we again quote the ninth and tenth verses of the fifth chapter: "Thou hast redeemed us to God . . . out of every kindred, and tongue, and people, and nation: and hast made us unto our God kings and priests: and we shall reign on the earth."

If the Twenty-Four Elders are to have positions as kings and reign on the earth with Christ, then the Four Living Creatures will have authority as priests. Christ will also be the High Priest with the Heavenly New Jerusalem as the place from which He will perform His priestly ministrations.

As we continue to pursue this line of thought the links become stronger, and there emerges a wonderful pattern. Jesus is the Lion of the Tribe of Judah. The lion was the insign under which the tribe of Judah marched and camped. So, He is associated with the Twenty-Four Elders as their King sitting on the throne of His father David, ruling from the earthly domain forever.

The Lion as the semblance of the first of the Four Living Creatures of the fourth chapter also shows Him to be linked with the company so pictured. There is this difference: to the Twenty-Four Elders He is King, but to the Four Living Creatures He is High Priest.

Summing up, we learn both companies picture redeemed ones of the earth. The Twenty-Four Elders represent Old Testament saints, and the Four Living Creatures New Testament saints. Further, since this last company is said to be closest to the throne of all redeemed ones, it is only natural to identify them as the Bride of Christ and her attendants.

HEAVEN'S EARTHLY PATTERN

In order to become better acquainted with this heavenly spectacle it is necessary to go back to the Old Testament and study more fully the arrangement of the encampment of Israel in the wilderness under Moses. The pattern for this camp was revealed to the lawgiver by Jehovah Himself, and was to be a replica of the heavenly abode. In proof of this, Hebrews 8:5 says, "... Moses was admonished of God when he was about to make the tabernacle: for, See, saith He, that thou make all things according to the pattern shewed thee in the mount."

Since it is certain that Moses did make everything according to the divine pattern, and that pattern was the heavenly tabernacle, this earthly copy can be studied and a great deal learned about the original. A brief description of the camp of Israel in the wilderness would show, in the center, a tent or tabernacle fifteen feet wide by forty-five feet long. This structure was enclosed by a court seventy-five feet wide by one hundred feet long. In front of this court was the camp of Moses, Aaron and the priests. The three families of the Levites occupied the other three sides. Around all this was the camp of the other tribes.

A detailed description of this encampment of Israel should begin at the very center—the Most Holy Place of the Tabernacle. This chamber was fifteen feet wide by fifteen feet long. Originally, the Most Holy Place contained the ark of the covenant, the mercy seat with the overshadowing cherubims, the golden pot of manna, Aaron's rod that budded and the tables of stone. In this Most Holy Place God met with Aaron. It was here this earthly high priest sought an atonement for his sins and the sins of the people. Between this chamber and the Holy Place was a thick veil through which none but the High Priest could enter the Most Holy Place, and that only once a year.

After this description of the Most Holy Place, comes the other room in the tabernacle—the Holy Place. It was fifteen feet wide by thirty feet long. This was the part of the tabernacle where the lesser priests ministered. In it were found the table of the shew bread, the golden altar of incense and the seven-pronged golden candlestick.

In the outer court the congregation came to have the priests offer their sacrifices. In this enclosure were located the brazen altar and the laver. Sacrifices were burned on this altar and the laver was used for the priests' washings.

Around all this were the camps of the priests and Levites. There were three families of Levites—the Kohathites, Gershonites and Merarites. However, from the family of the Kohathites were taken the families of Moses and Aaron. This latter group, which included Aaron's sons the priests, made up the fourth contingent. Their camp was immediately in front of the tabernacle, and the three families of the Levites (excluding the families of Moses and Aaron from the Kohathites) had places on the other three sides.

The camps of the tribes completely encircled all this. In front of the outer court—with the camp of the Priests in between—was the camp of Judah, facing east. In the camp with him were Issachar and Zebulun. The camp of Reuben was on the south with the Kohathites in between. With him were Simeon and Gad. The west camp was for Ephraim, Manasseh and Benjamin—with the Gershonites between them and the court. Dan had the north camp and shared it with Asher and Naphtali. It was separated from the court by the camp of the Merarites. More will be said about this heavenly scene in the fifth chapter.

GOD'S REDEMPTIVE PLAN

God's plan for the restoration of man is divided into three phases. The first was from Adam to Abraham; the second from Abraham to Christ; the third from Christ until all sin is put down and everlasting righteousness brought in. Some may object to the call of Abraham as being the dividing point of the Old Testament aspect and say the flood marked the division. But the great deluge came only 1,656 years after the creation of man. According to the generally accepted chronology in Genesis, Abraham left Ur about 2,024 years after the creation of Adam. So if this call is accepted as the dividing line, the 2,000-year dispensation will be off by only about twenty-four years.

During this first period God dealt with man individually. In it is found Abel's "more excellent sacrifice," Enoch's godly walk and translation and Noah's perfection in his own generation. Also, there was Adam's expulsion from Eden, wicked Cain's unacceptable sacrifice-offering and murder of Abel. In all these cases God dealt with individuals, with very little emphasis on mankind in general. Although in the judgment of the flood it seems had man listened to Noah, he could have been saved from its waters. But there seemed to be no group effort in worship. From the record one gathers that Cain's offering was for himself alone. Likewise, Abel's sacrifice atoned only for himself. Enoch walked with God, but it seemed he walked alone.

From the flood to the calling out of Abraham was a period of some 368 years. We have no indication that God dealt with man in relation to his basic spiritual needs any differently than He did before the flood. The change really came with the calling out of the great patriarch. The Scofield Bible divides the time from the expulsion to the end of the final millennium into six dispensations and calls them the dispensations of Conscience, Human Government, Promise, Grace and Kingdom. However, these are but subdivisions of these three features of God's redemption plan.

In the second phase of His dealing with man, God called Abraham out, separated him from his country and his father's house, sent him on a journey to an unknown destination and with his posterity determined to make a great nation. From that nation God's plan was to provide salvation for all the human race through Jesus Christ. Abraham's posterity failed miserably, but in spite of their stubbornness, self-exaltation and countless failures, the plan of salvation was carried out. Jesus did come, die on the cross and atone for man's sins.

The last part of God's plan was instituted when Jesus Christ came to earth, made the supreme sacrifice at Calvary, rose from the dead, ascended to heaven and sent back the Holy Spirit. This last will continue until all sin is put down.

* * * * * * *

Remember, the scene here in this fourth chapter is the Court of Tribulation Judgment. Although terrible things were to transpire shortly, there is an overriding joy on the part of those who are to participate in this action. In spite of the horrible ordeal which is to take place on the earth, this elation is felt because it has become apparent that man's redemption is about to be completed. In viewing this fearful time of sorrow, one may lose sight of the supreme object involved. One is apt to forget that this divine visitation is just a night-marish chapter, its purpose being to put down all sin and bring in the eternal ages.

The actions of the Tribulation Court could be likened to an earthly court of the modern day in its efforts to clean up a city which has been brought under the absolute control of criminal elements. Good men have to step forward and furnish evidence upon which the court can act. Fearless prosecutors have to risk the wrath of entrenched lawlessness and fight for the right of the public. Sincere judges and juries have to weigh the evidence and make just decisions if such influences are to be eliminated.

This is the picture of our modern day world. The criminal rule, activated by Satan, demons, fallen angels and wicked men has almost taken over. Forces of depravity are so strong that decency and godliness are in danger of completely disappearing from the earth. No doubt man has now reached the place equal to the antediluvian world in violence and the city of Sodom in wickedness.

Looked at from a natural standpoint, the Great Tribulation may seem unjust. Why would God allow all this to come upon mankind? We do not have all the answers to this question, but from present developments in the field of weapons of war one may safely say that this will be a perod of mercy as well as judgment. Man is determined on a course of total self-extemination, and unless something stops him his grand finale will be complete race suicide.

Modern weapons being what they are, man IS capable of destroying himself. This is one of the grave concerns of world leaders today. They know that should a major conflict break out and nations fight to their full capacity, all kinds of awesome devices of desolation would be let loose. The atomic bomb, the hydrogen bomb, the cobalt bomb; the laser ray; biological, germ and gas warfare, plus many weapons of which the public has scarcely dreamed would be brought into play.

With all these instruments of extinction let loose, everyone might not be killed, but the aftermath of such a holocause would be the contamination of land, sea and air with deadly radiation. This would result in the death of other multiplied millions. It also would result in making the human race mostly sterile. Very few of those who survived such an ordeal would be capable of having children (according to many present-day scientists). This would mean that when a person died, there may be no one born to replace him. One by one, man would die off. But God does not intend to let man destroy himself. He will allow the Tribulation to bring things to a halt. Looked at in this light, one can clearly see mercy mixed with judgment.

In Noah's day, before the last righteous person was to disappear from the face of the earth, God sent the flood and saved this godly man and his house. And just as God had to send the confusion of tongues at the tower of Babel and scatter the people in order to stop man in his mad attempt to thwart God, just so He has to send the Tribulation before man annihilates the human race. Also, as there were not enough righteous people in Sodom for God to spare her in Lot's day, he had to call this "Righteous" man out of the city before he sent fire and brimstone in a mighty conflagration. So when the present world gets fully ripe for judgment, Christ will come and take His bride from the earth and judgment will swiftly follow.

The saints of God, under the figure of the Four Living Creatures, have important parts in directing these judgments. The Four Horsemen are sent to the earth in the sixth chapter at their bidding. This is just one of the many duties they will perform .

CHAPTER FIVE

THE TRIBULATION JUDGMENT COURT
(Continued)

"And I saw in the right hand of him that sat upon the throne a book written within and on the backside, sealed with seven seals. And I saw a strong angel proclaiming with a loud voice, Who is worthy to open the book, and to loose the seals thereof? and no man in heaven, nor in earth, neither under the earth was able to open the book, neither to look thereon. And I wept much, because no man was found worthy to open and to read the book, neither to look thereon" (Revelation 5:1-4).

Try to imagine a vast rectangular plain, stretching for hundreds of miles in each direction. In the center we see a level area, large enough to accommodate the Tribulation Judgment Court and the Sea of Glass in front of the throne. From the outer edge of this smaller area we see the surface sloping gradually upward until at its outer borders it reaches the altitude of lofty mountains.

In appearance this might be said to resemble a huge athletic arena of modern times. The sloping sides of this would be the grandstand and bleachers, with the level part as the playing space. This is the Heavenly Mount Zion John sees in the fourteenth chapter. Let the Twenty-Four Elders be placed in the grandstand and bleachers. Down on the playing field proper where the action is will be located the Four Living Creatures.

The similarity between the Tribulation Judgment Court and a modern athletic arena is only that of relative dimensions. To get a better picture we must go again to the description of the wilderness camp of Israel as it relates to the heavenly pattern. In the discussion of the fourth chapter a description is given of the camp itself with the arrangements of the tabernacle, court and camp of the tribes. In this fifth chapter parallels will be drawn between its activities and the heavenly camp.

As was seen in the previous chapter, in the Most Holy Place of Israel's tabernacle was to be found the mercy seat. This was where God sat (symbolically) and before Whom Aaron appeared once a yeart to make a blood-sacrifice for his sins and the sins of the people. In the heavenly Holy of Holies God the Father is seated on the rainbow-encircled throne with Jesus Christ as our High Priest ministering in our behalf. This gives a picture of where our Saviour appeared and offered His own blood after it was spilled at Calvary.

In the Holy Place of the wilderness tabernacle lesser priests performed their ministry. They used the golden seven-pronged candlesick, the table of shewbread and the altar of incense in this service. Also, they executed the priestly functions when the people brought their sacrifices into the outer court for offerings to God. Assisting in all this, and caring for the tabernacle and its furniture, were the three families of the Levites. The Four Living Creatures perform similar functions in the heavenly sanctuary.

That the companies represented by the Living Creatures themselves are not all equal in rank and importance is borne out by the analogy of the priests and Levites and their work. In the task of moving the camp to a new location, each family of these Levites had certain responsibilities. The priests were to carry the oil for the light, the anointing oil, the sweet incense and the daily meat offering. The Kohathites had charge of the worship furniture of the tabernacle, such as the ark of the covenant, the mercy seat, the table of shewbread, the seven-pronged candlestick, the golden censers, etc. After the priests went in and prepared these articles for moving, this family was to carry them on their shoulders. The Gershonites were to take care of the curtains, cords, and other materials making up the walls and partitions. They were allowed two wagons and four oxen for transportation. The Merarites were given four wagons and eight oxen to carry the boards, staves and other heavy paraphenalia.

Added to the figures of this Tribulation Judgment Court as in a measure paralleling the modern athletic arena and the wilderness camp of Israel, there is yet another to which it can be likened—a modern American courtroom. God on His throne as the judge on the bench; Jesus Christ as the

Lion of the Tribe of Judah as the prosecuting attorney; the Four Living Creatures as the staff of this Attorney; the Twenty-Four Elders as the jurors; the Little Book as containing the indictments upon which the court must act; the Dragon, the Beast and the False Prophet and a world of degenerate men as the criminals before the bar of eternal justice.

That the Four Living Creatures are to be administrators of the judgment is pictured by the calling forth of the Four Horsemen at the opening of the first four seals on the Little Book. Also, one of these Living Creatures gives to the seven judgment angels the golden vials "full of the wrath of God" which are poured out upon the earth in the seven last plagues.

But back to the text. The court is in session. The participants are arraigned. But before there are any legal proceedings a worship service must be held. We are told the Living Creatures give honor and glory and thanks to the One on the throne—God the Father. The Elders fall down, cast their crowns before the throne and worship God as Creator.

THE LITTLE BOOK

The first order of business after this service has to do with a Little Book. It is sealed with seven seals. Just what is the significance of this Little Book? Let us see what the record says about it, and go on from there.

First, it is now in the hands of God on the throne. It has been in the archives of heaven all these weary centuries since far off Eden.

Second, it is little. In the account of the Great White Throne Judgment, John saw "The books" out of which the dead were judged, "According to their works." Also, he saw another book. "The Book of Life." Those whose names were not found in this Book of Life were cast into the Lake of Fire. No doubt the word "Little" is here used for a comparison with other books that were not little. The Book of Life is a great book. In it will be found the names of every person whose right it is to enter heaven. The other books mentioned contain the life history of every man, woman and child. Those in the Book of Life will receive rewards based on the contents of these books. Those whose names are not in the Book of Life will receive punishment according to information found in these books.

Third, it is sealed with seven seals. Since seven is a number denoting completeness, it means the sealing is complete. In ancient Israel it was the custom to have two copies of any legal document. One copy was open and available for anyone to see and read. The other was sealed and could be opened only by judicial act, and that by a person with the proper authority. This could be said about the Bible as the open record, and this "Little Book" as the sealed record.

Fourth, it can only be opened by the proper person. John wept much because no one seemingly could be found worthy to break the seals, open the book and reveal its contents. In the simplest terms, it is like our postal system today. First class, registered and insured mail is not to be opened or tampered with by anyone but persons authorized to do so. Severe penalties are meted out to those who disregard these postal regulations. Only one person, the Lion of the Tribe of Judah (Jesus Christ) has this right and this book will remain with all its seven seals intact until that time when God hands the Little Book to His Son and the seal-breaking begins.

Sixth, at the breaking of each seal there is great activity on the earth, mostly in the form of chastisements of the earth-dwellers.

Seventh, when the seals are all finally broken, the "Mighty Angel" (Jesus Christ) comes down from heaven, sets His right foot upon the sea and His left foot upon the earth, and formally takes possession.

Looking at the foregoing in an inverted order, it becomes apparent that the Little Book has to do with the planet on which man lives, and the question as to whom it really belongs.

* * * * * * *

In order to lay a little background, let us digress somewhat and look at this planet a little. There are many mysterious things about our earth. Scientists tell us it is billions of years old. Some say the universe is expanding, others say it is shrinking and dying. Some say that once upon a time many billions of years ago, there was a huge mass of hot gas thrown out from the sun. As the gas swirled around in space it collected bits of meteorites and other waste material of the universe, until finally there was a solid crust around this mass of hot gas. They point to the eruption of volcanoes as this gas breaking to the surface, bringing with it molten lava. Others disagree and say the core of the earth is nickel. On and on the theories run.

To the Bible believer much of this is sheer nonsense. After all their fine spun theories of the creation of the earth, the Bible still says, "In the beginning God created the heavens and the earth." Let the scientists fling their astronomical figures around like tennis balls if they so desire, the Bible still says, "In the beginning God...."

It is widely accepted as a fact by many who accept the plenary inspiration of the Scriptures that the earth was created some six thousand years ago. They go to the average Bible and see at the top of the column in the center of the page "4004 B.C." But this center column is not part of the inspired record. This is the figure chronologists have come up with as the date of the creation of man. And the dispensational interpretation of the Bible events appear to agree with this as the time when man first appeared on earth.

But what about the earth itself? Was it created only six thousand years ago? A careful reading of the first two chapters of Genesis will fail to bear this out. As some have pointed out, between the first and second verses of the first chapters of Genesis is room for any age figure anyone might suggest. Whatever this figure might be, the final authority says, "In the beginning God...."

Look at the next few verses. Forget for the time being everything you have ever heard about them, and take the words just as they come from the inspired recorder. The second verse says, *"The earth was without form and void; and darkness was upon the face of the deep, and the Spirit of God moved upon the face of the waters."* In this second verse we find the earth *already here*. But it was a formless void. Not only that, but *the deep was here,* and *water was here!*

In the twelfth chapter of this present study will be found an account of Satan as Lucifer under the heading of "The Trail of the Serpent." Fuller disclosures of his footprints will be found there. Suffice it to say here that from many veiled references to this slimy creature, it appears this planet was his habitation before his fall. When he fell there was a great cataclysmical judgment visited upon the earth. Evidence of such calamities are found in many places in the form of strange formations of the earth's surface which can be explained only as resulting from some such action.

For instance, in the Swiss Alps there is an example of rock folding on a gigantic scale. A picture was published recently with this explanation: "This particularly impressive fold . . . offers a striking evidence of the power exerted by the mountain building forces in the course of the earth's history. Such folding has often occurred where stratified rocks of various types ... were compressed and forced up into ridges which ultimately became our mountains." Although rejected by most modern day scientists, one explanation of the one time convulsions of our terrestrial ball could be that this happened at the awful time when Lucifer was dethroned.

When we come to the second verse of Genesis one, we find the earth and its atmosphere all jumbled together. The earth was here but it was a formless void. The sea was here but it was covered with darkness. Water was here in the atmosphere as well as in the deep.

After the moving of the Spirit of God upon the waters, the first thing God did was to speak light into existence. If we accept the teaching there was absolutely nothing here until God began to move, as recorded in this second verse, then we run into difficulties. The record says God created light the first day, but did not create the sun, moon and stars until the fourth day. If this is the case, from where did this light come? If we will accept the proposition that the creation was really a RE-creation and a RE-setting in proper order of all things pertaining to our earth, then everything will fall into its natural sequence.

The paragraph heading in the Scofield Bible says the sun, moon and stars *became visible* on the fourth day. This would be the natural order then: the darkness was dispelled and light was allowed to break through the first day, but fog and mist still kept the heavenly from being visible on the earth. Thus the rotation of the earth allowed a day and night to be observed.

In the second day there was a further action when the waters "above the firmament" and the "waters below the firmament" were divided. The third day saw the land appear, as the waters were drained off and gathered into the area called the seas. Also, this day saw the appearance of plant life. And it was only on the fourth day that the sun shone, and the fourth night that the moon and stars appeared. Animal life appeared on the fifth day, and man was created on the sixth.

After going off in this lengthy tangent to lay some ground work, the Little Book will be studied further. Since the earth was given to Lucifer he has claimed possession even after having been ejected from his exalted position. To him, man is the intruder. This is one of the many reasons he has such animosity toward the human race. God's plan has been to replace his angels with man. And as "Perfect Man" Jesus Christ will also fill the place on this earth vacated by this monster.

Thus the battle rages. Who owns the earth? The Little Book holds the answer. It is now kept in the archives of heaven. Chapter by chapter, the book has been compiled. In it the fall of Lucifer is recorded. In it will be found the fall of man. Also, in it will be found a sort of index to the books out of which the wicked dead will be judged at the Great White Throne Judgment. The whole sorry record of fallen men and angels is outlined.

The foregoing is just half the picture. There is another side. In it the plan of man's redemption is recorded. The ministry, death and resurrection of Jesus Christ find a large place here. The account of the battles and triumphs of God's people hold a prominent place. Its full contents will not be disclosed until the last seal has been broken, the last trumpet blast sounded and the last woe visited upon unregenerate humanity. More will be said about this Little Book when the tenth chapter is reached.

* * * * * * *

After this somewhat extended discussion on the Little Book, we now return to the scene before us. As the fifth chapter opens we find God on the throne. He is holding this Little Book in His right hand. A "Strong Angel" seeks someone to break the seals, open the Little Book and reveal its contents. Heaven, earth and under the earth are searched, but it looks as if no one will be found worthy to do this.

There is a pause in the action. Angels hover over the scene in perfect silence. Elders and Living Creatures become absolutely motionless. The Apostle John is overcome with grief; tears flow freely from his saintly eyes. He wonders if the Little Book will ever be opened and its contents revealed. Upon observing this, one of the Elders tells him not to weep. Someone worthy has been found—"The Lion of the Tribe of Judah." The seer looks in the midst of the throne, the Living Creatures and Elders. He beholds a "Lamb slain from the foundation of the world." This Lamb takes the Little Book out of the right hand of the One on the throne.

What is this Little Book? It is the title deed to this earth! This is what man forfeited in Eden. This is what will be redeemed legally when all the seals have been broken and the Mighty Angel of the tenth chapter sets "His right foot upon the sea, and his left foot upon the earth." But it will become an actuality only after everything connected with the sounding of the seventh trumpet shall have transpired.

In connection with this Little Book and its place in the plan of the redemption of mankind, a few words will be given about it.

CHRIST, OUR KINSMAN REDEEMER

God's design for man's redemption is prefigured in the Law of Moses. This law said an Israelite could not be held in perpetual servitude. He could not be permanently dispossessed of his land. Even though he sold himself or his land to a fellow Israelite there were provisions whereby everything could be redeemed.

The law itself is found in Leviticus: "And if a sojourner or stranger wax rich by thee, and thy brother that dwelleth by him wax poor, and sell himself unto the stranger or sojourner by thee, or to the stock of the stranger's family; After that he is sold he may be redeemed again. One of his brethren may redeem him: Either his uncle, or his uncle's son, may redeem him, or any that is nigh of kin unto him of his family may redeem him; or if he be able, he may redeem himself" (Lev. 25:47-49).

An example of the outworkings of this law is given in the book of Ruth. You remember Naomi with her husband

and two sons, went into the land of Moab. While there the sons married Moabite girls. Husband and sons died in the land. Naomi, with her daughter-in-law Ruth, returned to Bethlehem in the land of Judah.

In endeavouring to earn a livelihood for herself and her mother-in-law, Ruth met the wealthy Boaz. This man desired to make the Moabite girl his wife. He was a near kinsman of Ruth's dead husband. Thus he was eligible to play the part of a kinsman redeemer. Let the writer of this book of romance himself tell how the law of redemption was carried out.

". . . And now, my daughter, fear not; I will do to thee all that thou requirest; for all the city of my people doth know that thou art a virtuous woman. And now it is true that I am thy near kinsman: howbeit there is a kinsman nearer than I. Tarry this night, and it shall be in the morning that if he will perform unto thee the part of a kinsman, well: let him do the kinsman's part: But if he will not do the part of a kinsman to thee, then will I do the part of a kinsman to thee as the Lord liveth."

Then we have where Boaz went through the necessary procedures to establish his right as a kinsman redeemer. *"Then went Boaz up to the gate . . . and behold the kinsman of whom Boaz spake came by. . . . And he said unto the kinsman, Naomi, that is, come again out of the country of Moab, selleth a parcel of land, which was our brother Elimelech's. If thou will redeem* (*buy*) *it, redeem it; but if thou wilt not redeem it, then tell me, that I may know: for there is none to redeem it beside thee; and I am after thee. . . . And the kinsman said, I cannot redeem it, lest I mar mine own inheritance: redeem thou my right to thyself; for I cannot redeem it. . . . And Boaz said unto the elders, I have bought all that was Elimelech's and all that was Chilion's and Mahlon's, of the hand of Naomi. Moreover, Ruth the Moabitess, the wife of Mahlon, have I purchased to be my wife, to raise up the name of the dead upon his inheritance, that the name of the dead be not cut off from his brethren"* (Ruth 4:1, 3, 4b, 6, 9, 10a).

Another example is found in the thirty-second chapter of Jeremiah. The prophet's cousin, Hanamell, had a field which he wanted to sell. According to the law of Moses, only a near kinsman was eligible to purchase it. Jeremiah, being an acceptable purchaser, was instructed of the Lord to buy the field.

From this law and these examples, together with references to the subject here and there throughout the Scriptures, there emerges a beautiful outline of God's plan for the redemption of the human race, and the earth upon which it dwells.

Briefly, there are four qualifications for one to be eligible as a kinsman redeemer. He must be a near kinsman; he must be willing to redeem; he must be able to redeem by having the purchase price; and he must be free to redeem.

In studying this plan of God it is necessary to find out just what condition fallen man is in, how he got that way, and who would be the proper person to play the part of the redeemer.

Man's fall is recorded in Genesis where that first pair met Satan in the form of the serpent, yielded to his temptations, ate of the forbidden fruit and brought sin and ruin upon all succeeding generations.

It was here that man forfeited his inheritance (this earth), and Satan corrupted man's soul and usurped his domain. Here is where this conflict of the ages began. Holy God and sinful man must find a common meeting place where divine justice and inherent sinfulness can be reconciled.

This is illustrated in Israel's law of redemption. The qualifications set forth in Israel's law give a picture of the redemption of man and the earth on which he lives. But just who in all the universe can fulfill such requirements?

The first necessity was that the redeemer must be a near kinsman. Even God the Father Himself does not have this qualification. He is not our kinsman according to the flesh.

Next, the redeemer must be willing to perform this service. When Moses told God to blot his name out of the book of life along with the rebellious Israelites in the wilderness if He were going to do this to the rebels, he proved he was willing to be their redeemer. Likewise, Paul, who could wish himself accursed for the sake of his brethren according to the flesh, showed there was at least one other person who could fit such a category. But these were not qualified.

As the third thing necessary was that one must have

the redemption price, sufficient for all mankind. This is where all but Deity is ruled out.

The last requirement is that he must be free to redeem. Since all men are born in sin, it follows that no sinful man could be free to redeem another sinful human.

You see what a dilemma is presented here. God Himself could not redeem us. Although He created us, He is not our kinsman according to the flesh. Although some man may be willing to die for other men's sins, his own sin-infected blood would not be sufficient to remove his sins and those of others.

So, to sum up: God was not eligible as a redeemer. Man does not have the redemption price, nor is he free himself. There is only one solution—God must become man, but at the same time remain God.

No wonder the seemingly futile search was made in the fifth chapter of the Revelation. BUT A REDEEMER WAS FOUND! He is Jesus Christ, the Son of God—"Very God and Perfect Man." He fulfilled the requirements of being a near kinsman according to the flesh. This is the one over-riding ground for His coming to earth in the form of man.

He was willing to be our Redeemer. He proved this by His life, death and resurrection on earth. His love for mankind was equalled only by that of God the Father. He had the redemption price—His own precious blood, which He shed freely at Calvary. He was free to redeem. He alone of all humanity was born without sin. His blood was pure—sinless. So it alone could be used as an innoculation to destroy the virus of sin in our own contaminated blood.

* * * * * * *

After Christ takes the Little Book, there is another and greater worship service. In the fourth chapter these Elders and Living Creatures fall down and worship before God on the throne. In this chapter the Lamb is the One to whom they pay divine homage.

These Elders and Living Creatures have harps with which they make sweet music. Also, they have golden odor-filled vials. These contain the prayers of saints. These prayers will be answered as the events of the end-time unfold. No doubt the great burden of these petitions will be that "the kingdom of God should come, and the will of God be done in earth as it is in heaven."

Finally, both groups burst forth in a song of praise to

the Lamb. The message of the first stanza of this song has to do with Christ's worthiness to break the seals of the Little Book and reveal its contents. The second tells of the crucifixion. The third speaks of redemption. The fourth deals with the kingship and priesthood of the saints. The fifth and final stanza reaches a grand climax in the anticipation of the reign of the saints on earth.

John is filled with holy gladness when he hears this song. A little later hosts of angels began their lovely declamation of Christ's worthiness. They do not seem to sing as do the other groups. They speak out in mighty poetic tones. It takes but a few seconds to read in the Bible what these angels say, but no doubt these words are just the titles of the different verses of this heavenly poem. As with the others, the first verse has to do with Christ's worthiness. The second verse says He is worthy to receive power. The third speaks of the riches of which He is worthy. The fourth speaks of His wisdom. The fifth speaks of his strength. The sixth gives Him honor. The seventh ascribes to Him glory and the final verse tells of His worthiness to receive blessings.

At this point the worship service is just getting started. After the Living Creatures, Elders and angels play on harps, sing lovely songs and recite heavenly poetry, there is a pause. The groans of creation cease for a time. The whale, hundreds of fathoms below the surface of the ocean stops his restless moving. Wild animals of the jungle become quiet and forget to seek their prey. Domestic animals likewise become motionless. Birds in flight become still, gliding through the air. The whole creation waits in unexplained anticipation.

This silence does not last for long. Soon *"Every creature which is in heaven and on the earth and under the earth, and such as are in the sea"* burst forth in glad praise in expectation of the time when they, like man, will be redeemed from the universal curse. They ascribe blessing and honor and glory and power to God on the throne and to the Lamb for what is soon to transpire. All who enter into this service ascribe to God and the Lamb worthiness to receive honor, power, and glory. The Four Living Creatures pronounce the benediction and the scene closes with the Twenty-Four Elders prostrate in worship to *"Him that liveth forever and ever."*

CHAPTER SIX

THE TRIBULATION JUDGMENT COURT
(Concluded)

BREAKING OF THE SEALS

"And I saw when the Lamb opened one of the seals, and I heard as it were the noise of thunder, one of the four beasts (Living Creatures) *saying, Come and see"* (Revelation 6:1).

The sixth chapter records the beginnings of the Great Tribulation proper. As it opens we find the rapture over and the Bride gone. The Judgment Court is in session. The Little Book is in possession of the "Lion of the Tribe of Judah" (Christ). The worship service is finished. Everything is in readiness for the wheels of divine justice to start grinding out their full measure of retribution.

The Lion of the Tribe of Judah has now begun operations. He is tearing the seven seals from the Little Book. He is to reveal to the world its true possessor. The Four Living Creatures are playing their part in the performance. They are much interested in these events. These proceedings hold them fascinated unto the end. They call forth the first four judgments on the earth as the first four seals are broken.

The significance of numbers in Scripture is illustrated in the process of the opening of these seven seals. Seven is the number combining heaven and earth. There are the four of earth and the three of heaven. This pattern is followed here. The action following the breaking of the first four seals is directed by the Four Living Creatuers as they call forth the four horsemen. The influences let loose as revealed in their riding forth stems from the activities of man, as he is moved on by such forces. The tenuous peace, wars, famine and death are in a great measure the results of man's actions.

The breaking of the last three of these seals lets loose on the world forces controlled entirely by spiritual powers —both divine and diabolical. While the martyrs seen at the breaking of the fifth seal became martyrs as a result of man's activities, this scene is one in which divine influences play a major role. The sixth seal discloses cosmic disturbances on a scale never before experienced. The results of the opening of the seventh seal is the breaking down of the partition between the spirit world and the physical world. In this activity, man is just a pawn.

* * * * * * *

Centuries and millenniums have come and gone since sin first entered into the world and infected mankind. And failure is written largely on all efforts to cure the awful malady of evil. Because of man's inherent sinfulness, animal sacrifices have claimed their millions of unwilling victims. Prophets have thundered out their message of doom to mankind in calls to repentance, with only limited success. Christ has come and done His work of redemption. The Gospel has been preached throughout the world. But man still lives on in rebellion against God. The only thing left is judgment.

In the second Psalm God promised Christ that He would give Him the heathen for His inheritance, and the uttermost part of the earth for His possession. Also, that He (Christ) would break them with a rod of iron, and dash them in pieces like a potter's vessel. Saints of God, as represented by the overcomers in the church of Thyatira, also were promised power over the nations, and they, too, would rule them with a rod of iron and break them in shivers like a potter's vessel. The time has now come. The breaking and dashing to pieces will soon begin. This is necessary before a benevolent rule will become a reality. Only the Great Tribulation will make this possible. But after this will come the wonderful Millennium during which Christ shall reign with His people from earthly Jerusalem.

SEAL ONE—THE WHITE HORSE

"And I saw, and behold a white horse, and he that sat upon him had a bow; and a crown was given unto him: and he went forth conquering and to conquer" (Rev. 6:2).

Here Christ opens the first seal on the Little Book. When He does, the first Living Creature, described as like a lion, calls forth a White Horse, whose rider has a bow in his hand and a crown on his head. He rides out as a continuing conqueror.

In endeavoring to understand this scene, remember that these four horses and their riders form a group. Rules for understanding their significance must apply to all. It is easy to see that the Red, Black and Pale Horses and their riders personify War, Famine and Death. But what about the White Horse?

Since the color of the other three horses serves as an indication of their work and activities, the same must apply to the shade of this first horse. In the Bible white stands for righteousness, purity, holiness, peace mercy and many other like attributes. So, to be consistent, this creature must be identified from attributes to which his shade points.

There are those who see in the White Horse a deceptiveness, marking him as an evil personification. Some go so far as to make this rider the personal Antichrist. Others go to the opposite extreme and recognize him as Christ Himself. Both interpretations are wrong. When this rider is made out as an individual and the other riders are made out as symbols, the rules of interpretation are ignored.

Let the shade of this horse and the equipment and activities of this rider find natural interpretation in the generally accepted symbolism of the Bible, and some of the difficulties will be cleared up. So, from the foregoing, it appears that this first horse and rider picture a benevolent force.

If the text be allowed to interpret itself, this explanation of the White Horse has ample support. It is when plain words are not allowed to tell their story that many questionable devices have to be employed to make a theory stand up.

This White Horse rider has a bow. Usually the bow is associated with warfare. But the bow has at least two other connotations, according to the Bible—the bow in the clouds forming the rainbow, and the bow as the Word of God as noted in Habakkuk 3:8, "Thy bow was made quite naked . . . even thy word." Thus there are three meanings in Scripture for the bow—as the rainbow, as the Word of God and as signifying warfare.

In the fourth chapter John sees "A rainbow about the

throne." In the sixth chapter he sees a bow in connection with the White Horse. There could be an indirect connection here. With all this in mind it is concluded that this White Horse represents God's mercy in time of tribulation. Here we have a view of God's plan for getting multitudes ready before the world is completely engulfed in the Great Tribulation. David sings, "I will sing of mercy and judgment" (Psa. 101:1). The Bible reminds us in at least twenty-six places that God's mercy endureth forever.

It is not far-fetched to see in the symbol of the bow a three-phase interpretation. This rainbow of God's never-ending mercy arching the dark clouds of the coming Tribulation; the Word of God as breaking into shivers man's rebellious nature, causing multitudes who have missed the rapture to turn from their evil ways; the bow of remedial judgment God uses so often and so successfully in allowing personal calamities, etc. In support of this Isaiah tells us, "When thy judgments are in the earth, the inhabitants of the world will learn righteousness" (Isa. 26:9).

The rider on the White Horse has a crown given him. A crown signifies rule and authority. Just when this crown will be given to him we are not told. But the simplest and most logical explanation is that it is given just prior to his riding forth. Whatever he will be doing will be at the behest of the One giving him the crown. As this is an action directly from heaven to earth it is felt this crown is given by Christ Himself, and represents the authority of heaven.

The purpose of the judgment instigated by the rider on the White Horse is remedial and not punitive. It takes place in order that man may make a choice at this late hour whether to turn to God or not.

The last thing to be noted is that the efforts of this White Horse rider will be successful. We are told that "He went forth conquering and to conquer." This sets the tone for God's remedial judgments for the entire Tribulation Period. This means that, overshadowing the awful calamities visited upon mankind, will be the brooding presence of God's Holy Spirit, with His never-exhausting supply of mercy toward those who will turn from their wickedness.

There is a question as to just how long these four horsemen will ride. Will each have a time to ride, marked off in days, months or years; or will the influence continue throughout the entire period? This could be interpreted either one or both ways. All during the period there will be God's mercy, war, famine and death. But possibly there will be a time in the early part of the Tribulation when each of these influences will be a major factor in determining the course of events.

In dealing with humanity in judgment God always takes care of His own. We have examples of this even in the antediluvian age. Before God sent the flood He translated Enoch, and instructed Noah to build the ark for the saving of his household. So, before the beginning of the Great Tribulation proper God will transport His Bride and the Bridal company to heaven, and they will miss the entire period of judgment. The work of the White Horse rider is to get multitudes of "left" ones ready for whatever their lot may be in the Tribulation—enduring, sealing, rapturing or dying.

After the first shock caused by the disappearance of multitudes of individuals from the earth as a result of the rapture, the world settles down to its regular routine, and the work of the White Horse Rider is swallowed up in the overall picture. Merchants will return to their merchandising; industrialist will begin running their factories at full capacity. Politicians will resume their campaigning and scheming. Many churches will conduct services as usual, giving only lip-service to Christ, while engaging in their own selfish pursuits. Newspapers, television and radio stations will turn to more recent events and the rapture will have been almost forgotten.

SEAL TWO—THE RED HORSE

"And when he had opened the second seal, I heard the second beast say, Come and see. And there went out another horse that was red: and power was given unto him that sat thereon to take peace from the earth, and that they should kill one another: and there was given unto him a great sword" (Revelation 6:3, 4).

In the continuing action Christ opens the second seal. The second Living Creature, who is described as like a calf, calls forth the second horse and rider. This time the horse is red. This symbolizes war and bloodshed in every area of life.

The first thing noticed about the Red Horse is that his rider is given the power to take peace from the earth. This would indicate that, relatively speaking, there will be a period of peace during the time of the White Horse. Of course, the peace will be only relative. Compared to the conditions at the time of the Red Horse it will be a period of peace. However, this previous period is of short duration.

The present turmoil and violence throughout the world give a little preview of what will happen when the rider on the Red Horse comes forth. Right now the nations of the world are like a putrifying mass of corruption in a seething cauldron of decaying flesh, ready to boil over at the slightest increase of heat. Today's world is an armed camp. China with three quarters of a billion people is threatening to break out of her boundaries and start foraging on her neighbors. Not only that, she has her agents throughout the world, fomenting revolution. Russia, with almost a quarter of a billion, has her guns trained on the trouble spots of the earth. She is ready to protect her interest and impose her way of life on people wherever possible. The United States and her allies are armed to the teeth. They expect trouble any time. Lethal weapons are everywhere. Mustard and nerve gas are stored and ready for instant use should the occasion arise. Biological and germ warfare are much in the thinking of military men. Rockets are being manufactured and deployed at strategic places, ready to become operative at a moment's notice. Above and beyond all these are the bombs—atomic, hydrogen, cobalt, etc. And worse of all there is the laser beam.

The United States and her allies have recently been at war with the Communist countries. Armies of the large countries have not actually been meeting on the battlefields of the world, but weapons of war were furnished the smaller nations to carry on the struggle. Russia and China furnished war supplies to North Vietnam. The United States furnished war material to Israel with which to fight the Arabs; Russia does the same thing for the Arabs.

All this can mean but one thing. After Christ comes for His Bride and the short period of tenuous peace is over, all the danger spots of the earth are apt to explode at once. This will probably happen when the rider on the Red Horse takes peace from the earth.

This will be different from anything the world has ever experienced in the past in the way of warfare. It will not be just nation against nation; it will be man against man. Black men and white men will be at war with each other. Everyone will take up arms against his imagined oppressors. Patriotism and national loyalty as now known will be things of the past. These things are shown by the statement, "...Power was given him ... to take peace from the earth, and that they should kill one another."

The rider of this Red Horse will have in his possession a "Great Sword." Just what this sword represents is a matter of conjecture. Under present conditions it could be a so-called "Peace keeping" arm of the United Nations. In theory, this UN peace keeping army was involved in Korea and intangled in Vietnam, with the United States bearing the major responsibility for both operations. Whatever the meaning of the "Great Sword," it will be used in wholesale slaughter.

SEAL THREE—BLACK HORSE

"And when he had opened the third seal, I heard the third beast (Living Creature) *say, Come and see. And I beheld, and lo a black horse. And he that sat on him had a pair of balances in his hand. And I heard a voice in the midst of the four beasts say, A measure of wheat for a penny, and three measures of barley for a penny; and see thou hurt not the oil and the wine"* (Revelation 6:5, 6).

After the Red Horse has come and gone, Christ will break the third seal. The Living Creature, described as like a man, will call forth the third horse. This horse is black—signifying famine. Already famine on a world-wide scale is being predicted by the experts. They say it will come in the 1980's. If these men are right, this could well be the famine under the symbol of the Black Horse. Right now there is a world-wide shortage of food. Millions of people go to bed hungry every night, and starvation is a way of life for whole populations on some parts of the globe.

This voice in the midst of the Four Living Creatures speaks of wheat, barley and oil and wine. In John's day these were staple products of every day living. They characterize the necessities and luxuries of life. Ordinarily wheat and barley were not expensive products. When there was a good supply they were correspondingly cheap, but under the hoofs of the Black Horse one will pay dearly for these common food necessities.

In the time when this was visioned the penny or denarius was worth about twenty cents in American money. This was about the daily earnings of a laboring man or soldier. This measure was about a quart. Hence, a quart of wheat for a day's labor, and three quarts of barley for a day's labor. This rider has a pair of balances in his hand to measure the wheat and barley, showing their great scarcity.

There is a difference of opinion among writers as to what the phrase, "See thou hurt not the oil and the wine," means. One thought is that these luxury items will be out of the reach of most of the people of that day. Another thought is that there will be a shortage of these items—"So just forget about them." Possibly both are right. Because ordinary food is so scarce it will take all the money people can get to purchase it. What luxuries there are will be entirely out of the reach of most people.

SEAL FOUR—PALE HORSE

"And when he had opened the fourth seal, I heard the voice of the fourth beast say, Come and see. And I looked, and behold a pale horse: and his name that sat on him was Death, and Hell followed with him. And power was given unto them over the fourth part of the earth to kill with sword, and with hunger, and with death, and with the beasts of the earth" (Revelation 6:7, 8).

As a natural consequence of the going forth of the riders on the Red and Black Horses, the man on the Pale Horse will be called forth. This will be done by the fourth Living Creature, like unto an eagle. You will notice a natural sequence in the riding of these four horsemen. Under the White Horse peace of a sort prevails for a time. But with the coming of the Red Horse is soon broken and war starts. This naturally causes a shortage of food. Almost always in wartime there are shortages of the necessities of life. Witness America's shortages in the two world wars. Rationing was the order of the day. When armies are locked in mortal combat there are not enough people left free to grow and process sufficient food. Add to this the possibility of a crop failure for a year or two because of drought or insects, and you will find the food supply short indeed.

This is when Death begins to reap his grisly harvest as a result of war and famine. Also, wild beasts are allowed to multiply in some sections of the world and become a menace to man. Disease is the natural result of war and famine. When this man on the Pale Horse rides forth he will be given power over the fourth part of the earth. The sword, hunger, beasts and disease will take their toll.

SEAL FIVE—SOULS UNDER THE ALTAR

"And when he had opened the fifth seal, I saw under the altar the souls of them that were slain for the word of God, and for the testimony which they held: And they cried with a loud voice, saying, How long, O Lord, Holy and True, dost thou not judge and avenge our blood on them that dwell on the earth? and white robes were given unto every one of them; and it was said unto them, that they should rest a little season until their fellowservants also and their brethren that should be killed as they were, should be fulfilled" (Revelation 6:9-11).

During this time of great trouble, those Christians who have failed to make the rapture will be subjected to severe persecutions, Satanic forces will seek to blame them for all the troubles of the world. As a consequence, multitudes will be slain. This martyr group is seen when the fifth seal is opened. John sees them as disembodied souls. They are under the heavenly altar. In the Jewish economy this place under the altar was where the blood of the sacrificial victims ran out.

These "Souls" do not understand why their blood is not being avenged. True, they have missed the rapture, but now they have made up for any shortcomings by dying the martyr's death. Why should not something be done for their vindication? Instead of vengeance being poured out on their executioners, these "Souls" are given white robes and told to "Rest a little season." They are informed that others like themselves are to be killed during this awful ordeal, and they, with all the other future martyrs, will come up as a group at the proper time.

SEAL SIX—COSMIC DISTURBANCES

"And I beheld when he had opened the sixth seal, and, lo, there was a great earthquake; and the sun became black as sackcloth of hair, and the moon became as blood; and the stars of heaven fell unto the earth, even as a fig tree casteth her untimely figs, when she is shaken of a mighty wind. And the heavens departed as a scroll when it is rolled together; and every mountain and island were moved out of their places. And the kings of the earth, and the great men, and the rich men, and the chief captains, and the mighty men, and every bondman and every free man, hid themselves in the dens and the rocks of the mountains; And said unto the mountains and the rocks, Fall on us, and hide us from the face of him that sitteth on the throne, and from the wrath of the Lamb: For the great day of his wrath is come; and who shall be able to stand?" (Rev. 6:12-17.)

The actions produced by the opening of the first five seals are brought about somewhat through the instrumentality of men. The uneasy peace is broken by war, which is shown by the second seal. As a consequence of the opening of the second seal, war, famine and death are brought about. Now we come to the opening of this sixth seal. Under it is seen the quaking earth, the blackened sun, the bloody moon, the departing heavens, the shaking mountains and the moving islands. These disturbances of nature are the direct actions of Almighty God, and man has nothing whatsoever to do with them.

The effect of this awful cataclysm is seen when kings of the earth, great men, rich men, chief captains, along with ordinary men, cry for rocks and mountains to fall on them and hide them from the face of an angry God. Finally, man is made to realize these things are evidence of divine judgment. But rocks and mountains will not hide man from God. Each must stand before Divine Justice and give a personal account for himself. In this period men will want to hide from God, but few will want to repent.

CHAPTER SEVEN

THE ONE HUNDRED AND FORTY-FOUR THOUSAND ISRAELITES

"After these things I saw four angels standing on the four corners of the earth, holding the four winds of the earth, that the wind should not blow on the earth, nor on the sea, nor on any tree. And I saw another angel ascending from the east, having the seal of the living God: and he cried with a loud voice to the four angels to whom it was given to hurt the earth and the sea, Saying, Hurt not the earth, neither the sea, nor the trees till we have sealed the servants of God in their foreheads" (Revelation 7:1-3).

The Tribulation rushes on with undiminished fury toward its awful climax at Armageddon. Devastating judgments have left the world prostrate. How much more can man endure and still retain any semblance of sanity? How much more can the earth suffer before it disintegrates? War, famine, death and convulsions of nature have made a shambles of everything thought stable and permanent.

Added to these are even greater calamities to come. Four judgment angels are poised and ready to call forth sorrows which will immerse the earth in a fiery baptism. Also, they are prepared to announce a black-out of the sun, moon and stars in an Egyptian night even surpassing the darkness of Pharaoh's kingdom during the ninth plague ordered by Moses.

Suddenly a halt is ordered by an angel with the "Seal of the living God." He commands these angels to hold back the winds of destruction. Hold back the hail, fire and blood, they are told. Do not burn up the trees and grass. Do not let the sea water become blood. Do not destroy the ships. Do not contaminate the rivers and fountains with wormwood. Hold back the darkness. Let the heavenly bodies give their light. Say nothing about the three terrible woes yet to come.

The reason for holding all this in abeyance is that there is a group of people who must be protected from these winds of destruction. They are introduced in this chapter. There are one hundred and forty-four thousand of them. Who are they? Why anyone would try to make them out as being any other than whom John records them to be is hard to understand. They are Israelites—twelve thousand from each of the ancient tribes. They are not just Jews, since the Jews are mainly descendants of Judah, Benjamin and Levi, but from all the tribes.

By a careful reading it will be observed that while there are twelve tribes mentioned, they do not follow the exact order of the births of the twelve sons of Jacob. Also, it will be seen that Dan is left out entirely, while Joseph comes into the picture to be substituted for Ephraim. Going back to the account of the birth of these twelve sons in Genesis, and the meaning of each name, it can be understood why Dan and Ephraim were left out. According to Lehman Strauss, the reason Dan was left out of the Revelation roster is that he was an idolater. Dr. Seiss says that since Dan means *judging,* and judging has no place in the activities of the one hundred and forty-four thousand, to include his tribe here would not be appropriate. Seiss also explains why Ephraim was left out. He says the word "Ephraim" means *increase* or *growth by multiplication,* and this company includes exactly one hundred and forty-four thousand—no more; no less. They will never be increased nor decreased.

The above mentioned writer has taken the meanings of the twelve tribes mentioned here and has strung them together in the same order as Revelation gives them, and has come up with this interesting combination: *"Confessors or praisers of God, looking upon a Son, a band of blessed ones, wrestling with forgetfulness, hearing and obeying the word, cleaving unto the reward of a shelter and a home, an addition, son of the day of God's right hand, begotten in the extremity of the age."*

These are to receive the seal of the living God in their foreheads. This seal has to do with setting them apart from the rest of Israel and enabling them to face the terrible times ahead. Two references are found which throw light on this sealing. Paul, speaking to the Ephesians says, *"Also, after that ye believed, ye were sealed with that Holy Spirit of promise, which is the earnest* (pledge) *of our inheritance until the redemption of the purchased possession"* (Eph. 1:13, 14). Continuing in the same book; *"Grieve not the Holy Spirit of God, whereby we are sealed unto the day of redemption"* (Eph. 4:30). Scofield points out the fact that the Holy Spirit Himself is a seal. "A seal in the symbolism of Scripture signifies (1) A finished transaction; (2) Ownership; (3) Security."

From these words one is led to understand this seal is "The Holy Spirit of promise." This seal was stamped upon the one hundred and twenty disciples in the upper room in Jerusalem on the Day of Pentecost. Here are a few salient facts about that event: *"They were all in one accord and in one place ... sound from heaven as a rushing mighty wind ... filled the house ... appeared cloven tongues as of fire ... sat upon each of them ... all filled with the Holy Ghost* (Spirit); ... *began to speak with other tongues."*

This phenomena was repeated at the household of Cornelius, at Ephesus and other places as recorded in the book of Acts. According to the tenor of Paul's writings, it was a normal experience for the early Christians. And it is a normal experience for millions of Christians today.

From the foregoing it seems reasonable that this is the experience by which and with which the one hundred and forty-four thousand Israelites will be sealed. It is a spiritual experience which raises them to the highest plane of holy sainthood. Their description as given in the fourteenth chapter corresponds to this. *"They are not defiled; they are virgins* (holy); *they follow the Lamb. They are without fault. They are without guilt."* If it seems far-fetched that spiritual experiences will be received during the Tribulation, remember, God does not turn the world over to Satan in this period. The Holy Spirit does not leave the earth (as some contend). Men can and will be converted and receive spiritual blessings all during the Tribulation. If this were not the case, then why would God allow the Tribulation anyway? Why would He not just consign all the wicked to hell and the Lake of Fire, unless He had provisions for penitent souls to find escape?

The sealing of the one hundred and forty-four thousand takes place just prior to the opening of the seventh seal. This opening not only is the signal for fiery judgments, darkness and woes, but marks the beginning of the seven year reign of the Beast or Antichrist. This reign begins with the signing of the seven year covenant with Israel. And, since the one hundred and forty-four thousand are of Israel, the great burden of their ministry will be to expose and denounce this seven year covenant as "A covenant with death and an agreement with hell."

Their activities bring forth determined opposition from the newly instituted government of Antichrist, and extreme embarrassment for Israel. However, neither the Antichrist government nor Israel can harm them; they have the seal of the living God in their foreheads, and are miraculously preserved until their work is finished. They will then be raptured to heaven under the figure to be discussed at a later time.

THE WHITE ROBED PALM BEARERS

"After this I beheld, and lo, a great multitude, which no man could number, of all nations and kindreds, and peoples, and tongues, stood before the throne, and before the Lamb, clothed with white robes, and palms in their hands; And one of the Elders answered saying unto me, What are these which are arrayed in white robes? and whence came they? And I said unto him, Sir, thou knowest, And he said unto me, These are they which came out of great tribulation, and have washed their robes, and made them white in the blood of the Lamb" (Revelation 7:9, 14).

After John sees the sealing of the one hundred and forty-four thousand on earth, his attention is turned again to heaven, and the activities going on there. He beholds an innumerable company "Before the throne and before the Lamb." This group of people wear white robes and carry palms in their hands, and are from "All nations, and kindreds, and peoples, and tongues." They are "Before the throne and before the Lamb," and "are they which come up *out of great tribulation* and have washed their robes, and made them white in the blood of the Lamb."

These are not the Bride and her company. She is already in heaven—seen under the figure of the Four Living Creatures. They are not martyrs because the martyrs are identified as the "Souls under the altar" under the fifth seal. And they are distinct from the one hundred and forty-four thousand as the text plainly shows. In brief, they are a company of God's people who are raptured from the earth before the opening of the seventh seal, and the beginning of the most horrible part of the Tribulation.

Notice the Antichrist as the Beast is not mentioned in connection with this company. This indicates they have reached this state before the Antichrist appears. Remember, the Beast does not appear until the beginning of the last seven years of the Tribulation, and is not fully revealed until three and one-half years later.

Some teach that there will be exactly seven years from the catching away of the Bride until Armageddon. For this to be the case it would mean at the catching away of the Bride the Antichrist would have everything all ready for signing the seven year covenant with Israel. Internal evidence in Revelation indicates there will be an indeterminate period between the rapture and the beginning of the Antichrist's reign. Just read the text and accept it for just what it says.

The "Souls under the altar" show that there was a great slaughter of God's people up to this time. However, nothing is said about the Antichrist. This white robed, palm bearing multitude are said to "Have come out of great tribulation," but nothing is said about the Beast. It is not until the fifteenth chapter that a group is introduced who had "Gotten the victory over the beast, and over his image, and over his mark, and over the number of his name." All this tends to prove that a period of great judgment will take place before the appearing of the Antichrist. In fact, to let the Bible interpret itself one would be inclined to say the Beast or Antichrist does not appear until the opening of the seventh seal. And even then he is not fully revealed until the seventh trumpet is sounded.

There will be a great harvest of souls during the first part of the Tribulation. Some will be killed as we saw under the fifth seal. But some will be raptured during the Tribulation. This company seen in the latter half of this chapter is one such raptured group.

Up to this point in Revelation, five companies of God's people have been seen. They are the Bride and the Bridal company, as symbolized by the four Living Creatures; the Old Testament saints under the figure of the Twenty-four Elders; the Tribulation martyrs, some of whom are seen as "souls under the altar," under the fifth seal; the one hundred and forty-four thousand Israelites, and this innumerable multitude of Palm Bearers. As the Tribulation grows progressively worse, still other companies will be raptured out just before some awful judgment is to be meted out.

Notice where this company is. They stand before the throne and before the Lamb. Notice their clothing. They are robed in white. Almost without exception when white is used in the Bible in a symbolical sense, it stands for purity. In Revelation this is especially true. The overcomers in Pergamos were promised a white stone, and in it a new name. The worthies of Sardis were to walk with Christ in white. The Laodiceans were counselled to buy white raiment to cover their nakedness. The golden-crowned Twenty-Four Elders were clothed in white raiment. White robes were given to the "Souls under the altar" at the opening of the fifth seal. At the marriage of the Lamb His Bride will be arrayed in fine linen, clean and white, denoting her righteousness and purity.

Besides all this, there is the white head and hair of Jesus as shown in the first chapter; the white horse of the sixth chapter; the white cloud upon which sat the Son of Man in the fourteenth chapter; the seven angels with the last plagues clothed in pure and white linen. The Great White Throne judgment in the twentieth chapter completes the picture.

Members of this company have palms in their hands. Palms or palm trees were much in evidence all through the history of the ancients. The *International Standard Bible Encyclopedia* tells us: "The palm is a tree which from earliest times has been associated with the Semitic people. In Arabia the very existence of man depends largely upon its presence.... It is only natural that such a tree should have been sacred both there (Arabia) and in Assyria in the earliest ages.... Among the Hebrews it was extensively used as a decoration of the temple." Psalm 29 says, "The righteous shall flourish like the palm tree."

At Jesus' triumphant entry into Jerusalem the week before His crucifixion, multitudes strewed His pathway with palm branches as they took up the cry, "Hosanna; blessed is the king of Israel, that cometh in the name of the Lord." The scene here in this seventh chapter is reminiscent of the earlier one, "Salvation to our God which sitteth upon the throne, and unto the Lamb," they cry with loud voices.

Here we find this company in heaven, in a wonderful worship service. In unison they take up the cry, "Salvation to our God which sitteth upon the throne and unto the Lamb." One reading this may get the impression that this cry is given once and no more. But no doubt this is just the subject matter of this great worship service. Notice, too, that they express themselves with loud voices. They are so overcome with joy that their pent-up feelings can find expression only in this way.

Some of these worship services of Revelation are by one group alone; others are held in which more than one group are involved. Some of these services include all of heaven's hosts and all earthly creation. This white-robed, palm-bearing multitude and the angels participate in this service. For an audience they have the Elders and Living Creatures.

The angels here prostrate themselves before the throne in worship. The outline of this service is something like this: "Amen, let it be so; Blessing be unto our God forever and ever. Thanksgiving be unto our God forever and ever. Might be unto our God forever and ever. Honor be unto our God forever and ever. Power be unto our God forever and ever."

This glorious company is caught away from earth to heaven before the Antichrist begins his bid to be god of the world. They have gone through much sorrow. Some of the group may have been professors of religion at the time of the first phase of the rapture, but just like the foolish virgins in the parable in the twenty-fifth chapter of Matthew, they have gone to the Source of supply and have had their oil replenished.

Others in the group possibly were unconverted at the first phase, and were made to grieve when some of their loved ones mysteriously disappeared. When they realized what had happened they made the necessary preparation so when the call came from heaven for the palm-bearing multitude to "Come up higher," they were permitted to join the glad throng.

Now this assemblage will never hunger any more. It will never have the sun's scorching rays fall upon it any more. It will forever be fed and led to fountains of living waters by the Lamb. Tears will never fall from its eyes; God will have wiped them all away.

CHAPTER EIGHT

OPENING OF THE SEVENTH SEAL

"And when he had opened the seventh seal, there was silence in heaven about the space of half an hour" (Revelation 8:1).

Thundering voices, powerful doxologies, loud singing of songs of high praise and sweet music from celestial harps have been ringing out in heaven's domain ever since the divine spectacle of the end-time began to unfold. In the beginning of this chapter the tempo changes. The thundering voices are stilled; harps are laid aside and absolute silence reigns for "About the space of half an hour." Everything is awaiting the pleasure of the Lamb to reveal what the opening of the last of these seven seals on the Little Book will bring forth.

As one by one the preceding seals were broken, conditions on the earth worsened. War, famine, death and the disturbances of the elements, are like the stepping of a colossus in gigantic strides, bringing certain destruction. What awful things are yet to be revealed, all creation wonders. In this holy hush, beings of the empyreal land fold their wings and redeemed ones from the earth stand in awe and await the end of this interlude. The time has now come to disclose its final secrets.

CHRIST AS HIGH PRIEST

"And I saw the seven angels which stood before God; and to them were given seven trumpets. And another angel came and stood at the altar, having a golden censer; and there was given unto him much incense, that he should offer it with the prayers of all saints upon the golden altar which was before the throne. And the smoke of the incense which came with the prayers of the saints, ascended up before God out of the angel's hand. And the angel took the censer and filled it with fire of the altar, and cast it into the earth: and there were voices, and thunderings, and lightnings, and an earthquake. And the seven angels which had

the seven trumpets prepared themselves to sound" (Revelation 8:2-6).

At the end of this thirty minutes of silence seven angels are seen standing before God—each with a trumpet—ready for action. However, before a note is sounded another angel appears. His duties are that of a priest. Evidently this is Christ Himself.

As the great High Priest He is here offering up to God the prayers of all the saints. Who are these saints? There is a two-fold answer to this question. First, they are the saints of all ages, beginning with righteous Abel and continuing to the last prayer to be prayed. These prayers have come up as a memorial before God. "Unanswered yet, the prayers your lips have pleaded," sang the poet. But they will be answered "Sometime, somewhere." "Right has been on the scaffold and wrong on the throne" so long that some may have despaired. Even so, there is coming a time when every wrong will be made right, and the Great Bookkeeper will strike a just balance. So, do not despair, Christian friend; your unanswered prayers will come up in remembrances when our High Priest presents them before God.

Second, and of even greater concern here, are the prayers of the saints still on earth at the point where this High Priestly function is taking place. From internal evidence it seems certain that at least some of these saints are those who suffer the distresses brought about by the opening of the first six seals right along with the rest of mankind. At least part of the prayers of the martyrs under the fifth seal seems to have been answered when they are told to "Rest a little season," etc. Yet there are the prayers of others who were not martyrs. War, famine, death and disturbances of nature caused these suffering. Also, in a very real way the saints must have been made aware that a great many of their number had been caught away and were identified as the Palm Bearers "Before the throne and before the Lamb," seen in the seventh chapter. Then there are the one hundred and forty-four thousand converted Israelites. Although miraculously protected from the Tribulation sorrows, no doubt they pray many of these prayers for the success of their ministry. Then there are the two witnesses. Certainly they were in constant contact with the heavens through prayer.

The results of the answers to these prayers at this particular time is seen in the actions of this angel. At the beginning he took the incense-filled golden censer, offers it with the prayers of all saints upon the golden altar, and allows the perfume-laden smoke to ascend before the heavenly throne. As if in answer to these prayers, he picks up the golden censer and again fills it. Only this time it is not the sweet-smelling incense. This time he fills it with fire from the altar before the throne. Instead of an oblation in worship, this time he casts fire and censer both into the earth.

Like a gigantic explosion the earth responds with voices, and thunderings, and lightnings, and an earthquake. Angry voices arise from millions of ungodly throats in defiance of God and His judgments. The roll of omnious thunder reverberates throughout the universe. This is preceded by lightning which dazzles and blinds. The earth begins to quake. All creation is in convulsive agitation. This over, the angel retires to the background and the seven trumpet angels prepare for their work.

THE TRUMPET JUDGMENTS
THE FIRST TRUMPET

"The first angel sounded, and there followed hail and fire mingled with blood, and they were cast upon the earth: and the third part of trees was burned up, and all green grass was burned up" (Revelation 8:7).

The first three trumpet judgments are fiery ordeals. This first one comes with hail, mingled with blood. The fire from the censer of the priestly angel was just a token and prediction of what was to follow. The falling of hail calls to mind the seventh judgment upon Pharaoh and the Egyptians. Not only hail, but thunder and fire accompanied this ancient plague. Imagine such a storm: Thunder, lightning, hail, all combine to terrify the Egyptians. Men and cattle in open fields were destroyed. Crops were ruined. Trees were broken. When this calamity was over Pharaoh's people looked upon a land of utter desolation.

This Egyptian plague is only a small sample of what will come from the trumpet-sounding of this first angel. We do not know all the effects of this divine visitation. Since there are indications that there will be people saved all during these troublous times, this plague as well as the others may well be the means of turning many to God in their hour of desperation. Mankind in general, though, will go on in wickedness.

The hail, fire and blood cast upon the earth will produce great distress. All green grass will be burned up. One third of the trees will be destroyed. Think of what this will do to the earth! If all grass is destroyed, it will seriously affect animal life, both domestic and wild. Think of the deaths! Think of the unbearable stench arising from the decaying carcasses of these animals!

THE SECOND TRUMPET

"And the second angel sounded, and as it were a great mountain burning with fire was cast into the sea: and the third part of the sea became blood: And the third part of the creatures which were in the sea, and had life, died: and the third part of the ships were destroyed" (Revelation 8:8).

The sounding of the second trumpet will be the signal for a third part of the sea to become blood. All sea life in the affected area will die. These bloody waters will be of such a nature that ships caught in them probably will disintegrate.

There will be an intensifying progression in the judgments to be visited upon mankind during this period. War, famine and death multiplied into calamities seemed harsh as the four horsemen ride. However, these were things which have afflicted the human race to a greater or lesser degree all through history. These present trumpet judgments are taking on more of the nature of the unearthly. There have been disturbances in the heavens all through time, but not on the scale found under the seventh seal. We here come to things never before experienced by man.

THE THIRD TRUMPET

"And the third angel sounded, and there fell a great star from heaven, burning as it were a lamp, and it fell upon the third part of the rivers, and upon the fountains of waters. And the name of the star is called wormwood: and the third part of the waters became wormwood; and many men died of the waters, because they were made bitter" (Revelation 8:10, 11).

Pollution of the waters of the sea is one thing, but pollution of the fresh waters of the earth is quite another. One third of sea life may die, ships may be destroyed and their occupants perish, but these things may not seriously affect the bulk of humanity. On the other hand, when one third of the rivers and fountains of water turn to the bitterness of wormwood, most all of mankind will be affected one way or another. The wormwood here is absinth. "It is a bitter, intoxicating and poisonous herb. It produces convulsions, paralysis and death," we are told.

What is meant by the great star falling from heaven is nowhere told. Some have suggested a meteor. This is a possibility. With man's probe into outer space, who knows what disturbances he will create. Or it may be a man-made satellite, placed in orbit around the earth as a military weapon. It could be filled with poison, which when released would contaminate everything it touched.

If this is a man-made star it may be placed in orbit as a deterrent to war, or as a threat by one nation to keep in subjection other nations. It could be made to hurtle to earth in some military retaliation. Or, it could develop a malfunction and accidentally get out of control. On the other hand, it could be something with which man has nothing to do. Whatever the circumstances surrounding it, the results will be the same—death on a wholesale scale.

THE FOURTH TRUMPET

"And the fourth angel sounded, and the third part of the sun was smitten, and the third part of the moon, and the third part of the stars; so as the third part of them was darkened, and the day shone not for a third part of it, and the night likewise. And I beheld and heard an angel flying through the midst of heaven, saying with a loud voice, Woe, woe, woe to the inhabiters of the earth by reason of the voice of the trumpet of the three angels which are yet to sound" (Revelation 8:12,13).

War, famine, death, voices, thunderings, lightning, burning grass and scorching trees, bloody seas and bitter waters mark the progress of this period of God's retributive judgment. Now we come to the sounding of the fourth trumpet which heralds the darkness of the sun, moon and stars. For a third part of the day there is no sun shining in the sky.

For a third part of the night there is no moon nor stars shining. The universe itself seems to have gone wild.

With all the severe plagues already visited upon mankind thus far in the Tribulation, the worst is yet to come. John saw and heard an angel flying through the midst of heaven, announcing yet greater terrors. Three frightful woes are to be visited upon unregenerate man before this time of sore trial shall have an end. These woes will increase in severity as one after the other they take place. They will come as the three other angels sound their trumpets.

CHAPTER NINE

THE FIRST TWO WOES

"And the fifth angel sounded, and I saw a star fall from heaven unto the earth: and to him was given the key of the bottomless pit. And he opened the bottomless pit; and there arose a smoke out of the pit, as the smoke of a great furnace; and the sun and the air were darkened by reason of the smoke of the pit. And there came out of the smoke locusts upon the earth: and unto them was given power, as the scorpions of the earth have power. And it was commanded them that they should not hurt the grass or the earth, neither any green thing, neither any tree: but only those men which have not the seal of God in their foreheads. And to them it was given that they should not kill them, but that they should be tormented five months: and their torment was as the torment of a scorpion when he striketh a man. And in those days shall men seek death, and desire to die, and death shall flee them. And the shapes of the locusts were like unto horses prepared unto battle; and on their heads were as it were crowns like gold, and their faces were as the faces of men. And they had hair of women, and their teeth were as the teeth of lions. And they had breastplates, as it were breastplates of iron; and the sound of their wings was as the sound of chariots of many horses running to battle. And they had tails like unto scorpions, and there were stings in their tails: and their power was to hurt men five months. And they had a king over them, which is the angel of the bottomless pit, whose name in the Hebrew tongue is Abaddon, but in the Greek tongue hath his name Apollyon" (Revelation 9:1-11).

Four trumpet blasts have already reverberated throughout the universe, announcing the blighting of the earth with hail, fire, blood, bitter waters and darkening skies. These evil times are only introductory to the real troubles. After the judgment inspired by the sounding of the fourth trumpet, John sees and hears "An angel flying throughout the midst of heaven." In thunder tones he speaks of three woes yet to come.

A great part of the book of Revelation is taken up with the final phase of the great controversy between God and Satan. This started when Lucifer attempted to dethrone Deity in the dim aeons before man made his appearance on the earth.

As has been stated elsewhere, God acts according to set laws of justice, judgment and mercy. In keeping with these laws He even allows Satan to inflict great sorrows upon mankind. The last three of these seven trumpet judgments are illustrative of this. The first four of these seven judgments are God-inspired. Hail, fire, blood, bitter waters and the darkened heavens come, giving God the first round.

Satan is then given his turn. He uses forces at his disposal in bringing these three woes upon humanity. The first woe brings the infernal locusts, the second the infernal cavalrymen and the third the infernal beast.

With the sounding of the fifth trumpet in this chapter, there appears to be a breakdown of the barrier between the spirit world and the material world. In this case it is the barrier to the world of wicked spirits which is broken down. It is not known just how thin is the veil between these two worlds, but God in His wisdom has placed such a veil.

During the Tribulation, and particularly the latter part of it, hellish forces become more and more prominent. Demons from the pit join demon-possessed men and together they "Soften up" the human race in preparation for the final take over by the great superman—Antichrist.

Just what are demons anyway? According to Dr. Seiss, heathen authors held they were "The spirits of mortals when separated from their earthly bodies ... mostly souls of heroes and distinguished persons who have departed this life. The ancient philosopher Philo held they were the souls of dead men." Josephus states that the Jewish belief was they were the spirits of the wicked dead. The early Christian fathers agreed with the heathen and Jewish writers on this, he says. Seiss sums up the Jewish and early Christian belief in these words, "They are ... invisible spiritual beings, unholy in character, belonging to the kingdom of evil, and having a vicious and pernicious penchant to interfere in the affairs of mankind in the flesh."

As to how these demons operated in Jesus' time this authority states, "These wicked spirits incorporated themselves in the bodies of living men, intruding themselves between the soul and the nervous organism, getting possession of men's physical powers, measurably superseding the wills of those affected, so as to speak and act by means of human organs."

In our day many do not believe there is such a thing as demon possession. What the Bible calls demon possession is only mental or nervous derangement, it is contended. However, if there is to be any firm ground upon which to stand, it must be the Bible. Its authority and teachings must be accepted. And on this subject it is in harmony with the general teachings of the ancient philosophers and Jewish scholars.

Christ had a lot to say about demon-possession. Many of His recorded miracles had to do with freeing men from their fiendish power. Remember the demonized man of Gadara; the dumb man possessed with a demon; the little boy whom the demons caused to fall into the fire and into the water. These are just a few cases with which Jesus dealt.

It is stated that Satan is the prince of the power of the air. He has his emissaries everywhere. When man so gives himself over to work evil, he is in danger of becoming possessed by evil spirits. Besides demons, Satan has at his disposal millions of fallen angels. Much has been said about these angels in other places in this study. In it will be found a detailed account of Lucifer and the evil angels. So only a brief resume will be given here. When Lucifer fell he took a third of heaven's angels with him. Where are they now? Peter (II Pet. 2:4) says they have been *"Cast down to hell, and delivered . . . into chains of darkness to be reserved unto the judgment."* Jude (6) says this about them when he states that *"The angels which kept not their first estate, but left their own habitation, he hath reserved in chains of darkness unto the judgment of the last great day."*

In this chapter are found three orders of wicked beings —the "Star" fallen from heaven, which seems to be identical with the king of the bottomless pit, and perhaps Satan himself; the four angels bound in the river Euphrates and the two hundred million cavalrymen. Remember, the locust-like creatures and the horses of this army have their counterpart in like creatures on earth. They are incapable of either good or evil, but are manipulated by a higher order of beings.

The Middle East is the cradle of civilization. The Garden of Eden was located here. This is where Satan first met and corrupted man. The tower of Babel was erected in this area. Man's first rebellion against God took place here. A great portion of ancient civilization's history centers around the Euphrates and the Tigris, the Nile and the Jordan. Therefore it is quite possible that this region will be infested with the powers of Satan more than other regions of the earth.

Looking ahead a little into the Revelation one finds more and more of this sort of thing. Under the sixth trumpet are seen four angels, commanding an army of hell's cavalry. The Great Red Dragon is introduced in the twelfth chapter. The Beast and False Prophet appear in the thirteenth chapter. This unfolding revelation of diabolical forces is in line with the general progress found in the book.

Simultaneously with the sounding of this fifth trumpet, "A great star from heaven fell." Who is this great star from heaven? Indications are that he is a fallen being. The Revised Version of the Bible uses the word "Fallen" (not fall as the Authorized Version has it). If this is the correct translation it implies that John did not see the actual fall, but this "Star" had already fallen.

Satan is the prince of the powers of the air. Paul tells us that *"We wrestle not against flesh and blood, but against spiritual wickedness in high places."* The Greek word used here for this is *eupourois* and means "Above the sky, celestial, heavenly or heaven, or high." Clearly this describes Satan's present sphere of operation.

This "Star" is given the key of the bottomless pit. With it he opens this infernal place. When he does, there arises a smoke, darkening the sun and the air. Imagine a smoke so dense that it resembles that belching forth from the throats of millions of air-polluting furnaces of the modern day. It causes, as Joel (2:2) puts it, *"A day of darkness and gloominess, a day of clouds and thick darkness."*

Coming with this smoke are myriads of denizens of the abyss. They are shaped like locusts, have the battle stance of horses, wear golden crowns, have the faces like men, hair like women, teeth like lions, breastplates of iron, and wings that sound like many chariots of horses running to battle. Their scorpion-like tails are used to torment men for five months.

The likeness of horses prepared for battle suggests great strength and determination as well as immense size. The crowned head indicates authority. The face of a man points to their intelligence and purpose. The teeth of a lion warns of their great power to inflict terrible punishment. The breastplate of iron testifies to their impregnability against attack. The whirring of their wings creates a din calculated to drive fear into the stoutest hearts. Their scorpion-like sting drives their victims almost insane with pain.

Turn such creatures loose upon the earth and place over them a leader from the pit and it adds up to the most diabolical judgment yet visited upon the human race. The name of the king of these locust-like creatures is given both in the Hebrew and Greek languages. The word "Abaddon" in Hebrew means "A destroying angel," and Apollyon in the Greek means "A destroyer." Thus in both languages it is the same—a destroyer. Also, as the name is designated in both Greek and Hebrew, it is evident that both Jew and Gentile are represented in this vile creature's name.

Keep in mind that in all these judgments God and Satan are both working—God in His omnipotence, but Satan only as God allows. Satan has no thought nor desire to work out God's will, but unconsciously he is doing so in the Revelation.

These locusts are forbidden to hurt the grass, other vegetation, trees and the servants of God who have the seal of God in their foreheads. The only ones having the seal of the living God in their foreheads at this time are the one hundred and forty-four thousand Israelites introduced in the seventh chapter. These locusts are not to molest them.

Men will be tormented for five months with these hell-spawned monsters. Here is the sting of death, but no death. Here is the pain of death, but no death. Here is the desire for death, but no death. Such awful agony will be experienced by humanity under this judgment that men will seek death but it will flee from them.

THE SIXTH TRUMPET—SECOND WOE

"And the sixth angel sounded, and I heard a voice from the four horns of the golden altar which is before God, saying to the sixth angel which had the trumpet, Loose the four angels which are bound in the great river Euphrates. And the four angels were loosed, which were prepared for an hour, and a day and a month and a year, for to slay the third part of men. And the number of the army of horsemen were two hundred thousand thousand: and I heard the number of them. And thus I saw the horses in the vision, and them that sat upon them, having breastplates of fire and jacinth, and brimstone: and the heads of the horses were as the heads of lions; and out of their mouths issued fire and smoke and brimstone. By these was the third part of men killed, by the fire, and by the smoke and the brimstone which issued out of their mouths, For their power is in their tails: for their tails were like serpents, and had heads, and with them they do hurt. And the rest of the men which were not killed by these plagues yet repented not of the works of their hands, that they should not worship devils, and idols of gold, and silver, and brass, and stone, and of wood: which neither can see nor hear, nor walk. Neither repented they of their murders, nor of their sorceries nor of their fornication, nor of their thefts" (Revelation 9:13-21).

In spite of all the fearful judgments already suffered, mankind sinks lower and lower into sin and degradation, bringing this second woe. When the sixth angel sounds his trumpet, a voice is heard from the golden altar. This is the altar of judgment. It is the same golden altar seen in the eighth chapter upon which incense is offered with the prayers of the saints.

These incense-laden prayers ascended up to God, Who is sitting upon His throne. Mention here of this altar would indicate that at least some of these prayers are now to be answered. Since every God-honoring prayer is prayed in the spirit of "Thy kingdom come, thy will be done in earth as it is in heaven," it naturally follows that this is the great burden of the prayers to be answered at this particular time. The earth must be cleansed of the usurpers before the kingdom of God can come and the will of God be done on earth. Although brought on by the forces of the pit, this judgment brings God's kingdom one step nearer realization.

The sixth angel is given the task of loosing the "Four angels which are bound in the great river Euphrates." In view of the available evidence it would appear that these four angels are from that group who *"Kept not their first estate, but left their own habitation* ... (and are now) *reserved in everlasting chains under darkness; unto the judgment of the great day"* (Jude 6).

There is a significant statement in the above quotation from Peter and Jude. It is that they are "reserved . . . unto the judgment of the great day." Being bound they are not free to do as they desire, but await the loosing for this particular time.

These four angels are held in readiness for a certain hour, day, month and year. Some would add all this up and say this judgment would last for thirteen months, one day and one hour. Perhaps the five tormenting months of the locust plagues is the reason for this interpretation. However, it is the point of time and not its duration that is seen here.

If these four angels are of the fallen group, then these horsemen may well be the spirits of the uncounted hordes who have fallen in battle near here. The riders here seem to guide and direct these hellish horses, but they themselves do not seem to use weapons. It is the horses that do the killing. There are those who see in the symbols of war in Revelation, present day man-made implements of destruction. They see the airplane, armoured tanks, atomic bombs and other paraphernalia as filling these descriptions. But since weapons of warfare become obsolete so quickly it could well be that by this time in the history of things our present engines of annihilation will have been replaced with others so far removed as to have no relation whatsoever with these symbols.

In his vision John sees these horses as having lion-like heads. From their mouths issue forth streams of fire, smoke and brimstone. The breastplates of the men reflect these same elements, but in a seemingly harmless way. Not so with the horses. With their stiffling flames they destroy one-third of mankind. In addition to the wholesale slaughter is the awful pain they inflict with their serpentine tails. From a close reading of the text it would seem certain that the serpent bite of these tails causes great pain, but not necessarily death. If this be true, then in addition to one-third of the human race being wiped out, multiplied millions of others may suffer from their poisonous bite.

Even at this late hour there is a call to repentance. Those who were bitten by the serpent-like tails of these horses, but did not die, and those who witnessed the deaths and sufferings of others from the fiery blasts of these horses, should have taken heed. But they did not. The record says they repented not.

What were the sins of these unrepentant men? First, they were worshipping devils. This is the worst indictment to be brought against any person—to actually worship the Devil. Mention here of this should not seem strange. Men are now worshipping Satan. There is in existence in these United States what is called "Satan's Church." Not long back over television one of the "Ministers" of this church recited a prayer, modelled after our Lord's Prayer. In it he substituted Satan for God, reference to heaven he changed to hell, and God's kingdom to Satan's kingdom.

The practice of witchcraft and astrology is becoming more and more common. There are many self-styled witches even in this day. A few years ago a person who believed in astrology would be laughed to scorn. Not now. It is becoming fashionable. Hundreds of newspapers publish daily horoscopes. And multiplied thousands, if not millions, consult them before making major decisions.

Also, the ancient signs of the Zodiac are seen everywhere. Many people believe the sign of the Zodiac under which they were born has a lot to do with their personality and chance in life. The only difference in our day and that of this coming day is one of degree. We have everything now they will have then, only on a more limited scale.

These men not only worship devils, but idols of gold, silver, brass, stone and wood. They seemed to have been completely steeped in false worship. Not only their worship, but their other sins brought forth the cry from the four horns of the golden altar for punishment. They were murderers. Now murder has been common throughout history ever since Cain slew his brother Abel. Mention here indicates a multiplication of this terrible crime. Over thirteen thousand people were murdered in the United States alone in one year. This is an increase of some thirteen percent over the previous year. Should this rate of increase continue for a few years the United States will have reached the place to where the blood of their victims will cry out from the ground for vengeance. What will it be under the sixth trumpet?

The second sin mentioned here is sorceries. This is just another facet of devil worship. It is aligned with witchcraft, astrology, spiritualism and the like.

Fornication is the third sin with which they are charged. This is defined as immoral relations between the unmarried. This also has been a sin of mankind through the ages. The reason it is mentioned here is that it has become one of the predominant evils of that day. This vice has mushroomed in the last few years. Increased sexual knowledge, the prevalent permissive attitude toward these illicit relationships, and surer means of contraception, have all contributed to its rapid spread. What will conditions be in a few years if God does not send His judgments to call a halt to man's toboggan slide to perdition?

The final sin is theft. A few generations ago the boast was "A man's word is his bond," and that was the prevailing standard. Things have changed. Now it takes the eternal vigilance of every agency of government to maintain any semblance of honesty in our body politic. It is not uncommon to read of the embezzlement of vast sums by high government officials. As one example, in a recent general election it was generally conceded that the candidate for governor of a certain state lost his bid for election because high state officials of his own party were involved in a web of theft. Links between underworld characters and state officials are uncovered quite frequently.

Dishonesty in public officials is just one phase of the practice of theft. Many of the money games so popular a few years ago on televisions turned out to be "Rigged." Before the game ever started it was determined by the operators who would be the winner. Instances of athletes having been bribed by gamblers to manipulate the scoring have been disclosed quite often. Added to all this are the operations of the out and out criminal elements. The statistics on this are appalling. The figures for a recent year reveal that there was an increase of over twenty-two percent in robbery, seventeen percent in major larceny and eleven percent in auto theft, in the United States alone. Projected into the future a few years, these figures will reveal a situation in which no personal property will be safe. With all the cases of murder, sorceries, fornication and theft we know about, one wonders just how many more are never brought to light.

The present picture is indeed very dark. Yet if one will forecast the future a little, it will be shown why the four horns of the golden altar before God's throne will cry out for vindication when the sixth angel sounds his trumpet.

Chapter Ten

THE LITTLE BOOK OPENED

CHRIST TAKES POSSESSION

"And I saw another mighty angel come down from heaven, clothed with a cloud: and a rainbow was upon his head, and his face was as it were the sun, and his feet were as pillars of fire: And he had in his hand a little book open: and he set his right foot upon the sea, and his left foot on the earth, And cried with a loud voice, as when a lion roareth: and when he had cried seven thunders uttered their voices. And when the seven thunders uttered their voices, I was about to write: and I heard a voice from heaven saying unto me, Seal up those things which the seven thunders uttered and write them not" (Revelation 10:1-4).

Who is this "Mighty Angel" John sees coming down from heaven? All evidence points to him as being Jesus Christ Himself. Notice His description:

He is clothed with a cloud—Clouds are the vesture-material of Deity. God appeared on Mount Sinai in a "Thick Cloud." His presence in the form of a cloud covered and protected the wilderness camp of Israel in the day time until their journey was to be resumed. When Jesus left the earth at His ascension a cloud received Him out of the sight of men. Matthew, Mark and Luke all see Him "Coming in the clouds of heaven with power and great glory." In the first chapter of Revelation the prophet sees Christ "Coming with clouds." In the fourteenth chapter "One like the Son of man" is seen sitting upon a cloud, which, with other evidence, proves this to be Christ.

He has a rainbow upon his head—The mighty angel is wearing as a tiara a rainbow. The rainbow speaks of God's mercy in time of judgment. After the great deluge God showed Noah the rainbow as the sign of His covenant between Himself and all living creatures that the earth would no more be destroyed by water. When Noah looked out of the ark at the end of the flood upon a world of utter desolation, only the rainbow of promise enabled him to start a new life, and through his sons, found a new race. John saw the Occupant of the Tribulation Judgment Throne as a Being of terrible majesty, but encircling this throne was the emerald rainbow of promise and mercy.

His face as it were the sun—The face of Omnipotence is as the sun shining in his strength. Mortal eyes cannot look upon such and live. On Mount Sinai Moses was allowed to see only the "Back parts" of Jehovah. His contact with Deity brightened his own countenance so gloriously that the children of Israel could not stedfastly behold his face. Christ as the light of the world could be seen by man only in his fleshly body. On the mount of transfiguration the curtain was pulled aside for an instant and Peter, James and John were given just a little glimpse of their glorified Lord. Saul of Tarsus, on the Damascus road, saw the great light "Above the brightness of the sun," and in it Jesus speaking to him. By prophetic insight Malachi records that "The Sun of righteousness shall arise with healing in his wings.... And shall tread down the wicked." In proof that this promise will be fulfilled in the end-time, he goes on to say, "I will send you Elijah the prophet before the coming of the great and dreadful day of the Lord."

His feet as fiery pillars—On Mount Calvary the Romans nailed His unresisting feet to the rough upright beam which was to hold His body. Until all the blood was spilled out of His veins and all life drained from His body, Christ was to be held fast. His enemies did this—both Jew and Gentile.

Now they must behold these same feet. Not as feet of poor human clay, subject to all the hurts and bruises of mankind, but as fiery pillars of divine justice and judgment. John sees these feet in the first chapter as "Like unto fine brass, as if they burned in an oven." There they are seen as pillars of fire.

* * * * * * *

The Little Book opened—This is the Being with whom this judgment-bound world has to reckon. In the fifth chapter a "Little Book" is introduced. It is sealed with seven seals. It is the title deed to the earth. The "Lion of the Tribe of Judah" alone was found worthy to break the seals, open the Book and reveal its contents. Here these seals have all been broken. The last one ushers in the seven trumpet judgments. Six of these sore afflictions have already been visited upon mankind. The seventh seal was broken in the eighth chapter, and all following that chapter will be under this seventh seal. Five of the trumpet-judgments have come. The sixth one which started in the ninth chapter with the riding of the infernal cavalry, will be finished in the eleventh chapter with the slaying of the two witnesses.

The Mighty Angel takes possession of sea and earth—This mighty angel (Christ) in this chapter holds a "Little Book" in His hand. This is the same "Little Book" of the fifth chapter. Now it is open! Here He "Sets his right foot upon the sea and his left foot upon the earth." The word *set* used here carries with it the idea of permanency. No more will these fiery pillars be removed; they are planted to stay. Christ is here taking formal possession of the earth, sea and sky. The contents of the opened book prove His claim.

The roar of the Lion of the tribe of Judah—With His feet firmly planted on the sea and land, He issues a challenge to His enemies. He does this by giving a mighty lion-like roar. Jeremiah (25:30) prophesies that *"The Lord shall roar from on high, and utter his voice from his holy habitation: he shall mightily roar upon this habitation; he shall give a shout ... against all the inhabitants of the earth."* Hosea (11:10) speaks of the roar of God in these words, *"... The Lord ... shall roar like a lion, when he shall roar then the children shall tremble from the west."* Joel (3:16) says, *"The Lord shall roar from Zion, and utter his voice from Jerusalem; and the inhabitants of the shepherds shall mourn, and the top of Carmel shall wither."*

There is another creature lurking in the shadows. Peter describes him as *"Your adversary, the devil, as a roaring lion, walketh about, seeking whom he may devour."* He was once in heaven as the "Son of the Morning," or Lucifer. There has been a great controversy going on between Christ and this old evil lion ever since the rebellion of the angels, which resulted in the expulsion of this one-time archangel from the heavenly domains of God's throne. As Satan he still believes he will be the ultimate victor over Christ. This lion-like roar from the Son of God is His battle challenge to the roaring lion of all evil.

Roll of the seven thunders—As if to answer in sympathy, the roll of thunder is heard throughout the universe. John personifies this thunder and calls it the "Voice of the Seven Thunders." Now thunder is an awesome thing to hear. There is something ominous and mysterious about its sound. Also, there is a great uncertainty about its message. Does it herald the approach of a harmless thunder shower, or does it portend something hurtful? Does it announce the approach of a good rain, or does it warn of an approaching storm which will cause frightful devastation? Whether in a soft rain or a disastrous tornado, thunder is usually present.

In the Bible there are at least twenty-eight references to thunder. In nearly every instance it is connected in some way with divine judgment. God's voice is likened to thunder in at least thirteen places; nearly always it is associated with chastisement.

Thunder is first mentioned in connection with the seventh plague of Egypt. *"God shall thunder out of heaven upon his adversaries,"* Hannah, the mother of Samuel tells us. The Lord *"Thundered a great thunder"* upon the Philistines in giving victory to Israel at Eben-ezer. God showed His displeasure of Israel when they wanted a king by sending thunder and rain. *"The Lord thundered from heaven."* David sang of thunder after God delivered him out of the hand of Saul and all of his enemies. Job has much to say about God's power as evidenced by thunder. The Psalms are sprinkled with references to the thunder-like voice of God. Isaiah speaks of God's visit to Jerusalem with Thunder. Thunder is present in the seventh trumpet judgment and the pouring out of the seventh vial.

Speculation as to what these Seven Thunders uttered is foolish. John knew what was said, but was told not to write what he heard. Since God evidently desired that this remain secret their message must be left alone. However, by considering the place thunder has had in announcing judgments, and seeing that those announcements are usually made by the voice of God in thunder, it would not be presumptuous to suggest that these Seven Thunders were uttered by the throne-Occupant of the fourth and fifth chapters—or God Himself.

Why should this great thunder sound immediately following Christ's setting His feet upon the earth as symbolical of possession? It appears that this is God's way of giving a mighty amen to this action, and a mighty assent to what is to soon take place.

The earth-shaking roar of the Lion of the Tribe of Judah, and the deep peals of thunder in its seven-fold volume announce to all and sundry that a war of such magnitude as has never been fought since the dawn of creation is about to begin.

This will be a decisive war. It will bring to a head and settle once and for all the strife which started in the dim aeons before man ever made his appearance upon this planet. The principals will be Christ and the fallen Lucifer. Up until this time agents of both forces have borne the brunt of the action. As the seals of the "Little Book" were ripped from it, the Twenty-Four Elders, the Four Living Creatures and the four Apocalyptic horsemen were the front line soldiers on the side of heaven. Such powers as the infernal locusts and the infernal cavalrymen of the fifth and sixth trumpet judgments were hell's forces of counteraction. Now the real show-down is to begin in the eleventh chapter. Christ sends the two witnesses. Lucifer counters by having them slain. Christ wins the final round by resurrecting them in the sight of men. In the twelfth chapter, Lucifer in the form of the great Red Dragon seeks to devour the Man Child. Christ's answer to this is to send Michael the archangel and win the battle which results in the Dragon's being cast out of heaven, and becoming earthbound.

On and on the war rages. By way of anticipation the curtain is drawn back and the apocalyptical seer is allowed to get a little glimpse of future events. He is told by the mighty angel (Christ), that there will be no more delay. Events will follow one after another in rapid succession until everything connected with this will have taken place. He is told that when the voice of the seventh angel should begin to sound the *"Mysteries of God should be finished."*

"And the angel which I saw stand upon the sea and upon the earth lifted up his hand to heaven, and sware by him that liveth for ever and ever, who created heaven, and the things that therein are, and the earth, and the things that therein are, and the sea, and the things which are therein, that there should be time no longer. But in the days of the

voice of the seventh angel when he shall begin to sound, the mystery of God should be finished, as he hath declared to his servants, the prophets" (Revelation 10:5-7).

In reading the above verses some have come to believe that this marks the end of time. This is not the meaning here of the expression "*... There should be time no longer.*" This simply means that there will be no more delay. Everything associated with the end-time will hasten to its conclusion.

Under the sounding of the trumpet of the seventh angel everything yet connected with the Tribulation will have its fulfillment. In reading the account of the sounding of this trumpet, one could easily get the idea that these trumpet-blasts continue but a few moments, or possibly hours. Notice, in the seventh verse it says, "In the *days* of this voice of the seventh angel." These *days* will stretch out for at least something over three and one-half years.

However, the present events are taking place under the sounding of the trumpet of the sixth angel. The slaughter by the 200,000,000 infernal cavalrymen, the opening of the "Little Book," measuring the temple, the latter part of the ministry of the two witnesses and the great earthquake in which the tenth part of Jerusalem fall—all transpire under the sixth trumpet sounding.

JOHN AND THE "LITTLE BOOK"

"And the voice which I heard from heaven spake unto me again, and said, Go and take the little book which is open in the hands of the angel which standeth upon the sea and upon the earth. And I went unto the angel, and said unto him, Give me the little book. And he said unto me, Take it, and eat it up; and it shall make thy belly bitter, but it shall be in thy mouth sweet as honey. And I took the little book out of the angel's hand, and ate it up; and it was in my mouth sweet as honey: and as soon as I had eaten it, my belly was bitter. And he said unto me, Thou must prophesy again before many peoples, and nations, and tongues, and kings" (Revelation 10:11).

John's position in the Revelation is mostly that of an observer and recorder. However, he becomes actively involved in the action of the visions at different times. He is invited to come up to heaven in the fourth chapter. He weeps in the fifth chapter at the prospects of no one being able to open the Little Book. He stands upon the sand of the sea in the thirteenth chapter. He is carried away in the spirit into the wilderness in the seventeenth chapter to see the judgment of Babylon. He is carried away in the spirit *"to a great and high mountain"* that he might see the New Jerusalem in the twenty-first chapter.

In the latter part of this tenth chapter he becomes a participant in the action. He is told to "Go and take the little book, which is open in the hand of the angel which standeth upon the sea and the earth." This angel gives John the Little Book with the instructions to eat it up. He is told it will be sweet to his taste but bitter when digested.

Why the bitterness? Why the sweetness? When John contemplated the anticipated final results of the breaking of the seven seals, and when he saw the mighty angel take possession of the sea and the earth, it was "Sweet as honey." When he began to realize the awfu suffering through which humanity must go to reach the place of final blessedness, the sweetness of honey turned to the bitterness of gall.

Here John received an enlarged commission. He is told in the first chapter to "Write the things which thou hast seen, and the things which are, and the things which shall be hereafter," and send it to the seven churches of Asia. In the tenth chapter he finds the circulation of the message is to be larger. He is to "Prophesy again before many peoples, and nations, and tongues and kings." Certainly John was not to preach in person in the flesh to all these people. At the time of the Patmos visions he was an old man. After being released he would have only a few years left at most; certainly not enough time for a world-wide ministry. There is nothing in the record to warrant the assumption that he would be resurrected in the latter days for such a ministry. The only thing left is the dissemination on a world-wide scale of the contents of his visions. He must faithfully record them, and so identify himself with them until the sweetness of honey and the bitterness of gall are felt in his own spirit.

Chapter Eleven

MEASURING THE TEMPLE

In the Book of Revelation it will be noticed that before many climactic scenes everything comes to a standstill. In the fifth chapter there is a pause when it looked to John like there would be no one found who was worthy to take the "Little Book," break the seals and look thereon. This difficulty was eventually resolved and things began to move again. At the opening of the seventh seal there was a thirty-minute silence; then the action resumed. After the sounding of the sixth trumpet in the ninth chapter there was a long break in the trumpet-produced activities before the sounding of the seventh trumpet.

Whether the action of the latter half of the ninth chapter and that which takes place in the tenth chatper, and the eleventh chapter—through the twelfth verse—runs simultaneously or consecutively there is no sure way of knowing. Still, all must take place before the seventh trumpet is sounded.

The things going on here resemble the old-time three ring circus. You look at one ring and see things happening. You look at another ring and other things are taking place. In the third ring still other things are going on. While the two hundred million cavalrymen are riding, it is altogether possible the scene of the opened "Little Book" is also taking place. This eleventh chapter chronicles a number of periods of definite duration. The first is the treading down of Jerusalem by the Gentiles for forty-two months. Also the two witnesses are to prophesy for a like period.

MEASURING THE TEMPLE

"And there was given me a reed like unto a rod: and the angel stood, saying, Rise, and measure the temple of God, and the altar, and them that worship therein. But the court which is without the temple leave out, and measure it not; for it is given unto the Gentiles: and the holy city

shall they tread under foot forty-two months" (Revelation 11:1, 2).

In the first two verses of chapter eleven, John is again seen as a participant in the divine drama. He is given a reed-like rod, told to take this instrument and measure the temple of God, the altar, and those who worship therein. He is not to measure the court outside the temple. This is given to the Gentiles and these Gentiles shall tread the holy city under foot for three years and a half.

This scene presents many difficulties. Let us examine it and see if it cannot be placed in its proper perspective. If one accepts the teaching that events in Revelation come mainly in the chronological order in which they are recorded, then this scene is to be placed just before the Antichrist breaks his seven-year covenant with Israel. This covenant is political, and one in which the Jews are allowed to worship God, using their ancient rites. The temple here mentioned is in Jerusalem. In restoring their age-old rituals, naturally they leave Christ and the Gospel out. They go back to the time of the destruction of their temple by the Romans in A.D. 70, and start from there.

Paul states that "Blindness in part has happened to Israel." In their partial blindness they returned to their homeland and established their modern nation in 1948. After the destruction of the temple by Titus and the Romans in A.D. 70, their means of public worship has been restricted mostly to the synagogue. Now at this point in Revelation the temple has been rebuilt and their original method of worship restored. For some time they have been floundering in the deep waters of "Jacob's Trouble." True, the covenant they made with the Beast allows them religious privileges, but they have suffered everything others have suffered and more. In their sorrows they have sought their ancient Jehovah in their half-blinded way. God has taken knowledge of this all along. Their wailing at the old wall has not gone unnoticed by Him. He has not turned deaf ears to the sound of their mourning as for an only son. Their age-old cry for their Messiah reaches to the heart of God.

Many say this is the point which marks the close of the Gentile age, and the time which God turns again to the Jews, to deal with them as a nation. However, God has been dealing especially with Israel as a nation from the beginning of their present national existence. How else can one explain the miraculous way this tiny state has been able to exist. For every Israeli they have had at least a hundred enemies. Their modern wars find a parallel only in their Old Testament conflicts.

When John is told to "Measure the temple of God, and the altar, and them that worship therein," it is God's way of appropriating these things for Himself. Christ, in the guise of the "Mighty Angel," takes general possession of the sea and land, in the tenth chapter, but this is only in anticipation. Much has to be done before its usurpers are finally driven out. In the restoration of Temple worship God is recognizing it in a real way. Of course, this is not Christian worship; it is half-blinded people earnestly seeking after their God.

THE TWO WITNESSES

"And I will give power unto my two witnesses, and they shall prophesy a thousand two hundred and threescore days, clothed in sackcloth. These are the two olive trees, and the two candlesticks standing before the God of the earth. If any man will hurt them, fire proceedeth out of their mouths, and devoureth their enemies; and if any man will hurt them, he must in this manner be killed. These have power to shut heaven, and that it rain not in the days of their prophecy; and have power over waters to turn them to blood, and to smite the earth with plagues, as often as they will. And when they have finished their testimony, the beast that ascendeth out of the bottomless pit shall make war against them, and shall overcome them and kill them, and their dead bodies shall lie in the street of the great city, which spiritually is called Sodom and Egypt, where also our Lord was crucified. And they of the people and kindreds and tongues and nations shall see their dead bodies three days and a half, and shall not suffer their dead bodies to be put in graves. And they that dwell upon the earth shall rejoice over them, and make merry, and shall send gifts one to another; because these two prophets tormented them that dwelt on the earth. And after three days and a half the spirit of life from God entered into them, and they stood upon their feet; and great fear fell upon them which saw them. And they heard a great voice from heaven saying,

Come up hither. And they ascended up to heaven in a cloud; and their enemies beheld them. And the same hour there was a great earthquake, and the tenth part of the city fell, and in the earthquake were slain of men seven thousand: and the remnant were affrighted, and gave glory to the God of heaven" (Revelation 11:3-13).

Who are these two witnesses? The most common answer is Elijah as one, and either Enoch or Moses as the other. The Scriptural proof that Elijah is one is almost incontrovertable.

Elijah was perhaps God's greatest champion in the battle against idolatry. He seemingly dropped out of nowhere, confronted the wicked Ahab with his sins, and predicted a terrible drought as a punishment upon Israel. He challenged the false prophets of Baal to do battle on Mount Carmel. From this victory he went on to pronounce doom upon this vile king. He faced the bloody Jezebel and announced her approaching death, giving details such as that dogs would eat her flesh. He called fire down from heaven which consumed a total of one hundred soldiers and their two captains. Finally, he was transported to heaven without going the way of death.

Malachi prophesied that God would send *"Elijah the prophet before the coming of the great and dreadful day of the Lord."* There is a teaching that John the Baptist was, in fact, Elijah. Matthew (11:14) says, *"If ye will receive it, this is Elias* (Elijah) *which was for to come."* In Matthew (17:11, 12), Jesus says to His disciples, *"Elias* (Elijah) *shall come first and restore all things, But I say unto you that Elias* (Elijah) *is come already and they knew him not, but have done unto him whatsoever they listed."* From this the disciples understood that Jesus spoke of John. In Luke (1:17) we are told *"He* (John) *shall go before him* (Jesus) *in the Spirit and power of Elias"* (Elijah).

Using these references one would be inclined to agree that John was Elijah. However, a little closer look would change the picture. In speaking of John in Matthew (11:14) Jesus says *"If ye will receive it this is Elias* (Elijah." In the next verse (15) He cautions *"He that hath ears to hear, let him hear."* This indicates there is something below the surface of the simple statement. Also in Matthew (17:13) the disciples *understood* that Jesus spoke to them of John.

Notice when Elijah shall come: "Before the coming of

the great and dreadful day of the Lord." By no stretch of the imagination could the first coming of the Lord be called *"The great and dreadful day of the Lord."* It was just the opposite; it was a day of (comparative) peace.

The words of John himself should settle forever the issue. The priests and Levites from Jerusalem (John 1:21) asked the Baptist point-blank: "Art thou Elias (Elijah)?" John answered just as firmly "I am not."

John did come in the spirit and power of Elijah and did turn many hearts of the children back to their fathers, and vice versa, but it remains yet to be fulfilled the complete prophecy of Malachi. It will be during the great and dreadful day of the Lord—the Great Tribulation—that this will be completed. And as one of these two witnesses, he will do this by exposing the seven year covenant for what it really is, and the Antichrist for what he really is.

The second of these two witnesses is not so easily identified. Look at Enoch. He was one of the most outstanding characters of the antedeluvian world. In the midst of almost universal wickedness he lived a life so holy and walked with God so closely that he was translated *"That he should not see death."* The argument that he will be one of the two witnesses runs something like this: Hebrews says, *"It is appointed unto man once to die...." And Enoch never did die;* thus to fulfill this Scripture, he must return to earth to die. When he does, it will be as one of these two witnesses.

Just how valid is the application of the Scripture to the case of Enoch? If a literal interpretation of this passage is insisted upon, then it must apply to all men everywhere and in every age. Even so, according to the general belief held by those who accept the premillennial interpretation of the end-time Scriptures, there will be millions of people who will go to heaven in the rapture, and will never die. In proof of this Paul speaks in First Corinthians these words: *"...We shall not all sleep* (die), *but we shall be changed, in a moment, in the twinkling of an eye, at the last trump."*

There are just two things involved here: dying or not dying. Enoch went to heaven without dying; the ready saints will go to heaven in the rapture without dying. All others will die. There is absolutely no proof that Enoch's translation was any different from what will take place when the Bride of Christ is caught away.

So since about the only claim Enoch has to being one of the two witnesses is that he went to heaven without dying. The fact that his translation was practically identical with the coming rapture of the saints nullifies this claim.

What about Moses? He is one of the most outstanding characters of the post-deluvian world. He led the children of Israel out of Egypt to the borders of Canaan. He gave them the law from Mount Sinai at the instructions from God. He was with Elijah on the Mount of Transfiguration with Jesus. From Exodus 2:10 to Revelation 15:3 this man is mentioned almost eight hundred times. In predicting the first coming of Christ he tells the children of Israel in Deut. 18:17, *"The Lord thy God shall raise up unto thee a prophet from the midst of thy brethren, like unto me; unto him shall ye hearken."*

There are unusual circumstanecs surrounding his death. The record says God buried him. The exact location of this grave has always been a secret. Another singular thing about him is found in Jude (9) where Michael the Archangel and the Devil are disputing about his body. Of all the millions of saints from Abel onward why should the body of Moses alone be the subject of a dispute? The answer must be that the lawgiver had a ministry yet to be fulfilled.

In another place we stated that this verse finds a parallel in the twelfth chapter of Revelation. In Jude Michael, Satan and Moses are in the picture; in Revelation Michael, Satan and the Man Child appear. In Exodus Moses and Aaron confront Pharaoh with demands concerning the children of Israel. In Revelation it is the two witnesses who, with the Antichrist, make up the trio, and who are involved in the controversy over the seven year covenant between Israel and Pharaoh's counterpart.

As to the suitability of Moses' being one of these witnesses, look at his record. Every plague of the end-time is seen in miniature in those brought upon Egypt at the bidding of this man. From the foregoing the evidence for accepting Moses as one of these two witnesses should be sufficient.

Looking back to the sixth chapter of Revelation and the breaking of the first four seals, a parallel is found in the blowing of the first four trumpets. The four Living Creatures are active in this seal-breaking. War, famine and death are the main results. Four is the earthly number, and since the Living Creatures picture earthly things, it follows that it would be proper for them to be involved in the breaking of only four seals.

The first four trumpet-blasts bring forth calamities reminiscent of those called forth by Moses and Elijah. The hail, blood and fire of the first three and the darkness of the fourth, all came upon Egypt and backsliding Israel at the instigation of these Old Testament worthies.

This brings a thought missed by many writers concerning this last book of the Bible. Did the two witnesses have anything to do with sending these trumpet judgments? It is said that in describing them that they had power to devour their enemies with their fiery breaths. They had power to stop the rain from heaven. They had power to turn the waters into blood. They had power to smite the earth with plagues as often as they desired.

From internal evidence it seems the Antichrist made his really serious bid for power about the time of the blowing of the first trumpet. The seven year covenant gives the signal. Coinciding with this, these two witnesses began denouncing this covenant. The question is, did they use this God-given power, and was the results felt only locally, or was it felt worldwide? It would not be inconsistent with all the evidence to say they did use this power, and it was felt worldwide in these four trumpet judgments.

* * * * * * *

These two will prophesy one thousand, two hundred and sixty days, or three years and one half—using the prophetical year of three hundred and sixty days. It is only after their testimony has been thoroughly established that God allows them to be slain. About this time God raptures the one hundred, forty-four thousand Israelites out of the world, details of which will be given later.

When the two witnesses are slain the wicked of the earth rejoice. No more will they have to put up with their denunciations of the seven year covenant. No more will they have to fear the judgments these two cause to be brought upon mankind. While their bodies are lying unburied in the streets of Jerusalem a worldwide holiday is proclaimed. People rejoice, make merry and send gifts to one another to celebrate their deaths.

Little did the Beast and his henchmen realize what they had done. They saw only the defeat and death of two troublesome enemies. Heaven viewed these assassinations in a different light. Two of the greatest servants of God who ever lived were taken from their places of bliss and happiness in heaven and sent to earth for a ministry which could only end in death. They must suffer the combined wrath of the Antichrist and wicked men. They must stand in the face of all opposition and proclaim *"Thus saith the Lord."*

Heaven cried for vengeance. When the celebrations are at their height God steps in. The two witnesses are resurrected and ascend to heaven in the sight of men. The merrymaking turns to consternation. Fear grips the populace. The earth begins to shake and quake. Buildings began to crumble. Before the terrible tremers subside a tenth of the city of Jerusalem lies in ruins. Seven thousand men lose their lives. It is quite likely these men were leaders in this persecution and death of the witnesses.

* * * * * * *

One last word. The Beast is mentioned here in this eleventh chapter, but we are not formally introduced to him until the thirteenth chapter. So he has been rising to power for three and one half years before we see him coming up out of the sea. More about the breaking of this covenant and its results later.

SEVENTH TRUMPET—THIRD WOE

"And the seventh angel sounded; and there were great voices in heaven, saying, The kingdoms of this world are become the kingdoms of our Lord and his Christ; and he shall reign for ever and ever. And the four and twenty elders, which sat before God on their seats fell upon their faces, and worshipped God, saying, We give thanks O Lord God Almighty, which art and wast, and art to come, because thou hast taken to thee thy great power and hast reigned. And the nations were angry, and thy wrath is come, and the time of the dead; that they should be judged, and that thou shouldest give rewards unto thy servants the prophets, and to the saints, and to them that fear thy name, small and great; and shouldest destroy them which destroy the earth. And the temple of God was opened in heaven,

and there was seen in his temple the ark of his covenant; and there were lightnings, and voices and thunderings, and an earthquake and great hail" (Revelation 11:15-19).

This is the last trumpet. Paul describes the action here in First Corinthians (15:51, 52), this way: *"Behold I shew you a mystery; we shall not all sleep, but we shall be changed in a moment in the twinkling of an eye, at the last trump; for the trumpet shall sound, and the dead shall be raised incorruptible, and we shall be changed."*

As has been stated in another place, this is the finish of the rapture and the first resurrection—not the beginning. It would not be proper for this to be placed at the sounding of the first trumpet or any other than the seventh.

Jesus speaks of this in Matthew (24:31), *"And he shall send his angels with a great sound of a trumpet, and they shall gather together his elect from the four winds, from one end of heaven to the other."* This gathering has been going on ever since the rapture of the Bridal saints, and will be completed only with the sounding of this last trumpet.

The third woe, the blowing of the seventh trumpet and the final wind-up of everything connected with the Tribulation, begins here with the fifteenth verse. The message here is *"The kingdoms of this world are become the kingdoms of our Lord and his Christ; and he shall reign forever and ever."* Of course, this is anticipatory. Many things will have to take place before the beginning of Christ's reign on earth. But the action has started. The wheels are turning. Before they stop Jesus will have returned to earth with ten thousand of His saints as prophesied by Jude, the battle of Armageddon will have been fought and won by Christ, and the Beast and False Prophet will have been cast alive into the Lake of Fire.

Satan's time is getting short. In the next chapter (12) there is a great voice from heaven saying, *"Woe to the inhabiters of the earth and of the sea! For the devil is come down unto you, having great wrath, because he knoweth that he hath but a short time."* The anger of the nations reflect this. They are angry with God and everything else which keep them from going on in their wickedness unmolested. They are angry because of the plagues which have been visited upon them.

It is in expectation of all the great victories which are to come that another great worship service takes place in heaven. This time the Twenty-Four Elders lead. They leave their seats and fall on their faces before God. They give thanks to the Eternal God in advance for His coming reign.

These Elders are made to see the culmination of all the Tribulation period; the nations angry with God; the wrath of God poured out in a measure never before realized; the judgment of the wicked dead; the rewards given to the prophets, saints and all others who hold God's name in awe; the final destruction of the earth-destroyers who still are on earth at this time.

The chapter closes with a view of the heavenly temple. It is open and in it can be seen the ark of His testament. Lightnings, thunderings, quaking earth and falling hail appear in the picture to foretell of awful events yet to come—all under this seventh trumpet.

Chapter Twelve

THE WOMAN IN THE SUN

"And there appeared a great wonder in heaven; a woman clothed with the sun, and the moon under her feet, and upon her head a crown of twelve stars; And she being with child cried, travailing in birth, and pained to be delivered" (Rev. 12:1, 2).

This twelfth chapter opens with the appearance of a great "Wonder." The Greek word translated wonder here is *Semeion.* It means wonder, miracle, sign or token. The Revised Version of the Bible translates the word "Sign."

This wonder is in heaven. This is not the third heaven of Paul's visit. It is the starry heaven. In it are found the heavenly bodies here mentioned—sun, moon and stars. In this starry heaven appears a woman. This is not a literal woman, but the figure of a woman used to picture something else. This woman is clothed with the sun. Genesis records that God created the sun to be "ruler of the day." So the woman is wearing the rays of the sun as a garment of triumph. She is using the moon as a foot stool. The moon is the empress of night, so the woman has her feet on the powers of darkness and night. This woman has on her head a crown of twelve stars. She is with child. Birth pangs have seized upon her body. The time of her delivery has arrived.

Who is this woman? There are several teachings concerning her identity. One is that she is the church universal in its composite form. Not only is she the church of the last days, but she is said to be the church of all ages. Look at this from the chronological view. The rapture has already taken place (between the third and fourth chapters). The judgment court and the introduction of the "Little Book" occupy the fourth and fifth chapters. As the twelfth chapter is reached all the seals have been opened and the events of the last trumpet judgment are in process of occurring. Now to go back and view the church would throw everything out of its proper order. The church as an organism is never mentioned as such after the third chapter.

Some may see the woman as the church at the time of the rapture. However, the catching away of the Bride will leave only an empty shell of professed Christians. They will not be victorious; they will be defeated—though not destroyed. They will not be in the sun; they will not be standing on the moon, and they will not be crowned with stars. As individuals many of the left ones will prepare themselves and come up in later companies, but at this time this woman in no way fits the picture of the portion of the church left to go through at least a part of the Tribulation.

To understand what the woman personifies, it is necessary to understand the symbols surrounding her. These symbols are the sun, moon and stars. The combination of these celestial bodies is found in Scripture in at least six places. In four of them the literal bodies are in view. Deut. 4:19 contains God's warning to the children of Israel against worshipping them. Joel 2:10 speaks of a time during the Tribulation when *"The sun and moon shall be dark and the stars will withdraw their shining."* Paul, in speaking of the comparative glory of the celestial and terrestrial bodies, mentions the sun, moon and stars. The one hundred and forty-eighth Psalm uses the sun, moon and stars in a figurative sense as praising God.

So, in only two places is the combination of sun, moon and stars used symbolically. In Genesis 37:9, where Joseph has the dreams, the sun is made to picture his father, the moon his mother and the eleven stars as his brethren (Joseph himself being the twelfth star). This is the exact combination found in connection with this woman, even to the twelve stars.

There is no question but that Israel is in the picture in Genesis. Since the sun, moon and stars are symbols in the twelfth chapter of Revelation and the only other place in Scripture so plainly refers to God's ancient people, it naturally follows that this woman represents Israel. The sun is Jacob, the moon Rachel and the twelve stars are the twelve sons, and as such, progenitors of the twelve tribes.

THE MAN CHILD

"And she brought forth a man child, who was to rule all nations with a rod of iron: and her child was caught up unto God, and to his throne" (Revelation 12:5).

Another figure is a "Man Child." The birth of this child is an outstanding feature of the chapter. His identity should be determined before the events surrounding his birth are discussed.

Who is he? Like the woman, there is a diversity of opinion concerning him. One school of thought says he is the Bride of Christ. They get around Christ having a male Bride by explaining that the word here is used in the generic sense. They say the word is neuter gender and mean mankind. The Greek dictionary in *Strong's Concordance* does not seem to bear this out. Even if this word were neuter, there would be other difficulties. If it is accepted that the woman is Israel, that alone would preclude all possibilities of the Man Child being the Bride. Then, too, this is not the place to introduce the Bride. To make this the Bride and the "Catching up" as the rapture would result in confusion, and break the continuity of events.

Some say this is Christ at His birth and ascension. Granted the woman is Israel, making this figure out as Christ at His birth and the catching away as His ascension would not fit the scene either. Why would John be shown all the great earth-shaking events of the opening of the seals, and, without any previous preparation, be shown Christ in the flesh? The text states that this Man Child would "Rule all nations with a rod of iron." This, some say, is absolute proof that this is Christ. Wait; the same thing is promised the overcomers in Thyatira. So this shows it was not said exclusively of Christ.

There is one group which fits the picture perfectly. The time, place and circumstances are all right. Look back to the seventh chapter. There is a group of people who are sealed and divinely protected while on earth during the Tribulation. They are the one hundred, forty-four thousand converted Israelites. They are sealed and left here on earth. Now this same company is seen in heaven in the fourteenth chapter. When were they transported from earth to heaven? The logical place is in this twelfth chapter under the figure of the Man Child.

Those who object to this line of reasoning are pointed to the problem of just when the Bride of Christ will be caught away. Many say this will be between the third and fourth chapters. They reason (and correctly) that after the message to Laodicea no more is said of the church as such in the entire book. But in the fourth chapter we meet a group, whom they identify as those fitting the description of the Bridal saints—the Four Living Creatures. With this we agree. But the point is, there is as much evidence that the one hundred and forty-four thousand and the Man Child are identical as that the rapture takes place between the third and fourth chapters.

MICHAEL

Daniel, Jude and John all speak of Michael the archangel. In the tenth chapter of his prophecy Daniel speaks of a vision he had. In this vision he is told about Michael. This "Man," whose description fits no other but Christ in His preincarnate state, calls Michael one of the chief Princes. The purpose of this vision was to make Daniel understand what would befall his people in the latter days. At the close of this vision this "Man" calls Michael "Your prince." The vision is dealing exclusively with the people of Daniel (Israel). So Michael is the special champion of Israel. In the twelfth chapter of Daniel, verse one, are these words: *"At that time shall Michael stand up, the great prince which standeth for the children of thy people: and there shall be a time of trouble such as never was since there was a nation even to that same time: and at that time thy people shall be delivered, everyone that shall be found in the book."*

There is only one place in Revelation where Michael stands up for anyone. This is in this twelfth chapter. The reason for his standing up is to protect the Man Child. So, since he is to stand up for Daniel's people *"Whose names are written in the book,"* and since this is to be *"In the latter days"* and he is shown *"Standing up"* for the Man Child, the reasonable conclusion is that *"Those whose names are written in the book"* are the one hundred and forty-four thousand converted Israelites seen under the figure of the Man Child.

Another proof of the foregoing is to be found in Jude. In the ninth verse he says, *"Michael, the archangel when contending with the devil he disputed about the body of Moses, durst not bring against him a railing accusation, but said, The Lord rebuke thee."* These two scenes are almost identical. Here is found Michael, Moses' body and the Devil. In Revelation it is Michael, the Man Child and the Great Red Dragon. The analogy is too plain to be ignored. More will be said about Michael later in this chapter.

THE GREAT RED DRAGON

"And there appeared another wonder in heaven; and behold a great red dragon, having seven heads and ten horns, and seven crowns upon his heads" (Revelation 12:3).

A third figure is introduced in this chapter. He is called a great Red Dragon. This Great Red Dragon is Satan himself, as verse nine explicitly states. In this verse he is called *"That old serpent, called the devil, and Satan, which deceiveth the whole world."*

This serpentine creature has made a slimy trail through God's universe. He was defeated and cast out of heaven in the misty ages before man. So he took his spite out on Adam and Eve and the human race. He was defeated at the cross, so he has directed his hatred toward the church. He was defeated here in the twelfth chapter, so he takes out his animosity on the Woman and the Remnant of Her seed.

In order to give some background material and make the scenes in this chapter clearer, some details of Satan's defiling path and successive falls will be given in. . . .

THE TRAIL OF THE SERPENT

Sometime back in the ageless eternities all of God's creation was filled with peace and serenity. Celestial beings went about their heavenly ministrations with poise and gladness. Cherubims flew throughout the universe with lightning-like rapidity, in service to the throne of Jehovah. Seraphims kept up their incessant cry, reminding all creation that God is holy! holy! holy! Archangels marshalled their obedient hosts, ready for any need Deity might have.

For how many millenniums of man's time this continued it is not known. However, it is known that this tranquility suddenly was broken. Absolute obedience to God had always been taken for granted. Never had there been a question of love and loyalty in all creation. Never had the heavenly hosts been tested.

God's ways are past finding out; His sovereignty is unquestioned. So we can only surmise as to the root cause of the rebellion in heaven's ranks. Did God allow this in order to test the angelic hosts? From the imperfect light available on the subject this seems to have been the case.

Lucifer was one of a trinity of archangels. The other two were Gabriel and Michael. Of the three, Lucifer appears to have been the most outstanding. He was known as the "Son of the Morning." He had one-third of God's angels as his obedient subjects.

Let Ezekiel (28th chapter) describe him: *"Full of wisdom.... Perfect in beauty.... Every precious stone was thy covering.... And gold.... The workmanship of thy taberets and of thy pipes was prepared for thee in the day thou wast created. Thou art the anointed Cherub. Thou wast upon the holy mountain of God; thou hast walked up and down in the midst of the stones of fire."*

From this description a little glimpse of the beauty and majesty of this strange creature is seen. Nevertheless it was this very beauty and majesty that caused his downfall. In the fifteenth verse of this twenty-eighth chapter of Ezekiel we are told: "Thou wast perfect in all thy ways *till iniquity was found in thee."*

Details of this iniquity are found in Isaiah 14: "Thou hast said in thine heart, *I will* ascend into heaven. *I will* exalt my throne above the stars of God: *I will* sit upon the mount of the congregation; *I will* ascend above the heights of the clouds: *I will* be *LIKE THE MOST HIGH."*

Ezekiel tells more about this when he says, "Thine heart was lifted up because of thy beauty, thou hast corrupted thy wisdom by reason of thy brightness; thou hast defiled thy sanctuary by the multitudes of thy iniquities." When this iniquity (lawlessness) was brought to light for all heaven to see, Lucifer headed a rebellion. He used his third of the angels in an attempt to dethrone Majesty.

The outcome of the revolt is described by the Prophets Isaiah and Ezekiel: *"I will cast thee to the ground, I will lay thee before kings that they may behold thee. I will bring forth a fire from the midst of thee and it shall devour thee.... Thou shalt be brought down to the sides of the pit."*

Some may object to the use of Ezekiel's writings in describing the unfallen Lucifer. They may contend this is speaking of the king of Tyre. True, this does describe a mortal ruler, but as Scofield points out, "The language goes beyond the king of Tyre to Satan, inspirer and unseen ruler of all such pomp and pride as that of Tyre."

His first fall changed him from Lucifer, "Son of the Morning," to Satan, the avenger and accuser. From here can be traced his slimy route until he finally lands in the Lake of Fire. In his unfallen state Lucifer's throne is believed by many to have been this earth. Before the account of what happened in Genesis, chapter one and verse two, this planet is said to have been his home. The great war in heaven affected all the universe. The earth went through some mighty convulsions before man arrived. A careful study of the first few verses of Genesis will reveal that verse one records the original creation of the earth. When verse two is reached it is found that the earth was here, but *"without form and void . . . darkness was upon the face of the deep."* The waters were already here when the Spirit of God moved on them to bring order out of chaos.

Many mysterious geological formations can only be explained by some such occurrences. Two instances of this are found close to home. In the Arbuckle Mountains of Oklahoma there is a stretch of mountains some miles long that has parallel rows of jagged rock sticking up out of the ground. They look as if man had placed them there, though they are a natural formation. It appears that deep down in the earth an upheaval took place ages ago which broke layers of horizontal rocks and forced them to the surface in a vertical position where they now protrude. Also, in the Ozark mountains of Missouri and Arkansas fossils of marine life are found in abundance. This region is hundreds of miles from where such present day life is found.

When Adam and Eve took up residence in the Garden of Eden, according to the record, one of the first creatures they met was the serpent. Failing in his attempt to dethrone God, Satan began to work to destroy man.

Why does Satan have such enmity against the human race? One theory which seems quite plausible and one which will answer many questions is this: God's purpose in creating man was twofold. The first was to replace the angels lost in the rebellion of Lucifer with another creature —man. After the ranks of heaven have been filled with glorified saints of God, the second purpose will be to allow the perpetual generations of man.

This is in line with God's plan for the perpetuation of family life. In the Hebrew economy the rule of the Old Testament in connection with this was that should a man die childless, his brother was to marry his widow. This first male heir was considered as belonging to the dead man. Others born to the live brother were his own heirs.

Now the angels do not propagate themselves. They are sexless. Their number does not increase, nor does it decrease. Although one-third of the angels fell, they still exist in their fallen state. The creatures to replace them in God's kingdom perhaps will be the glorified saints of God. In their glorified state they will not multiply, but their number will always remain the same. They will not be angels but glorified humans.

Men living on earth in the flesh at the close of the millennium will go on multiplying just as natural man has always done. The difference is they will never die. They will finally fulfill God's plan for the human race. This plan was interrupted in Eden when man fell. It will be resumed by man when the eternal ages begin.

God respected the angel's free will and allowed one-third of them to follow Lucifer. He did not force obedience on any of them. However, when two-thirds remained true to God, their test was over. They proved their love and loyalty. They never again will be subjected to such an ordeal.

Likewise, God allows man his freedom of choice—serve God or Satan. This is why man was allowed to be tempted in Eden. It was a test of obedience. The well-known story is told in few words. Man was tempted by Satan to disobey God; he fell, was driven from the garden, and ever since, has come into the world with the seeds of rebellion and disobedience against God in his heart. By rights man should have been punished by being bound in chains as were the fallen angels. This is where Christ comes in. Although death was pronounced against all mankind, God in His infinite love, provided the wonderful plan of redemption.

Satan is the great adversary of man; he seeks to thwart him at every opportunity. Only the grace of a loving heavenly Father prevents this. In all history this serpent can be seen lurking and slinking in the background. His efforts in Eden did not result in a complete victory, so he found a likely subject for his purposes in Cain. Abel's was the line through whom the Redeemer was to come. Cain's jealousy-inspired murder of his brother Abel before he had a son prevented this. Satan was defeated here because God gave Adam and Eve another son, Seth, through whose line would come the Satan-bruiser.

Before the flood, man became so evil that God in His wisdom and fairness, knew He would have to destroy him. Satan almost won the victory here. However, enough godly people were found (Noah's family) whom God preserved and started the race over again with only eight people.

Satan was the prime mover in building the tower of Babel. Counteract God's plan, was the object. The deification and worship of man was another tool of the arch-deceiver. After they were long dead, many men (and women) were worshipped under the figures of mythological entities.

Another time Satan nearly won the battle. Man was steeped in the worship of idols, and the heavenly bodies. To counteract this God called Abraham out and started over again. When Satan inspired Pharaoh to destroy all the males among the Hebrew babies he was again in a fair way of winning. Moses was God's answer here. Time and again it looked as if Satan were going to be the ultimate conqueror. Since God acts only in accordance with certain rules, and this arch-deceiver knows these rules, many times the margin between victory and defeat has looked very narrow. Just after Eden the heredity line of the Messiah was almost extinguished. At the flood it got down to eight people. One time it rested only in King David, and Saul was seeking his life. Another time it rested on little one-year old (king) Joash, whom the bloody Athaliah thought she had slain. Little eight-year old Josiah was the only hope of the royal house of Judah to keep the seed alive when he came to the throne.

The greatest battle of all had to do with Jesus Christ as the Messiah. It was God's plan of redemption for Christ to die on the cross. Satan knew this, therefore he made every effort to prevent it. He inspired Herod to kill all the little boy babies of Bethlehem. This wicked king was only interested in destroying a possible rival to his throne. Satan had a different motive; he wanted to bring about Jesus' death by means other than crucifixion on the cross.

On the Mount of Temptation Satan's purpose was to induce Jesus to bypass the cross and accept the kingdoms of the world on terms contrary to God's will and purpose. Failing this, he constantly tried to bring about Jesus' death at the hands of mortal enemies. In the Garden of Gethsemane Christ's flesh had to be strengthened by the angels for the coming ordeal; otherwise, there would have been no Calvary.

* * * * * * *

In this twelfth chapter, Satan, as the Great Red Dragon, suffers his second fall. The first one was from the heaven of God's throne to the starry heavens. From the starry heavens he is here plunged to the earth. His third fall will be from the earth to the Bottomless Pit. His fourth and final one will be when he is "loosed for a little season," at the end of the Millennium and then cast into the Lake of Fire.

MICHAEL THE ARCHANGEL

"And there was war in heaven: Michael and his angels fought against the dragon; and the dragon fought and his angels" (Revelation 12:7).

In the study of the Man Child it was learned that Michael is the special champion of Israel. Also, that he will stand up for the children of thy (Daniel's) people during a *"Time of trouble such as never was since there was a nation."* This time is declared to be *"In the latter day."*

In the present chapter this archangel is seen meeting the Great Red Dragon head-on in a terrific battle. He has his soldier-angels and the Dragon has his. The angels here are of two classes: the angels of heaven and the fallen angels.

It is quite likely these two armies have met before. These were likely the ones who fought in the battle in which Lucifer was defeated and banished from God's heaven. Jude mentions the fallen angels in the sixth verse, *"And the angels which kept not their first estate, but left their own habitation, he hath reserved in everlasting chains under darkness unto the judgment of the great day."*

A careful reading of the verse will show these fallen

angels have been in chains *"Unto the judgment of the last great day."* It is also part of the *"Judgment of the great day."* It is altogether in keeping with this scene to assume these fallen angels to have been released in preparation for this specific battle.

In describing this great conflict a few words from Seiss' Apocalypse are in order: "The beings engaged are all spiritual.... The battle therefore must needs be spiritual and not physical. There is no taking life—no killing—no bloodshed—no slaughter.... All the strength of hell and heaven is measured; but it is moral, intellectual, spiritual strength. The cannonading is thought, argument, subtile accusations, and defense. It is the war of mind with mind, of malignant and hellish intellect inflamed with desperate hate and anger against the intellect, reason and right of heaven."

This is in keeping with the scene in Jude where Michael and the Devil dispute about the body of Moses. This is a forensic argument, as has been stated in another place. God works according to set laws which He Himself has decreed. Satan here is claiming God is not consistent with Himself in the bodily resurrection of Moses before the general resurrection.

The case of Michael, the Great Red Dragon and the Man Child is a parallel one. The Man Child is caught up to heaven as soon as he is born. This provokes Satan to do battle with his well-known adversary, Michael. The arguments cover about the same ground. There is one difference in the two scenes. Michael only invokes the rebuke of Jehovah in the first one, but here he does battle proper. This mighty angel prevails, and the Dragon and his angels are defeated and cast down to the earth.

The region in which this battle takes place is in the heaven of the stars and planets, as was shown in the previous discussion. Thus Satan becomes earthbound. It is a great victory when the one who accuses the brethren before God day and night is driven earthward. While Michael and his hosts seem to have fought the battle, some of God's people are also involved. These *"Overcome him* (Satan) *by the blood of the Lamb, and by the word of their testimony,"* and because *"they loved not their lives unto the death."*

As a result of this wonderful triumph, the dwellers in heaven are made to rejoice. Just the opposite is true in relation to the earth-dwellers. *"Woe to the inhabitants of the earth and sea,"* John says, *"because the devil is come down unto you, having great wrath because he knoweth he has but a short time."* Even though Michael has won a significant conquest, Satan will yet bring upon mankind the greatest woe—the Antichrist.

* * * * * * *

When Satan is cast to earth, and barred from the heavens he does not give up. The first thing he does is to take out his wrath upon the woman. After the catching away of the Man Child and the great war in heaven which follows, the woman is seen on earth. In spite of the fact that he failed to devour the Man Child the Dragon still believes he can destroy the woman. To prevent this, she is given *"Two wings of a great eagle"* with which she flies into the wilderness, where she is protected for three and one-half years. The effort to crush the woman by *"Casting out of his mouth water as a flood,"* proves to be futile. She is not now standing in the sun with the moon under her feet, yet she is the victor.

"THE REMNANT OF HER SEED"

"And the dragon was wroth with the woman, and went to make war with the remnant of her seed, which keep the commandments of God, and have the testimony of Jesus Christ" (Revelation 12:17).

After all the Dragon's efforts to subdue the woman fail, he does not give up. He finds a new victim—*"The remnant of her seed."* Who compose this company? If the woman is, indeed, the nation of Israel, then this company is also of Israel. There are some things said about this remnant which are significant, and should aid in the search. First, this group keep the commandments of God. So we know they are God-fearing Israelites. Second, they have the testimony of Jesus. This proves they are followers of Christ.

In following a logical line of reason one would say the woman is the Nation of Israel, while this group is composed of converted Israelites, whether identified as citizens of the nation or Israelites (Jews) whose earthly citizenship might be in any number of countries. They are distinct from the one hundred and forty-four thousand as the context shows.

There are two worlds involved in this twelfth chapter—the natural and the spiritual. Michael and the Great Red Dragon and their hosts are of the spiritual world. Although shown as symbols, the Woman, Man Child and the Remnant are of the natural world.

It has been shown what takes place in the spiritual realm. However, the material activities are somewhat obscure. At this point all the seals have been broken, and the last trumpet blown. If the chronological order is the right one, then the blowing of the last trumpet signals the beginning of the last or third woe. Everything from Revelation 11:15 on is included in this.

In point of time, this is just before the beginning of the last three and one-half year reign of Antichrist as god of the world. A great number of things transpire just at this point. One of these is the breaking of the seven year covenant with Israel by the Beast. Indeed, the scene in the heavenlies could well be a spiritual view of this very act. When this covenant is broken the Beast turns against Israel and inaugurates a severe persecution. This could well be where the Israelite government goes underground (symbolized by the woman) and flees to the Sinai desert, where her friends sustain her.

Here God is following a pattern we have seen before. He raptures some, gives divine protection to some, but allows some to suffer and even give their lives. He raptures the Bride before the opening of the Tribulation. Before the opening of the seventh seal He raptures the company of Palm Bearers in chapter seven. Before Antichrist takes his seat as god of the earth the one hundred, forty-four thousand are raptured.

He gives divine protection to the one hundred, forty-four thousand when He seals them in the seventh chapter. He protects the two witnesses during the first half of the reign of the Beast. He protects the woman in the wilderness during the last half of the rule of Antichrist.

With the Man Child in heaven and the Woman divinely protected, the wrath of the Great Red Dragon is turned upon the "Remnant of her seed." It is stated that the "Dragon . . . went to make war with the remnant of her seed." This war is inspired by the Great Red Dragon, and executed by the two Beasts of the thirteenth chapter.

Chapter Thirteen

THE ANTICHRIST AND HIS KINGDOM

"And I stood upon the sand of the sea, and saw a beast rise up out of the sea, having seven heads and ten horns, and upon his horns ten crowns, and upon his heads the name of blasphemy. And the beast which I saw was like unto a leopard, and his feet were as the feet of a bear, and his mouth was as the mouth of a lion, and the dragon gave him his power, and his seat and great authority. And it was given unto him to make war with the saints, and to overcome them; and power was given over all kindreds, and tongues, and nations. And all that dwell upon the earth shall worship him, whose names are not written in the book of life of the Lamb slain from the foundation of the world" (Revelation 13:1, 2, 7, 8).

The first three and one-half years of the reign of the Antichrist are shrouded in mystery. He is first mentioned in connection with the Two Witnesses in the eleventh chapter. These two had a three and one-half year ministry before being slain by the Beast. Thus, the beginning of their witnessing would coincide with the beginning of the reign of Antichrist and his signing of the seven year covenant with Israel. But what will be taking place at the point he begins his rule? It has been noted several times that just before a particularly severe judgment is to be visited upon the earth God devises means of protection for His people. This is what happens in the seventh chapter. Just before the breaking of the seventh seal one hundred and forty-four thousand Israelites are sealed for their protection as has already been noted (but left on earth). Also, an innumerable company of white-robed Palm Bearers appear in heaven, having come up out of Great Tribulation (nothing mentioned about the Beast). So it would appear that the opening of the seventh seal will signal the beginning of Antichrist's bid for universal control.

If this is the proper interpretation of the record, then these first three and one-half years cover the time of the first six trumpet judgments. Hail, fire, blood and bitter waters are the order of the day. Stygian darkness adds to the horror. Hell-spawned creatures from the bottomless pit come to torment man. Add to all this the awful slaughter by the infernal cavalry of 200,000,000 horsemen and a picture of the true conditions will begin to emerge.

In an effort to illustrate what might be taking place during this time, a fictional sketch has been prepared. It seeks to follow what details are given in Revelation; it fills in with fiction where these details are lacking. Please accept this for what you think it is worth.

ABDULLAH—OR THE MAN OF SIN

Washed by the blue waters of the Persian Gulf on the east, and completely surrounded otherwise by modern Arab nations, a certain tiny country appears to be a mere toe-hold of land, seeking a place in the sun in the southern section of what was once Old Babylonia. Slightly larger than the State of Connecticut, this relatively new Arab state stands fifth in world production of Petroleum. It has less than half a million people to share this great wealth, consequently, its citizens enjoy a tax-free economy.

During World War Two there was born in this little country a boy which we will call Abdullah. This Abdullah came from a very poor home. Oil was just beginning to be exported, so the nationwide affluence of later years was then unknown. Abdullah was a strange boy. His father, Sabah, would look into his dark, brooding eyes, and wonder what the future would hold for his offspring. His mother would experience a vague uneasiness when she would try to imagine his life as a grown man. This only child remained aloof from others of his own age. He seemed to live in a world apart.

As the boy grew, the father began to see the great possibilities lying dormant in him. Also, as the oil fields of the country become such a great source of wealth, Sabah realized a share in this good fortune. His minor government job, the salary from which barely kept his family fed and clothed when Abdullah was born, now had become one of importance and very profitable.

Like a good father, Sabah wanted only the best for his son. As the years went by Abdullah became more and more withdrawn and remote. Many times the father did not know what to make of the boy's moods. At the same time his keen intellect was there for anyone to see.

"Why am I not like other people?" Abdullah would say to himself. "I do not care for sports; I do not care for girls; I do not care to be around other people at all."

If Abdullah lived a life of withdrawal it was not one of unreality. His life was very real; but it was a life of books, governments, world affairs and history. He would eagerly devour huge volumes on great world rulers. The Pharaohs of Egypt, Darius the Mede, Cyrus the Persian, Alexander the Greek and the Caesars of Rome were his constant companions.

A study of the rulers of Old Babylonia was a special delight to him. "Just think," he would daydream. "Only a short distance north of here is where old Nebuchadnezzar ruled ancient Babylon. That Belshazzar was a coward; if he had not been so busy having a good time at those drunken parties, he might have kept his kingdom." In this seemingly idle daydreaming the young student would picture himself in the role of a great world ruler.

Sabah's prosperity allowed him to send his son to the best schools and universities. England, France, Germany, Russia and America all were made to contribute to the young man's liberal education and general fund of knowledge.

Government, history and politics were the subjects most greedily devoured in his insatiable appetite for knowledge. From a student he graduated to professor. From professor in a local situation he became a lecturer. The lecture halls of most of the great universities were open to him. Fortunate indeed was the student who was permitted to sit in on one such lecture.

It was not long until world leaders began to hear of this young man. From the lecture platforms of the universities he went on to become a consultant to governments. His uncanny ability to size up a situation and offer a solution made him welcome in the higher ranks of world leaders.

While outwardly he was just a consultant and a "Trouble shooter," for those enmeshed in problems beyond their capacity to solve, underneath he was forever planning, scheming and awaiting the day when his services would be sought on a world-wide scale.

His broad education, his professorship at major universities, his lecture tours, his role as a consultant to governments all combined to give him an insight into his life-long ambition. He aspired to be a world leader himself. More than that, in his wildest imaginings he saw himself as *THE* world leader!

His first real, definite step in this direction was when he became a special consultant to the World Organization of Nations. Working quietly and without fanfare, he ingratiated himself into the inner sanctums of that august body. He cultivated the acquaintance of every person of importance connected with the organization. Ambassadors to this organization from the leading countries were courted. This intense young man was seen everywhere—in the halls, offices, corridors, grounds—everywhere. He was rapidly making himself indispensable.

Meanwhile world conditions were steadily deteriorating. Nation after nation was hovering on the brink of war with some neighbor. Famine, floods, and earthquakes were coming with ever-increasing frequency. About the time some major crisis was resolved, another would develop. The world was being driven inexorably into a state where the only alternative to utter chaos was the formation of a strong world-wide government. Abdullah had prepared himself for just such a time.

It was in the year 19??. The World Assembly is just coming to order. The moderator bangs his gavel for attention. As quiet settles over that distinguished body, a deep voice is suddenly heard, asking for attention. A well-known individual is seen sitting in the seat of the delegate for a small Mid-East state.

Everyone knows him only as Abdullah, or "The Man." There is something about this Abdullah's voice and bearing which arrest attention. The moderator seems charmed by the man and allows him to speak. There seems to be a sinister magnetism about Abdullah which no one can quite describe nor pinpoint. His voice is powerful, but the facination is not limited to voice and figure. The eyes are dark and piercing, but they alone do not account for the eerie feeling generated. The figure is striking, but it does not appear to reflect his full personality. But as outstanding as his voice, eyes and figure are, his main attraction is the substance of his words. Let us listen in. Only a gist of what he is saying will be given; the total speech need not be quoted here.

"Mr. Moderator, delegates of this great body, visitors, ladies and gentlemen," he begins. "It is not my purpose or desire to disrupt the orderly business of this assemblage. Indeed, I am extremely interested in its continued functions and success. The survival of our world may well depend upon you who are gathered here today. It is for this reason that I persuaded the delegate from my country to allow me to substitute for him.

"All of you are aware of the deplorable conditions existing in our world. Wars and blood-shed have been the order of things for all too long. Famine has stalked our lands; death rides roughshod over our peoples.

"To you I appeal. You can put an end to most of this. You represent the real military strength of the world. If you will stand together, nothing can stop you."

Then Abdullah goes on to cover the entire world situation. It is a long speech. He concludes with the following surprising plea: "What you need is a leader; someone whom you can trust to bring order out of the present confusion. I am offering myself as this leader."

While this last statement astounds everyone; all felt what he had been saying made some sense. But that a man should say these things and at the same time have the affront to offer himself — only a consultant — as such a leader was unbelievable.

After he makes his proposals, he goes on to some specific conditions, and suggests solutions. At the end of his speech, the assembly votes favorable to seriously consider his proposals. It even hints at the possibility of accepting him as a leader. He is asked to address the assembly in the next session. Word of these developments reaches government leaders throughout the world. Consequently, at the next meeting every available seat in the vast hall is occupied by members of the world assembly representatives and other dignitaries from nearly every nation. They fly from everywhere to be present. In his second address he deals with details of major world problems. For each one he mentions he suggests a solution. Everything he says seems so right, but so strange. At the close he offers himself again—

on a trial basis. "Give me," he says "seven years in which to do this work. If I have not been successful by then, do with me what you will, and select whomsoever you will to succeed me."

To the casual visitor to this assembly session the foregoing would appear to be a spontaneous reaction on the part of that body to Abdullah's persuasive oratory. This is far from the truth. Instead, quiet negotiations had been going on secretly for many months. Leaders of the great powers had been meeting behind closed doors in an effort to resolve their basic differences and difficulties. Abdullah was the moving spirit behind these secret meetings.

Ever since the creation of the atomic bomb, these leaders had speculated about the possibility of man destroying himself with it. Since the first crude ones were dropped on Japan in World War Two, this bomb and others more frightful had been refined and perfected, and now they knew man did have the instruments of total destruction. They knew should the United States, Russia and Red China get into an all-out war and release their stockpiles of nuclear weapons the world would lie in shambles in just a few hours. They knew that if one-half the population survived the halocaust, the fallout from such a war, would likely render most of the remaining incapable of having children, and as men would die even from natural causes, there would not be enough children born to replace them.

It was in this atmosphere that, after some months of deliberations, debate and delay, the World Assembly agrees to Abdullah's proposals, and gives him this trial period in which to try to bring some order out of world chaotic conditions.

One of the last nations to come under this universal rule is Israel. She is somewhat cool to the idea of entering into any agreement which includes her age-old enemy, the Arab. But when Abdullah and those working with him make a solemn pledge to guarantee Israel's right to possess her nation without being molested, she too signs this covenant. This agreement is to be in effect for seven years.

Under ordinary circumstances the plan of the World Assembly to give Abdullah such wide powers would have been unthinkable. But these are not ordinary times. The world body has been wrestling with so many seemingly insoluable problems that it is a relief to find someone with so much confidence and self-assurance to put at the helm of the world ship of state.

During his rise to supreme power, Abdullah is known simply as "The Man." Not much is known about his background—only that he is from this small Arab state and has been a professor, lecturer and world consultant. He sells himself to the leaders of the world on the basis of what they think he can do, and not on who he is.

After signing the covenant Israel prospers greatly. Although many troubles still beset her, the great consolation to her is that she is to be left alone by those who had tried so long to drive her into the sea.

Not long after the seven year agreement between the nations of the world and "The Man," strange things begin to happen. Hail, fire and blood began falling out of the skies. Great fires rage throughout the world. Destruction of grass and timber causes great concern.

As if these things are not severe enough, there appears on the earth fierce locust-like creatures whose scorpion-sting makes men want to commit suicide. Many try to kill themselves because of this awful pain, but cannot do so. These creatures roam the earth for five months, then suddenly disappear.

During all this time there are those who recognize the seven year covenant with "The Man" for what it really is—"A covenant with death, and an agreement with hell." There are two men who denounce this world government, and especially the seven year covenant in no uncertain terms. They come to be known as the "Two Witnesses." They are always seen together. Some say they look like characters from Old Testament times.

There is also a group of Israelites who denounce this seven year pact. Their number is said to be one hundred and forty-four thousand. These have accepted Christ as their long-awaited Messiah. In addition to denouncing "The Man" and his covenant, they preach Jesus Chirst everywhere they go.

The Two Witnesses and the "one hundred and forty-four thousand" are quite successful in their efforts. Thousands all over the world are awakened to the sinister aspect of the covenant and "The Man" who is responsible for it.

These "Converts" also join in these denunciations. This opposition causes the rage of Abdullah to know no bounds. Every effort is made to have these trouble makers silenced. No plan is successful. There is something exceptional about this group of "one hundred and forty-four thousand." Each seems to have a spot in his forehead which glows at times. It is said by those who still believe in God that this spot is a seal and an evidence of their divine protection.

The success of the "Witnesses" and the "one hundred and forty-four thousand" is a source of genuine concern for the entire world government. They must be stopped! Too many are becoming disenchanted with the new order. A crackdown is ordered. Investigations are begun. A world wide inquisition on the scale of those of the middle ages is instituted. People are brought into court to account for their actions and attitudes toward the rule of "The Man." But with all this exertion there is a growing feeling that things are getting out of hand. Something drastic must be done.

It was at this juncture that a group of four remarkable men appear on the scene. They claim to be from the Middle East, near the Euphrates River, but no one seems to have ever heard of them. There is an aura of unreality about them, as though they came from another world. They come to the world assembly headquarters, sit quietly in seats reserved for visitors for a day or two, then leave. They are seen here and there all over the world, and at places so far apart that it seems impossible for them to be at so many places at once.

After a few days, strange things begin to happen. First, it is only rumors. In an out of the way place someone reports that an unearthly horsemen is seen. He has a fiery breastplate. He is riding a mount, the head of which is like a lion. From its mouth there comes fire and smoke. About the time one rumor is laid to rest with the explanation that it is only an hallucination of some drug-diseased brain, another starts. A prominent world leader avows he has seen such a creature. In a comparatively short time these creatures are seen everywhere.

Then the terrible carnage begins. These infernal horses have an incredible hatred for man. They rush through a crowd of people, blowing their fiery, sulphureous breath and lashing with their serpentine tails, and leave only corpses. Incomplete statistics reveal over a billion people are slain by these hellish horses. Eventually they run their course and disappear. Right in the misdt of this Abdullah is killed; whether by these horses nobody knows.

THE PERSON OF ANTICHRIST

"And I saw one of his heads as it were wounded to death; and his deadly wound was healed: and all the world wondered after the beast. And they worshipped the dragon which gave power unto the beast: and they worshipped the beast, saying, Who is likened unto the beast? Who is able to make war with him? And there was given unto him a mouth speaking great things and blasphemies; and power was given unto him to continue forty and two months" (Revelation 13:3-5).

When the Great Red Dragon is cast to earth (in the twelfth chapter) he finds his work cut out for him. The man of sin had done his work well. The four fallen angels and the diabolical cavalry also did their work well.

In the opening of this thirteenth chapter the first figure seen is a "Beast rising up out of the sea." Satan has to have some instrument through whom he can work after his fall shown in the twelfth chapter. He finds himself earth-bound. He must have a creature of earth. He is not long in finding such a one. This person is someone like the fictional Abdullah. Up until his death he will have a will somewhat of his own. Satan cannot possess him completely. But in bringing him back to life, the Great Red Dragon gains full control of all his faculties. Although leaders of the world are mourning the death of "The Man" and wondering where a replacement can be found, Satan knows this death will afford a great opportunity to display his own power.

Who is this Antichrist? This Beast? This "Man of Sin"? These questions have intrigued and baffled many who would interpret end-time prophecy. In studying the various writers on the subject one finds about as many candidates for this office as there are writers. Cain is the first in point of antiquity to be suggested as the Antichrist. Then there follows Nimrod, King Saul, Judas Iscariot to name a few characters found in Scripture. In history is found such names as Antiochus Ephipanes, Alexander the Great, Julius

Caesar and Napoleon. In more modern times such names as Mussolini and Hitler are on the roster.

Perhaps if the sacred records are searched and some of the qualification a being must have in order to fit the picture are found one can get at least some idea of the identity of this person. One of the qualifications is to deny the deity of Jesus Christ. I John 4:3 tells us, *"Every spirit that confesseth not that Jesus Christ is come in the flesh ... is that spirit of Antichrist."* Another of the requirements will be that this Beast or Antichrist will exalt himself as God. *"He sitteth in the temple of God, showing himself that he is God"* (2 Thess. 2:4). Still other qualifications and marks of identity will be his power, signs and lying wonders, and his ability to deceive. *"His coming is after the workings of Satan with all power and signs and lying wonders.... With all deceivableness of unrighteousness"* (II Thess. 2:9, 10). The name itself is another clue to his identity. He is ANTI-Christ—opposed to Christ. In order to reveal the Antichrist as the great imitator he is known to be, the following is offered:

CHRIST AND ANTICHRIST COMPARED AND CONTRASTED

CHRIST HAD A PRE-EXISTENCE BEFORE COMING TO EARTH. *"In the beginning was the Word, and the Word was with God, and the Word was God. The same was in the beginning with God.... The Word was made flesh and dwelt among us"* (John 1:1, 2, 14a). ANTICHRIST HAD A PRE-EXISTENCE BEFORE COMING TO EARTH. *"The beast thou sawest was* (before the time of John), *and is not* (was not at the time of John's writing), *and shall ascend out of the bottomless pit"* (Revelation 15:5b).

CHRIST CAME TO ESTABLISH A KINGDOM. *"Verily I say unto you, there be some standing here which shall not taste of death, till they see the son of man coming in his kingdom"* (Matt. 16:28). ANTICHRIST WII COME TO ESTABLISH A KINGDOM. *"And power was given unto him over all kindreds, and tongues, and nations"* (Rev. 13:7b).

CHRIST HAD A THREE AND ONE HALF YEAR EARTHLY MINISTRY. ANTICHRIST WILL HAVE A THREE AND ONE HALF YEAR REIGN of absolute supremacy. *"And power was given to him to continue forty-two months"* (Revelation 15:5b).

CHRIST WAS PUT TO DEATH. *"Pilate delivered him to be crucified"* (Matt. 27:26b). *"The soldiers led him away to crucify him"* (Matt. 27:31b). *"And they crucified him"* (Matt. 27:35). *"Jesus yielded up the ghost"* (Matt. 27:50). ANTICHRIST WILL BE PUT TO DEATH. *"And I saw one of his heads as it were wounded to death"* (Rev. 13:3a).

CHRIST AROSE FROM THE DEAD. *"And the angel said . . . I know that ye seek Jesus which was crucified. He is not here: for he is risen"* (Matt. 28:5, 6). ANTICHRIST WILL RISE FROM THE DEAD. *"The beast that thou sawest was and is not, and shall ascend out of the bottomless pit"* (Revelation 17:8). *"His deadly wound was healed"* (Rev. 13:2, 12). *". . . Them that dwell on the earth . . . shall make an image to the beast which had the wound by the sword and did live"* (Rev. 13:14b).

CHRIST IS ONE IN THE HOLY TRINITY. *"For there are three that bear record in heaven, the Father, the Word and the Holy Ghost"* (John 5:7). ANTICHRIST IS ONE IN THE UNHOLY TRINITY. *"And I saw three unclean spirits like frogs come out of the mouth of the dragon and out of the mouth of the beast and out of the mouth of the false prophet"* (Rev. 16:13).

CHRIST IS OFFERED THE KINGDOMS OF THIS WORLD BY SATAN, BUT REJECTS THE OFFER. *"The devil . . . showeth him all the kingdoms of the world and the glory of them, and saith unto him, All these will I give thee if thou wilt fall down and worship me. Then saith Jesus unto him, Get thee hence, Satan"* (Matt. 4:8, 9). ANTICHRIST IS OFFERED THE KINGDOMS OF THE WORLD BY SATAN AND ACCEPTS THE OFFER. *"And the dragon gave him his power, and his seat* (throne) *and great authority"* (Rev. 12:2b).

A final parallel is seen in the church and the image of the Beast. The church is the body of the second Person in the Holy Trinity—Christ. It is brought into existence by the operation of the third Person of the Holy Trinity—the Holy Spirit. The *IMAGE* of the second person in the unholy trinity—the Beast—is made by the third person of the unholy trinity—the False Prophet.

However, there is the greatest contrast between Christ

and Antichrist when it comes to the purpose and outcome of their respective ministries. Christ came to save; Antichrist will come to destroy. Christ came in love; Antichrist will come in hate. Chirst was revealed in meekness and lowliness; Antichrist will be revealed in arrogance and boastfulness. Christ came and brought life; Antichrist will bring death. Worshippers of Christ will live forever with Him in heavenly bliss; worshippers of Antichrist will live forever with him in the Lake of Fire.

HOW WILL ANTICHRIST COME?

There are several ways that Antichrist can make his debut. He can come and be reincarnated in the life of a new born baby. He can suddenly come as an evil spirit and possess the newly resurrected body of some modern, well-known world leader, or he can be resurrected as a full-grown man with all the attributes and characteristics which he had in a previous existence. Christ came as a baby, and lived the physical life of a normal person, and at the age of thirty began His public ministry. As the Beast is to be a counterfeit Christ, he could come by the same route.

However he comes he will be a person who is self-willed, self-magnified, blasphemous and one who prospers until his work is accomplished. *"The king shall do according to his will; and he shall exalt himself, and magnify himself above every god, and shall speak marvellous things against the God of gods, and shall prosper till the indignation be accomplished"* (Dan. 11:36).

Imagine a vile spirit whose sole reason for existence has been to shape the destinies of mankind through its wicked rulers. There is Nimrod the mighty hunter, whose kingdom sought to build the tower of Babel, thereby bringing the confusion of tongues and the scattering of mankind over the face of the earth. Add to him the spirit of the Pharaohs of Egypt who sought to exterminate the children of Israel by having all the male children put to death at birth. Place the spirit of Saul, the mad king of Israel, with them. Throw in Nebuchadnezzar whose great image so exalted him that he demanded divine homage. Then there is the spirit of the Caesars, the Herods, the Mussolinis, the Hitlers, the Stalins. Place these all together with the rest of Satan-inspired rulers. Merge them into one evil spirit. Allow this hellish spirit to enter into an already wicked, power-hungry ruler, and you have the "Beast rising up out of the sea." Who he is and how he will come no one has a sure way of knowing.

Just as Christ was the manifestation of the Holy Trinity while on earth, just so will the Antichrist in the flesh be the embodiment of the unholy trinity on earth during the Tribulation.

* * * * * * *

THE BEAST ASSUMES SUPREME POWER

"And I beheld another beast coming up out of the earth; and he had two horns like a lamb, and he spake as a dragon. And he exerciseth all the power of the first beast, whose deadly wound was healed And he doeth great wonders, so that he maketh fire come down from heaven on the earth in the sight of men. And he deceiveth them that dwell on the earth by the means of those miracles which he had power to do in the sight of the beast; saying to them that dwell on the earth that they should make an image of the beast, which had the wound by the sword, and did live. And he hath power to give life unto the image of the beast, that the image of the beast should both speak and cause that as many as would not worship the image of the beast should be killed. And he causeth all, both small and great, rich and poor, free and bond, to receive a mark in their right hand, or in their forehead: And that no man might buy or sell, save he that had the mark, or the name of the beast, or the number of his name. Here is wisdom. Let him that hath understanding count the number of the beast: for it is the number of a man; and his number is six hundred, three score and six" (Revelation 13:11-18).

About the time the Great Red Dragon brings the slain leader back to life (if this proves to be the Antichrist) great changes begin taking place. The Two Witnesses are slain. Gentiles begin over-running Jerusalem. The rapture of the one hundred and forty-four thousand Israelites had just previously taken place. The seven year covenant between Israel and the Antichrist is broken. The Israeli government flees to the wilderness. The mark and worship of the Beast are instituted. The Little Horn (Antichrist) plucks up three horns and begins a three and one-half year reign as absolute ruler.

In his rise to power the Antichrist will need all the assistance he can get. He will come to the scene quietly. He will be much sought after by the powers of the world for his great knowledge and the know-how of getting things done. He will come from a small people—we are told. He has a formula for world peace. But when he assumes full control he will declare the seven-year covenant with Israel null and void, and institute a plan to subjugate that tiny nation.

The world populace is so awed by the events of the day that it actually worships the Great Red Dragon as people worship God the Father. The Beast receives worship which should be accorded only to Jesus Christ.

Mankind wonders after the Beast. It feels he is invincible. The anti-God spirit rises to new heights in this period. The Beast blasphemes God's name, His abode and those who dwell there. He declares open war on all who recognize God.

In order to try to banish God and the thought of God from the minds of men, another Beast is brought forth out of the earth. This second Beast comes in subtility. He has horns and the appearance of an innocent lamb. However, he speaks like a dragon. So he is the mouthpiece of the Great Red Dragon. Speculation is rife as to who this second Beast will be. Let us just pass over this speculation and discuss the important thing—the place he will have in the Antichrist kingdom.

Now we have hell's trinity on earth—the Great Red Dragon, the Beast and the False Prophet. They lose no time in starting their operations. The first Beast controls the political and economic world; the second Beast the religious world. The Great Red Dragon is the unseen power behind it all. In spite of the awful wickedness of the day, some men still believe in and worship God. A few Christians and Israelites still refuse to bow down to the Nebuchadnezzar-like image.

The False Prophet (or second Beast) uses all the power of the first Beast. He has been given his power by the Dragon. The first thing he does with this authority is to force universal worship of the first Beast. He performs great miracles. He makes fire come down from heaven in the sight of men. They are deceived by this display of superhuman power. He has an image made of the first Beast. He gives life to this image. The image in turn has power. He decrees that all who refuse to worship the first Beast shall be killed.

Here is where the mark of the Beast comes into the picture. The language is somewhat obscure in the latter verses of chapter thirteen. It is not exactly clear who forces acceptance of the mark of the Beast—the False Prophet or the first Beast. Be that as it may, this is not as important as the action itself.

As a means of forcing universal obedience to Antichrist a mark is devised. It is placed either in the right hand or in the forehead. It is not known exactly what it is. Perhaps it is put on electronically, and can be seen only when it is subjected to some ray of light which will cause it to appear on the skin of the wearer. The record says it is "Six hundred, three score and six," or 666.

The kingdom of Antichrist will operate on at least three levels—political, commercial and religious. This mark of the Beast is the political and commercial angle. Those refusing the mark are barred from buying and selling in the world market places—at the corner grocery or the great world trade marts. On the religious level those who refuse to worship the Beast will be killed.

Many wonder what will happen to those who refuse to take the mark. An adult who knows that a person taking the mark will be doomed to hell, may reject the mark to the point of starving to death. But it may be a different story should this adult be a father or mother. When their small children cry for bread, many will take the mark. They know it will mean their eternal damnation, but to get their loved ones something to eat they take it anyway.

THE KINGDOM OF THE ANTICHRIST

Since the Antichrist and his kingdom both are in view in the text, it is sometimes difficult to understand when it is referring to Antichrist or when it is speaking of his kingdom. This is particularly true in Revelation thirteen, verse three, where these words are found: "And I saw one of his heads wounded to death; and his deadly wound was healed: and all the world wondered after the Beast."

Some say this speaks of Antichrist as an individual; others say it refers to his kingdom. Many who say it refers to an individual usually seek to find some great world leader of the past who has been slain in such a manner as to fit the description found in the Bible. When they do they seek to show that he will be brought back to life and energized by Satan.

On the other hand, those who interpret this Scripture as describing his kingdom, seek to find some kingdom of the past that has collapsed. Many times they wind up by talking about the revival of the Old Roman Empire.

Let us look at the first Beast of Revelation thirteen. He has seven heads. This is symbolical of the seven great empires over which the spirit of Antichrist has ruled or will rule. John identifies them when he says in the seventeenth chapter, *"And there are seven kings: five are fallen, one is, and the other is not yet come."* A glance backward into history will reveal the first six as Egypt, Assyria, Babylon, Media-Persia, Greece and Rome. The seventh world empire is identified by the ten toes of Nebuchadnezzar's great image found in the book of Daniel; the ten horns of the beasts of Daniel and Revelation, and the ten kings who rule with Antichrist. Also it will be noted that the above are the six empires that spanned the period of the existence of Israel, and who held that nation in subjection at one time or another. The Antichrist kingdom is the *eighth* and not the seventh.

The Revelation tells about both the last evil ruler and his kingdom. In speaking of the individual Antichrist, John says, *"The beast that thou sawest WAS."* Then the prophet says, *"And IS NOT"*—was not on earth at the time the apostle wrote. And he *"Shall ascend out of the bottomless pit."* Showing he was in the bottomless pit during John's day. And he *"Shall go into perdition."* This is proof that the Beast shall return to the abode of Satan after his kingdom is destroyed.

That he will have a kingdom is well authenticated in the Revelation. Chapter thirteen, verse two: *"The dragon gave him his power, and his seat* (throne) *and great authority."* Chapter seventeen, verse nine: *"There are seven kings* (kingdoms) *five are fallen,* (Egypt, Assyria, Babylon, Media-Persia, Greece) *and one is* (Rome) *and the other* (seventh) *is not yet come."* Chapter seventeen, verse twelve: *"The ten horns . . . are ten kings, which have received no kingdom as yet; but receive power as kings one hour with the beast."*

In verse three of this seventeenth chapter is found a woman sitting on a scarlet colored beast. In verse nine it is found that the woman is sitting on seven mountains (the above mentioned seven kingdoms). In verse fifteen the "waters" upon which the woman sitteth are said to be peoples, and multitudes and nations and tongues. Those who would identify the seven mountains in verse nine as the city of Rome and the scarlet woman as the Roman Church seem to fail to realize that by no stretch of the imagination could the seven small hills of Rome be called mountains. Neither could they say that the Roman Church, with less than twenty percent of the world's population in her fold, would fit the picture of the world-embracing church represented by this vile woman.

Many mistakes have been made by those who seek to identify Antichrist and his kingdom by pointing out individuals and countries as those of end-time prophecy. Witness Mussolini and his conquests. Many predicted that he would revive the Old Roman Empire. Some saw Hitler's rise to power as a portent of the establishment of the Antichrist kingdom, especially since he was the great persecutor of the Jews. Other earlier despots were thought to fit the picture of the coming world ruler. These have come and gone and have been mostly forgotten.

The Beast described in Daniel had ten horns. A "Little Horn" came up among the ten horns and subdued three of them. This left seven, but with the "Little Horn" there were eight. Revelation 17:11, speaking of the Beast says, *"He is the eighth and of the seven."*

John's description of this Beast is remarkably like the description of the beast Daniel saw. The Old Testament prophet saw one beast like a lion, another like a bear, another like a leopard, and the fourth beast so horrible as to be beyond description. Daniel sees this last beast as terrible, strong, possessing great iron teeth. What wild beast it could be likened to, Daniel was at a loss to say. Where Daniel saw four beasts, John saw only one. However, this one beast had all the features of Daniel's four. It is described as like a leopard, feet of a bear, mouth of a lion and empowered by the Great Red Dragon. Thus the spirit that energized the empires of Egypt, Assyria, Babylon, Media-Persia, Greece and Rome will be resurrected.

It is recorded that this Beast is the eighth and is of the seven. This kingdom will seek to rival the eternal kingdom of God. The Antichrist will seek to perpetuate it eternally with himself as god. All through this it is seen that Satan is the great counterfeiter. From the Bible record it is believed that man's total history from Eden to the Great White Throne Judgment is to last some seven thousand years. After this will come the eighth thousand years, ushering in the eternal ages. Satan's plan is to be the god of this eternal kingdom.

In speaking of the wounding to death and the subsequent healing in Revelation thirteen and three, is the Antichrist or his kingdom in view? If it is a kingdom, is it Rome? If it is speaking of a person, was the deadly wound inflicted upon some historical person in past ages, or was it suffered sometime during the Tribulation? On the answers to these questions depends the true interpretation of the record.

History generally points to 49 B.C. as the beginning of Rome as an empire, with Julius Caesar as the first emperor. The date of the division of the Empire into east and west is given as 376 A.D. The fall of the Western Empire as 476 A.D., and that of the Eastern Empire as 1453 A.D.

Why should Rome be identified by commentators with the Antichrist kingdom more than the five previous empires is something hard to understand. These empires all had these things in common. They were worldwide in their rule; manifested the same ruthless spirit; their rulers were worshipped as gods, thereby usurping the prerogatives of deity. Rome fell. Rome ceased to exist as an empire. Rome travelled the same road as the others and came to the same end. There is only one difference. It is the iron of the toes of Nebuchadnezzar's image, indicating continuing existence of the iron of Rome. But this iron was mixed with clay in the time of the feet and toes period. This would represent the rule of the ten kings of John's prophecy. This kingdom is said to be partly strong and partly broken. Other than this, everything else is just alike.

Now this seventh empire—the one to follow Rome—will be worldwide. Many writers limit this to the territory once controlled by Rome. This Roman Empire was limited mostly to those countries bordering on the Mediterranean.

This comprised most of the known world at that time. But since civilization has so greatly expanded, many other countries are as fully developed as the ones around the Mediterranean. May it not be assumed that the Antichrist kingdom will include the whole world?

Now for the seventh empire—the one of the ten toes, ten horns and ten kings. When he comes the Antichrist will find this kingdom in existence. In John's visions these ten kings had not received a kingdom as yet. Nevertheless, they are to appear in the end-time to receive power "one hour" with the Beast. It seems the logical explanation of this is that these ten kings are in a loose alliance for world rule. They establish this seventh kingdom, but are unable to handle the different nationalities and problems such a kingdom would present. They begin looking for a leader. This leader proves to be the "Little Horn" of Daniel's prophecy. He is given the reins and immediately deposes three of these kings. Thus, he becomes the eighth in two ways: when he deposes three of these kings, seven are left. He adds himself to them and this makes him the eighth of these kingdoms of the last days. He is ruler of the eighth world empire, and we are told he is the eighth and is of the seven.

The tenth verse of the seventeenth chapter further helps identify the Beast and his kingdom. It states there are seven kings—five are fallen, one is, and the other is not yet come. This one not yet come is this seventh and is the final world kingdom previous to the one Antichrist will establish. Perhaps this seventh will be the world organization about which men are now talking so much since the organization of the United Nations. This seventh kingdom is a composite picture of all the other seven. The Antichrist is not the absolute ruler of this kingdom as so many writers try to make him; but he is the absolute ruler of the eighth. The ten kings form the seventh and they give their power to the Beast; thereby causing a complete change and a new world empire. Those who say the Roman Empire will be revived as the seventh kingdom should change their program and make this the eighth if they are to place the Beast over the resurrected Roman Empire. Notice, it says he is the *eighth* and of the seventh—but *not* the seventh.

Right after World War Two there was a strong movement to bind the nations together in an effort at peaceful co-existence. One result of this was the formation of the United Nations Organization (later called the United Nations, or UN). Many prominent leaders of the day felt this body did not go far enough in its efforts to secure peace. Back in those days there was a magazine called THE FREE WORLD. Here are some excerpts from an editorial in the January, 1946, issue of this publication:

"If the UNO (now UN), fails, then not world government, but world anarchy and world war may follow." And in speaking of the staff of the Secretariat, the central agency including the chief administrative officers, the editorial goes on to say, "The staff may be chosen by standards of competence and loyalty to the UNO (UN) to the extent of an oath of exclusive allegiance to it." In other words, these workers would be loyal (says this writer) to the UNO (UN), regardless of the wishes of the government in which they hold citizenship. "Britain and America fear Soviet intentions ... the United States fears a strong UNO (UN).... Only by the transfer of sovereignty can war be prevented." The writer goes on in his plea to strengthen the UN, "To compel, by national legislation, the reference to the World Court *all* disputes, and the acceptance of the Court's findings ... to renounce as soon as possible, the use of the veto power." (The power by which one member of the Security Council can make void some action taken by that body.) Another writer in the same issue of the magazine stated, "World government ... has suddenly become the only alternative to atomic extinction." This magazine had connections in almost every country on the globe, and included among its contributors some of the leading statesmen of the day. Therefore, it reflected in a great measure what was being thought in official circles.

THE FREE WORLD did not become the power its promoters felt it would, and has ceased publication (according to present information). Yet, the seed thought of the one world government concept is not dead. The hardening of the lines between the Communist world and the Free world has only caused it to lie dormant. Now, it seems both camps want one world rule if they can do the ruling.

* * * * * * *

It is never safe to survey the world situation at any given moment and try to place it in a definite period of fulfilling prophecy. Others have done this and in a few years conditions in the world have so changed that their predictions are shown to be ridiculous. Witness Napoleon as the Antichrist; Mussolini as the Antichrist; Hitler as the Antichrist; Stalin as the Antichrist. At the same time world conditions are such at present that a broad outline would not be completely out of line. Without being dogmatic and leaving no place for a possible changing world climate, it appears that everything is in readiness for the rapid fulfillment of endtime prophecy.

The following may turn out to be just like so many other prognostications. But as a trial balloon—what about the world empire of Communism? Since World War One this ideology has engulfed almost a third of the population and more than one half of the land area of the earth. This is still a developing empire and growing at a rapid rate. In a little over fifty years it has reached and converted more people to its religion than Christianity has in almost two thousand years. It has used whatever means were at hand. If persuasion did not get results, force was used.

In Nebuchadnezzar's image the golden head of Babylon, the silver breast and arms of Media-Persia, the brass belly and thighs of Greece, and the iron legs of Rome, and finally, the Iron and Clay feet and toes of the seventh empire are seen. World Communism fits the picture of the feet and toes perfectly. Just as the Roman Empire was divided in 376 into east and west, represented by the legs of the image, just so is Communism divided. Russia and her satellites dominate Europe; China and her allies dominate Asia. While many people see this division as a good thing for the rest of the world, at the same time there is a general feeling that should war break out the Communist world might unite as one to defeat the Non-communist countries. This could end in the formation of the seventh kingdom.

The world empire is coming, and it may well be on the way toward concrete development now. Instead of a world-wide Communist take-over the UN may find its loosely knit organization and its lack of real power over the nations, present such drawbacks that a really representative world government will be substituted for the present organization. If this takes place, then it will take just one more step to place the affairs of this super-state into the hands of ten men. After some time these men face certain failure, so they select a leader, and it may well be the Antichrist himself. Time alone will tell.

On the other hand, the UN may die of its own weight and no world government come out of it. There may be an atomic war which will seriously depopulate the earth. This may make men see that they must get together in a real way. Then the ten kings may arise and select an administrator who will turn out to be the Antichrist. It is not worthwhile to make predictions in a dogmatic way. Too many Mussolinis have been deposed for one to be too sure of himself. But the above are POSSIBILITIES which might well take place.

Chapter Fourteen

THE ONE HUNDRED & FORTY-FOUR THOUSAND

(Seen in Heaven)

"And I looked, and lo, a Lamb stood on the Mount Sion, and with him an hundred and forty-four thousand, having his father's name written in their foreheads. And I heard a voice from heaven as the voice of many waters, and as the voice of great thunder: and I heard the voice of harpers harping with their harps; And they sung as it were a new song before the throne, and before the four beasts, and the elders: and no man could learn that song but the hundred and forty-four thousand, which were redeemed from the earth" (Revelation 14:1-3).

The introduction in the preceding chapter of the Beast out of the sea, the Beast out of the earth, and the animated image and mark of doom makes for blackness and darkness and unrelieved despair, unless followed by scenes such as are shown in the present chapter.

Everything is in contrast in these chapters. The Beasts come up out of the sea and earth, and the mark and image fill out the picture of diabolical materialism reaching its lowest depths. The scene of the Lamb and the "One Hundred and Forty Four Thousand" changes the picture to pure joy and happiness.

In the seventh chapter this group is sealed as a protection against the forces of the Antichrist. Here they are in heaven, as verse three makes very clear when it states, *"They sung a new song ... before the throne, and before the four Beasts and the Elders."* Also, the fourth verse says, *"These were redeemed from among men."* Somewhere between the seventh and fourteenth chapters they are transported from this earth to heaven. We feel there is only one place and one figure which fit this removal—the Man Child in the twelfth chapter.

The voice from heaven is as of many waters and great

thunder. Imagine the roaring of giant cataracts or mighty ocean billows, combined with the cannonading of the heavenly elements. Add this to the reverberating tones of one hundred and forty-four thousand harps, as they play the accompaniment.

The song they sing rings throughout the heavenly domain. It is a new song. Living Creatures and Elders help make up the silent audience. Although the latter could sing the *"Song of Moses and the Lamb,"* they are not permitted to join in this mighty anthem.

It is not recorded what the song is about, but from the position of the "One Hundred and Forty-Four Thousand" one is made to believe it has to do with their lives, their ministry as divinely protected evangelists during the rise to power of the Antichrist, and their rapture to heaven, with all the blessings received and anticipated.

This "One Hundred and Forty-Four Thousand" form a special company of redeemed ones. They are not the Bride or Bridal company symbolized by the Four Living Creatures. Neither are they of the Twenty-Four Elders representing the Old Testament saints. These groups are already in and around this throne before this special throng arrives.

There are seven things said about this group. 1. They are not defiled with women. 2. They are virgins. 3. They are followers of the Lamb. 4. They are redeemed from the earth. 5. They are the firstfruits unto God and the Lamb. 6. They are without guile. 7. They are without fault.

1. *They are not defiled with women.* Some have misunderstood verse four and sought to prove that members of this group had never married in their natural earthly lives. This is not necessarily the case. The Bible nowhere condemns proper marriage. This verse has a spiritual application and human marriage is not the subject. It is used only as a figure of speech and denotes the undefiled nature of these and means they were not guilty of practicing spiritual adultery—the word applied to unlawful association of married people.

2. *They are virgins.* Spiritual fornication in the Bible is used to illustrate the unlawful association of God's people with the sinful world or its sinful practices. It speaks of spiritual defilement. The word is different from adultery

in that it relates to the unlawful relationship between the unmarried.

As used in Scripture the word virgin means uncorrupted, pure, chaste. It was because this company had reached such a state that they were selected, protected and translated to their present heavenly estate.

3. *They are followers of the Lamb.* They were of Jesus' brethren, the Jews (more fully, Israelites). Jesus first came unto His own (people), but His own (people) rejected Him. In the earthly life of Jesus this caused Him great suffering. In Matthew 23:35-36 He laments, *"O Jerusalem, Jerusalem ... how often would I have gathered you together even as a hen gathereth her chickens under her wings, and ye would not.... Ye shall not see me henceforth, till ye shall say, Blessed is he that cometh in the name of the Lord."* Now these brethren (the One Hundred and Forty-Four Thousand) follow Him whithersoever He goeth.

4. *They are redeemed from among men.* This, as well as other indications, show they had reached the state of perfect redemption. Their race is over, their victory is won. They are now to bask forever in the presence of their Redeemer.

5. *They are the Firstfruits to God and the Lamb.* From a casual reading of the foregoing statements confusion could arise. In other places redeemed ones are shown to have already reached this state. However, if one will consider their particular relationship to Jesus it will become perfectly clear. THEY WERE THE FIRSTFRUITS IN THAT THEY WERE THE FIRST COMPANY OF GOD'S ANCIENT PEOPLE TO REACH THIS PLACE AS A BODY DISTINCT FROM ALL OTHER PEOPLE. Old Testament saints already here are both Jew and Gentile. Those coming from the Gospel dispensation are made up of both Jew and Gentile, blended together into one body, the church. Therefore, in this sense, the "One Hundred and Forty-Four Thousand" as a distinct body are the firstfruits to God and the Lamb.

6. *They are without guile.* Guile is the very essence of treachery, cunning, deceit and trickery. Jacob was noted for these traits, especially in his early life. Many of these traits are said to have been handed down to his descendants. So it is doubly significant that guile was completely absent from this company.

7. *They are without fault.* Pilate said at Jesus' trial, "*I find no fault in this man.*" This is just another mark of their Christlikeness, and worthiness to occupy this exalted place they held.

* * * * * * *

In the remaining part of this chapter we meet with six angels, a heavenly voice and one like the Son of Man. Angel One preaches the everlasting Gospel. Angel Two announces the fall of Babylon. Angel Three warns against the mark and worship of the Beast. Angel Four cries for the reaping of the harvest of the earth. Angel Five comes out of the heavenly temple with a sharp sickle in his hand. Angel Six cries for the reaping of the vintage of the earth.

ANGEL ONE—THE EVERLASTING GOSPEL

"*And I saw another angel fly in the midst of heaven, having the everlasting gospel to preach unto them that dwell on the earth, and unto every nation, and kindred, and tongue, and people, Saying with a loud voice, Fear God, and give glory to him; for the hour of his judgment is come: and worship him that made heaven, and earth, and the sea and the fountains of waters*" (Revelation 14:6, 7).

At this point the Bride of Christ is gone from the earth. Other companies, including the "One Hundred and Forty-Four Thousand" Israelites have their places in heaven. The Two Witnesses have been slain, resurrected and are now in heaven. The message of every Gospel preacher has been silenced by the Antichrist. What few God-fearing people are left on earth have to hide in dens and caves to escape the wrath of the Beast. Apparently not a voice on earth can be raised in behalf of God's program.

But God never has been without witnesses on the earth. He will not be so now. True, Antichrist has silenced all opposition. However, there is a voice raised which he cannot still. It is the voice of an angel. He comes preaching the everlasting Gospel. Out of heaven the voice comes; here the Beast has no authority.

Listen to the message this angel gives: "*Fear God*" he warns. There are some who say the church and the Holy Spirit will leave the earth at the rapture, and not a saved person will be left here. Then why "*Fear God*" if nobody is saved and nobody can get saved? Why "*give glory to God,*" if it will avail nothing as all who hear this message are doomed to land in the Lake of Fire? Only God's people *"Worship him."* Why then this admonition if there is none of God's people here? By reading the text just as it is written it becomes very plain that this angel is preaching the everlasting Gospel *"Unto them that dwell on the earth."* And the message is not to just one segment of the population; it is for *"Every nation, and kindred, and tongue and people."*

Could one dare say this preaching was ineffective? No; to do so would violate every principle of God's merciful dealings with man. This would be a cruel hoax perpetrated upon man in his direst extremity of suffering. No, this angel is offering salvation to all who will accept it. At this late hour God's mercy and love are still extended. And everyone who has not taken the mark of the Beast or worshipped his image has an invitation to partake of God's living water.

The thirteenth chapter introduces the mark and worship of the Beast, but no doubt some time will elapse between the time the decree for compliance is made and the time when it is completely enforced. Possibly it will be in this period that this *"Angel with the everlasting gospel"* will be flying through the heavens. That there will be a great harvest of souls as an outcome of the preaching of this angel, we are bold to state. They are found in chapter 15:1-4. More will be said about them at the proper time.

ANGEL TWO—FALL OF BABYLON ANTICIPATED

"And there followed another angel, saying, Babylon is fallen, is fallen, that great city, because she made all nations drink of the wine of her fornication" (Revelation 14:8).

There are two falls of Babylon, because there are two Babylons. One is mystical Babylon as a system; the other is a Babylon, a literal city. The ten kings as sub-regents of the Antichrist will hate Mystical Babylon and destroy her. But the kings of the earth will wail at the burning of literal Babylon. The first Babylon comes into remembrance for a final downfall in the seventeenth chapter. In the eighteenth chapter is described the final destruction of literal Babylon.

This second angel announces the fall of this wicked Babylon. This is an anticipatory announcement. The reason for her fall is given here, *"Because she made all nations drink of the wine of the wrath of her fornication."* The fall of mystical Babylon and of the literal city and her final destruction will be discussed later.

ANGEL THREE—DOOM OF THE BEAST-WORSHIPPERS

"And the third angel followed them, saying with a loud voice, If any man worship the beast and his image, and receive his mark in his forehead, or in his hand the same shall drink of the wine of the wrath of God, which is poured out without mixture into the cup of his indignation; and he shall be tormented with fire and brimstone in the presence of the holy angels, and in the presence of the Lamb: And the smoke of their torment ascendeth up for ever and ever: and they have no rest day nor night, who worship the beast and his image, and whosoever receiveth the mark of his name. Here is the patience of the saints: Here are they that keep the commandments of God, and the faith of Jesus" (Revelation 14:9-12).

Man has worshipped many things in his long sinful history. He has bowed down to stocks and stones in his quest for acceptance by some god. He has prostrated himself before idols of every kind, seeking to appease the imagined wrath of his gods. He has measured his length for many miles, trying to reach some supposedly hallowed shrine and gain the favor of a non-existent deity. All this comes to a head in the worship of the Beast.

By this time humanity as a whole will have rejected the true God and His worship. They will have come to *"love darkness rather than light, because their deeds are* (will be) *evil."* Then will be fulfilled to the last final letter the first chapter of Romans. God will have *"Given them up"* to lustful uncleanness, and the worship of the creature. He will have *"given them up"* to vile, unnatural affections, where men will lust after men, and women after women. And, finally, *"God will give them over"* to minds completely abandoned to *"Fornication, wickedness, malice, murder, deceit and malignings."* They will be "haters of God, boasters, and full of pride."

In a measure these people have been worshipping the Beast all along. Until now he has not manifested himself. And since they have turned away from the true God, it is an easy step to worship the Beast. Man has been preparing for this for a long time. Every time he has put the acquisition of creature comforts or selfish desires ahead of God, he has been forging another link in the chain which will eventually bind him fast to Satan.

The first two of the Ten Commandments strictly forbid the worship of any god but Jehovah. God is a jealous God; He alone must be worshipped. When man deliberately turns from the Lord God and worships the Beast, nothing but eternal destruction awaits. The wrath of God is poured out without any mixture of mercy, and the Beast worshippers shall be tormented with fire and brimstone. And the smoke of their torment ascendeth forever and ever, we are told. Thus the judgment is pronounced upon them who *"Worship the beast, and his image, and whosoever receiveth the mark of his name."*

Whether these six angels with their respective messages and ministries each occupy a period of time and then pass on, or they are all active at once, there seems to be no sure way of knowing. Be that as it may, we do know the first was an angel offering mercy, but warning of impending judgment. The second and third appear to amplify this message of coming judgment upon Babylon and the Beast worshippers. Babylon is to be destroyed and the Beast-worshippers doomed to eternal destruction in the Lake of Fire.

Here is another proof that there will be some of God's people still on earth at this period. They are told to be patient. And the proof of their patience will be that they refuse to be a part of Babylon and the kingdom of Antichrist. Rather, they will be keeping the commandments of God and the faith of Jesus.

THE HEAVENLY VOICE—THE BLESSED DEAD

"And I heard a voice from heaven saying unto me, Write, Blessed are the dead which die in the Lord from henceforth: Yea, saith the Spirit that they may rest from their labors; and their works do follow them" (Revelation 14:13).

This verse has been used countless times in funeral services to comfort the bereaved and give assurance that loved ones who die in the Lord are in a blessed state. This is quite proper, but the primary reference here is to members of a distinct group who die in a specific period. There is one word which holds the key to this explanation—*henceforth.* This word literally means *"From here on out."*

In the thirteenth chapter verse seven says, *"It was given unto him* (the Beast) *to make war with the saints, and to overcome them."* In the tenth verse it states, *"He that leadeth into captivity shall go into captivity; he that killeth with the sword must be killed with the sword."* The saints are admonished here to remember that the captors will themselves become captives, and those who wield the sword will themselves be slain with the same instrument.

In the war against the saints, the Beast will be the victor in that he will slay multitudes of those who refuse to worship him or take his mark. This will be a period of great trial for God's people. Places of worship will be closed, ministers' voices will be silenced. But God is not without methods of warning and comfort for them. The angel with the everlasting Gospel will be heard from heaven, the announcement of the impending fall of Babylon will hearten them to exercise faith and patience. The warning of the doom of those who worship the Beast or receive his mark will strengthen their determination to have no part of the program of the Antichrist. Finally, this voice from heaven speaking of the blessedness of those who die in the Lord *from here on out* gives them courage to persevere to the end.

In the fifteenth chapter is seen a company who had *"Gotten the victory over the Beast, and over his image, and over his mark, and over the number of his name."* This is the company who gained the victory and were raptured. These are seen on the Sea of Glass before the throne. Those whom the Antichrist overcame and killed are seen in the twentieth chapter where John *"Saw the souls of them which were beheaded for the witness of Jesus, and for the word of God, and which had not worshipped the beast, neither his image, neither had received his mark upon their foreheads or in their hands."* This last company comprises *all* the martyred dead of the Tribulation, and not just those killed by the Antichrist. Some were beheaded because they refused to cooperate with the Antichrist, but some were beheaded *"For the witness of Jesus, and the word of God"* before the Antichrist came to full power and was revealed as the Beast. This great group began to be gathered under the fifth seal and will be completed when the last saint has been martyred for his testimony.

ANGEL FOUR—THE HARVEST OF THE EARTH

"And I looked, and behold a white cloud, and upon the cloud sat one like unto the Son of Man, having on his head a golden crown, and in his hand a sharp sickle. And another angel came out of the temple, crying with a loud voice to him that sat on the cloud, Thrust in thy sickle, and reap; for the time is come for thee to reap; for the harvest of the earth is ripe. And he that sat on the cloud thrust in his sickle on the earth; and the earth was reaped" (Revelation 14:14-16).

Beginning with the sixth verse, there are five scenes in this chapter—the angel with the everlasting Gospel, the angel announcing the fall of Babylon, the voice from heaven proclaiming the blessedness of the dead who die in the Lord *"From here on out,"* the Son of man and the attendant angel announcing the harvest of the earth, and the two angels urging the gathering of the *"Clusters of the vine of the earth."*

Some commentators see the harvest and the gathering of the vintage as referring to one and the same thing—Armageddon. A close look will bring to light a vast difference. A study of the Scriptures will show that the word "Harvest" used in its symbolical sense, can refer to gathering either the wicked or the righteous into their final abode.

In the Old Testament the word "Harvest" is used figuratively several times. In Jeremiah 51:33 the prophet says the daughter of Babylon is like a threshing floor; it is time to thresh her, because her harvest time has come. Hosea 6:11 mentions a harvest set for Judah. Joel 1:11, in referring to the last days speaks of the perished harvest. And Joel 3:13, in a like vein, proclaims the great wickedness of the latter days and says to put in the sickle, for the harvest is ripe.

If these were the only references in the Bible to the word "Harvest" used in the figurative sense, it would be difficult to see anything but the harvest of the wicked here in these references. However, if one will look at the remaining Scriptures in which the word is used symbolically, it will be seen that there is a good harvest as well as a bad one. Only one Scripture in the Old Testament is used in the good sense. It is Jeremiah 8:20 where the seer says, *"The harvest is passed, the summer is ended and we are not saved."*

When we come to the New Testament it is a different story. The references are to the good harvest—at least in part. Both Matthew and Luke speak of the great harvest and few laborers. In speaking of the wheat and tares Matthew likens the natural harvest time to the end of the world (age) when the good and bad will be separated. Mark sees in the natural harvest a picture of the kingdom of God; John warns against any waiting for the harvest, saying the fields are already white unto harvest.

Further study of this picture of the end-time harvest in relation to the other scenes of the latter part of the chapter will disclose many differences. Three of the others are first announced by an angel; then the particulars of the vision are given. The harvest scene is different in that it introduces the principal characters first, then the angel, then his work.

In this scene the *"One like unto the Son of man"* is sitting on a white cloud. He is wearing a golden crown on His head and holding a sharp sickle in His hand. There is no question as to who this is. There is none *"Like the Son of man,"* but the Son of man—Jesus Christ.

A great part of the administration of the Great Tribulation punishment is meted out by the Living Creatures, the Twenty-Four Elders, or angels. Some of it is done, though, by Jesus Himself. As the Lion of the Tribe of Judah He takes the Little Book out of the hand of God on the throne, and, one by one, tears from it the seven seals. As the "Mighty Angel" of the tenth chapter He holds the now-open Little Book in His hand and *"Placing his right foot on the sea and his left foot upon the earth"* takes possession of this terrestrial ball. In the scene here He is described as *"One like unto the Son of man,"* sitting on a white cloud, wearing a golden crown on His head, and holding a sharp sickle in His hand. An angel comes out of the temple and announces that it is time for the harvest of the earth to be reaped.

What is this reaping? If we accept the explanation that it is Jesus Christ on the white cloud, then we must accept the fact that it is Jesus Christ here who does the gathering. Can we identify this mustering with the killing of millions of people as takes place at Armageddon? This does not quite fit the picture. This seems to be a benevolent operation. If we link this verse with verse thirteen, we can well see how this is so.

This group appears to be those who have gained the victory over the Beast. This follows a well defined pattern found in Revelation whereby just before some terrible event is to take place, God calls away a group to heaven. Witness the rapture of the Bride before the Tribulation itself; the great multitude standing before the throne in the seventh chapter; the catching away of the One Hundred and Forty-Four Thousand Israelites, represented by the Man Child in the twelfth chapter. Before the pouring out of the seven last plagues the company pictured by the harvest of the earth will be caught away.

ANGEL SIX—THE VINTAGE OF THE EARTH

"And another angel came out of the temple, which is in heaven, he also having a sharp sickle. And another angel came from the altar, which had power over fire: and cried with a loud cry to him that had the sharp sickle, saying, Thrust in thy sickle, and gather the clusters of the vine of the earth; for her grapes are fully ripe. And the angel thrust in his sickle into the earth, and gathered of the vine of the earth, and cast it into the great winepress of the wrath of God. And the winepress was trodden down without the city, and the blood came out of the winepress, even unto the horses' bridles, by the space of a thousand and six hundred furlongs" (Revelation 14:17-20).

The picture of the reaping of the vintage presents no great problems of interpretation. It emerges as a clear picture of Armageddon. This is another of those previews of things which happen later, but are announced beforehand. The actor in this scene is not, *"One like unto the Son of man,"* but *"Another angel from the heavenly temple possessing a sharp sickle."* The harvest of grain is bloodless, but the harvest of the vintage speaks of blood—a river of blood some 176 miles long, and up to the horses' bridles in depth. Further word about Armageddon awaits future chapters.

Chapter Fifteen

THE SEVEN LAST PLAGUES ANNOUNCED

"And I saw another sign in heaven, great and marvelous, seven angels having the seven last plagues; for in them is filled up the wrath of God" (Revelation 15:1).

As the Tribulation nears its end the activities are stepped up. The riding of the horsemen, the convulsions of the universe, the trumpet judgments bringing hail, fire, blood and Stygian darkness, the infernal locusts and the infernal cavalrymen are just stages in a softening up process to prepare for the pouring out of the seven last plagues seen in the sixteenth chapter.

The seven vials (bowls) of wrath complete the full measure of God's indignation toward hell's unholy trinity, and wicked man. In it is the fall of Babylon, the Battle of Armageddon, the casting of the Beast and False Prophet into the Lake of Fire, the binding of Satan and the consigning of him to the bottomless pit for a thousand years. These plagues will be discussed in detail in the next chapter.

SEA OF GLASS

"And I saw as it were a sea of glass mingled with fire: and them that had gotten the victory over the beast, and over his image, and over his mark and over the number of his name, stand on the sea of glass, having the harps of God. And they sang the song of Moses the servant of God, and of the Lamb" (Revelation 15:2, 3a).

John views this scene as a great and marvelous sign in heaven. Before he goes any further with the particulars of the vision he introduces a special group of saints. These compose a company of God's people who have been rescued from the earth and will not have to suffer further under the regime of the Beast. They are not martyrs, but have been caught away alive to heaven where they appear on the Sea of Glass.

A great harvest was reaped in the fourteenth chapter.

It was found this was a harvest of God's people who were caught away before the pouring out of the seven last plagues. So the first company of the redeemed we see after this is the group on the Sea of Glass. The connection seems unmistakable; this is the grain of that harvest.

This Sea of Glass first comes into view in the fourth chapter. It is "Like unto crystal," calm and unperturbed. In the present chapter great changes have taken place. The placidness of the crystal gives way to the flashing of amber flames as they dance and leap upward. In his first vision John sees no one on its crystal pavements. In this second look he sees it filled with a happy, shouting, singing, harp-playing group.

The scene finds its parallel in the victory celebration after the children of Israel had crossed the Red Sea. Moses and the people sang, and Miriam and the women made sweet music on their timbrels. Moses had stretched out his rod over the sea and the high-banked waters had levelled out. They filled the trough through which Israel had marched in the early morning watch. Pharaoh and his army had been caught in the engulfment. A screaming, struggling mass of horses and men gradually disappeared beneath the rushing waters. Many bodies were washed ashore.

At last Israel was free. No longer could Egypt hold them in bondage. Now they were headed for their Promised Land. In great waves of exulting joy these former slaves shouted, sang and rejoiced. Moses gave them a song of victory—the song of redemption. *"The Lord was their strength, their salvation and their God.... As a mighty Warrior He had cast Pharaoh, his captains and chariots into the Red Sea,"* they chanted.

Then as the Song of Moses grew more boisterous and the music louder they sang of *"The greatness of thine excellency, the breath of thy nostrils, the blowing of thy wind, the stretched out hand, all gave thee the victory."* On the other hand, they sang of God's goodness to them. *"In mercy thou hast redeemed and guided thy people toward thy holy habitation. But sorrow, amazement, trembling, fear and dread will take hold of our enemies,"* they shouted.

The foregoing gives but a faint comparison with the victory celebration indulged in by this group on the Sea of

Glass. Israel had a choice of freedom or slavery for a lifetime. These had a choice of eternal life or eternal death. There was the Beast over which they had gained the victory. There were the image, the mark and number of the Beast's name with which they had successfully contended. *"They loved not their lives unto death,"* so they were *"more than conquerors."* They were raptured from the earth before the grievous sore, the bloody waters, the scorching sun and the inky darkness were visited upon mankind under the seven last plagues.

They did not have to join issue with the frog-like spirits of the Dragon, the Beast and the False Prophet. They missed the bombarding of lightning induced thunder as the earth quaked, cities fell, islands disappeared, mountains sank and enormous hailstones rained down upon hapless humanity. While all this was going on they were singing the victors' *"Song of Moses and the song of the Lamb."*

This group had gotten the victory over the Beast, his mark and over the number of his name. Their position here gives added evidence that the events of the book of Revelation are generally to be taken in chronological order. A hasty glance backward will bring this out. The martyrs under the fifth seal (sixth chapter) were *"Slain for the word of God, and for the testimony which they held."* No mention is made of the Beast, simply because he is not revealed until the thirteenth chapter. Neither is anything said of the Tribulation as such. Now in the seventh chapter an innumerable multitude is seen *"Before the throne."* They are wearing white robes and holding palms in their hands. They came up out of great tribulation. No mention is made of the Antichrist (or Beast), because he had not yet been revealed. So three companies are dealt with here. First, those under the fifth seal. They were slain for "The Word of God, and their testimony." No mention of the Tribulation as such, nor of the Beast. Second, the white-robed palm-bearers come up out of great tribulation. No mention made of the Antichrist because he has not yet been made manifest. On the other hand, this third company was victor *over the Beast, his image, name and number,* showing they came up during the reign of the Beast as god of the earth.

These saints are playing on harps and singing the victors' *"Song of Moses and the song of the Lamb."* In Exodus is found the *"Song of Moses."* And since Paul stated in Corinthians that *"They* (Israel) *drank of that Rock that followed them; and that Rock was Christ,"* then it becomes apparent that the Lamb was also the inspiration for the ancient song. It is not only the song of victory, but also the song of redemption.

The victory of Moses and the children of Israel over Pharaoh and his army is a miniature picture of the triumph of this group over the Beast and his kingdom. For them the war is over. For them the final victory is won. Others will have to suffer the awful calamities yet to come, but these have reached their "Desired Haven."

"And after that I looked, and behold, the temple of the tabernacle of the testimony in heaven was opened: And the seven angels came out of the temple, having seven last plagues, clothed in pure and white linen, and having their breasts girded with golden girdles. And one of the four beasts gave unto the seven angels seven golden vials full of the wrath of God, who liveth forever and ever. And the temple was filled with smoke from the glory of God, and from his power; and no man was able to enter into the temple till the seven plagues of the seven angels were fulfilled" (Revelation 15:5-8).

There are three important series of God's judgments visited upon men for the purpose of breaking down their stubborn wills and assuring victory for His people—the plagues of Egypt under Moses, the seven trumpet judgments and the seven last plagues.

Blood, hail, fire, darkness, sores and death are the common ingredients of these periods of severe punishment. As terrible as were the Egyptian plagues, their effects were mild in comparison with the suffering under the blowing of the seven trumpets. Also, the trumpet judgments are not nearly so terrible as these seven last plagues.

The angels in verse one have control of these seven plagues which will be visited upon mankind. John saw this enactment as a sign in heaven *"Great and marvelous."* In verse five he sees the opened heavenly tabernacle of testimony. In verse six he sees this place as a temple. Out of it come these seven angels. He is careful to describe their attire. Their clothing is pure white linen, and their breasts are girded with golden girdles. The gold speaks of royalty, and the pure white linen speaks of purity. They are of the priestly order of heaven.

The Living Creatures again appear in this picture. One of them is in possession of seven golden vials (bowls), filled with the wrath of God. He gives them to the seven angels. This scene is so awe-inspiring that no one is able to enter the temple until the angels have poured out their vials upon the earth.

In chapter eleven, verse nineteen, is a resume of the disturbances of nature which will take place during the pouring out of these last plagues. The lightning, and voices, and thunderings, and an earthquake and great hail show the results from the vantage point of the earth. The eighth verse of this fifteenth chapter views it from heaven's standpoint. The temple here is filled with smoke. This calls to mind smoking Mount Sinai when Moses received the law. Also, it suggests Isaiah six in which the house of the Lord was filled with smoke. The smoke seen in the present chapter was from the glory of God and a visible evidence of His power.

This also is reminiscent of the time when Moses and the children of Israel had completed everything about the tabernacle in the wilderness. The record says, "*Then a cloud covered the tent of the congregation, and the glory of the Lord filled the tabernacle of the congregation, because the cloud abode thereon, and the glory of the Lord filled the tabernacle*" (Exodus 40:34, 35).

These seven plagues fill to the full God's wrath upon mankind. Six of them are recorded as finished in the sixteenth chapter. The wording of the description of the seventh plague is such that one sees a picture of continuing sore affliction right on to Armageddon.

Chapter Sixteen

THE SEVEN LAST PLAGUES

(Continued)

"And the first went, and poured out his vial upon the earth; and there fell a noisome and grievous sore upon the men which had the mark of the beast, and upon them which worshipped his image" (Revelation 16:2).

The action as a result of the trumpet judgments is just a little preview or sample of what happens when these seven last plagues are poured out. There is both a comparison and a contrast seen here. An attendant of the seven trumpet angels *"Stood at the altar ... was given much incense* (which he offered) *with the prayers of the saints upon the golden altar which was before the throne."* In contrast, there are no prayers associated with these last plagues.

This attendant of the seven trumpet angels took the censer which was used for the incense-laden prayers and filled it with fire of the altar and cast it into the earth. The reaction to this was expressed by *"Voices, and thunderings, and lightnings, and an earthquake."* The same reaction was seen in the seventh of these last plagues. However, added to this was *"The ... great city was divided into three parts ... cities of the nations fell ... Babylon came in remembrance before God, every island fled away and the mountains were not found."* Hailstones of a talent weight fell out of the heavens.

The *Authorized Version* of our Bible calls these vessels containing the wrath of God *"Vials." The International Standard Bible Encyclopedia* describes them as "A flat shallow bowl, shaped much like a saucer." No doubt they were essentially the same as the one used by the attendant to the trumpet angels. The difference being there was only one vessel used then, seven were used here.

There were seven areas affected by the last plagues—the earth, the sea, rivers and fountains, the sun, the seat of the Beast, the Euphrates River and the air.

THE FIRST PLAGUE

The first plague resulted in a *"Noisome and grievous sore"* coming upon those taking the mark of the Beast. The contents of this first bowl apparently could contain some element which, when coming in contact with the mark of the Beast upon the wearer, cause this sore.

This is called a *"Noisome"* sore. The dictionary defines "Noisome" as "Offensive or disgusting; evil smelling; stinking; fetid." Consider what the conditions will be when this sore develops from the mark of the Beast. It will be as if in this day everyone had a vile smelling cancer. The rich, the poor, the white, the black; the high-ups and the low-downs—all with this heavy burden. This was a grievous sore, and one which brought sorrow and pain. We do not know how long this plague will last. While this is the first plague of the series, we see those under the fifth plague suffering from sores. Perhaps these are the same old sores. And they may have lasted until the end of the Tribulation. The armies of Armageddon may, to a man, come to this battle suffering this awful stinking plague of sores.

THE SECOND PLAGUE

"And the second angel poured out his vial upon the sea; and it became as the blood of a dead man: and every living soul died in the sea" (Revelation 16:3).

In this day of pollution consciousness these last plagues should reveal what will prevail when the earth, sea and sky become completely polluted—with blood.

The account of these plagues moves quickly on. The problem of the grievous sores is left and other plagues occupy the scene. The second plague has to do with the waters of the sea. They become as the blood of a dead man. We are told that every soul in the sea died. The word "Soul" here means the animal principle only and does not refer to the immortal soul of man.

This plague is remarkably like the second trumpet judgment. With the blowing of this trumpet a great mountain falls into the sea. A third of the sea is involved, a third of the sea creatures perish and a third of the ships are destroyed. On the other hand this second plague wipes out every living thing in the sea. Keep in mind this difference;

in the second plague everything in the sea is touched, not just a third part.

THE THIRD PLAGUE

"And the third angel poured out his vial upon the rivers and the fountains of water; and they became blood. And I heard the angel of the waters say, Thou art righteous, O Lord, which art, and wast, and shall be, because thou hast judged thus. For they have shed the blood of saints and prophets, and thou hast given them blood to drink; for they are worthy" (Revelation 16:4-6).

This third plague is somewhat like the third trumpet Judgment. Then a third of the rivers and fountains of water were made unfit for use. This third plague is more severe. Now all fresh water becomes blood!

Blood is an element in nearly all acceptable sacrifices to God for man's sins. The blood of the animal sacrifice of Abel attested to his righteousness. From that time until the death of Jesus Christ on Calvary's cross blood made an atonement for man's sins. The shed blood of Christ became the substance of which animal blood was only the shadow. Now man is forgiven his sins only on the merits of the blood-sacrifice of Christ.

To reject the blood of Jesus Christ as the basis for forgiveness for man's sins is no light thing. The accumulation of this rejection has been building up ever since the blood became efficacious. At this point in the Revelation this rejection has become intolerable. So, man is given rivers of blood to drink. Fountains gush forth with it. It is not the fresh blood of animal sacrifice, rather it is the putred, stinking, coagulated blood of the long dead.

Not only is this blood given them to drink because of their rejection of Christ's blood, but because of the blood of millions and millions of God's saints and prophets whom ungodly men have slain. If the blood of all the righteous shed upon the earth from Abel onward was to be the basis of judgment of the Christ-rejecting Pharisees and Sadduces of His day, how much more shall all the blood of the righteous shed from Abel to Armageddon be charged against the kingdom of the Antichrist. Drink this blood, says the angel of the waters. You are worthy. And drink they must.

THE FOURTH PLAGUE

"And the fourth angel poured out his vial upon the sun; and power was given unto him to scorch men with fire. And men were scorched with great heat, and blasphemed the name of God which hath power over these plagues: and they repented not to give him glory" (Revelation 16:8, 9).

The fourth plague has to do with the sun. Men are scorced with its great heat. There is a wonderful thing about the sun. It is said to be some 93,000,000 miles from the earth. Yet its warmth makes possible life on our planet. Moved closer, it would scorch and burn, destroying all life—human, animal and vegetable. Moved farther away, everything would freeze. The temperature of the sun is said to be thousands of degrees hot. It is so hot that the earth has to rotate and give us days and nights, to keep it from burning everything to cinders. Likewise, the cycle of the seasons must be maintained. After months of hot weather we must have months of cold weather so the earth can cool off.

We are told that absolute zero temperature is around 550°. Without the sun everything would be absolute zero. So the solar system is like a giant rotisserie. A rotisserie, you will remember, is a device which has heat at one point, and at a certain distance away is an object to be cooked. The object is placed where it will rotate, so the food will be cooked properly on all sides. Should the rotation stop, the food would come out raw on one side and burnt on the other.

Somewhere between the 550° of absolute zero and the thousands of degrees of heat of the sun is just the right temperature. God has His hand on the thermostat, cooling and heating as only He knows how. It is very simple for God to rotate the solar system. All He has to do is move the earth closer to the sun to bring about conditions of the fourth plague.

Whether God increases the heat of the sun, or moves the earth closer, or uses some other method, the end result is the same: Men are literally scorced by the awful, burning rays. Under normal conditions they would cry out to God in repentance and plead for mercy. Not under the fourth plague; these depraved ones blaspheme the name of God.

Those who had worshipped the Beast and received his

mark had already sealed their doom for the Lake of Fire. But for those yet living who had not aligned themselves with the Beast here was their chance for repentance. If there were no chance for mercy and possibility of repentance even the mention of it would be a cruel travesty. This is just another proof that *"God's mercy endureth forever."*

THE FIFTH PLAGUE

"And the fifth angel poured out his vial upon the seat (throne) *of the beast; and his kingdom was full of darkness; and they gnawed their tongues for pain, And blasphemed the God of heaven because of their pains and their sores, and repented not of their deeds"* (Revelation 16:10, 11).

Under the fourth trumpet judgment, there was great darkness. The sun, moon, and stars were smitten. A third part of the day and a third part of the night were engulfed in darkness. The fifth plague also has to do with darkness. Where darkness prevailed only one-third of the time under the fourth trumpet blast, here everything is in total darkness in this plague.

Absolute, total darkness of the heavens is a condition almost unknown to man. When the sun is down and the night skies are blanketed with thick clouds there seems to be a little light coming from somewhere. But this will be TOTAL darkness. We are not told what will take place during this worldwide blackout, but our imaginations can fill it with every conceivable horror.

Since this plague is directed specifically at the throne of the Beast, mercy is not promised. The only repentance which could possibly be involved here is the change of mind about these judgments themselves. Although godly repentance which leads to salvation would be an impossibility, those of the Antichrist kingdom could say amen to their own condemnation. This they refuse to do. Although they recognize that these calamities come from God, all they have for Him is blasphemy, because of their pains and sores. Evidently they still have the sores they contracted in the first plague. Little by little everything is closing in upon the kingdom of the Beast. The end is almost in sight. Only the preparation for Armageddon and the battle itself remain to bring a finish to his regime.

THE SIXTH PLAGUE

"And the sixth angel poured out his vial upon the great river Euphrates; and the water thereof was dried up, that the way of the kings of the east might be prepared" (Revelation 16:12).

This sixth plague marks the beginning of the march of the world's armies to Armageddon and the final destruction of all hell inspired military power. This will be the last military battle ever to be fought on earth's soil. At the end of the Millennium there will be an abortive effort on the part of Gog and Magog to raise an army "As the sands of the sea," but God will step in and send fire down out of heaven and consume this would-be army.

The result of the pouring out of the sixth plague is the drying up of the waters of the river Euphrates. We have already come to this river once in our study. The result of the sixth trumpet judgment was the loosing of the "Four angels which are bound in the great river Euphrates." As an outcome of freeing these angels an army of 200,000,000 cavalrymen was let loose upon mankind. One-third of earth's population perish in this great catastrophe.

Many rivers in the world are longer and wider and deeper than the Euphrates, but few have a more colorful history. Somewhere in its vicinity was the Garden of Eden. On its banks Nimrod built the city of Babylon (Babel). Near its mouth lived the patriarch Abraham before journeying to Canaan. It was by its banks that the Hebrew captives hung their harps on the willows, unable to sing the songs of Zion in a strange land. Daniel and the three Hebrew children, and Nebuchadnezzar and Darius and Cyrus lived near its waters.

The modern Euphrates is some 1,700 miles long, and, at one point reaches a width of about twelve hundred feet. Its headwaters rise in Armenia and flow into the Persian Gulf. Under the sixth plague it is to be dried up. The reason: So the way of the "Kings of the east" might be prepared. As a military barrier it would pose a very small problem to a modern army. So, it must be that these kings of the east will have very crude equipment, or else the language is symbolical. In either case the result is the same: removal of the last restraining force, and allowing these kings of the east freedom to march to Megiddo.

The drying up of the river is just one more step in gathering the armies of the world to Armageddon. Verses thirteen through sixteen show that not only are these eastern kings ready to march, but the armies of the whole world are being prepared to march to that last great battle.

Immediately following the pouring out of this sixth plague (if not actually a part of the plague itself) John sees three unclean frog-like spirits come out of the mouth of hell's trinity—the Dragon, the Beast and the False Prophet. The drying up of the Euphrates clears the way for the eastern kings; these vile frog-like spirits, through their devilish miracles, entice the rest of the world's kings to bring their armies to the slaughter.

These wicked spirits completely captivate unregenerate humanity. This diabolical trinity knows it is fighting against God, but in presumption it is going to Armageddon even ready to fight against divinity. Lucifer once fought such a battle in the heavenlies and lost, but he is still the reprobate and will never give up until he is cast into the Lake of Fire.

These frog-like spirits go out to the earthly kings and make them believe there is victory to be gained. They prove their powers by their mighty miracles. Since these kings have rejected God's light, they are in complete spiritual darkness. Thus they are easy prey to Satan's wiles. The sixteenth verse shows the success Satan has. The armies of the world are converging on this one spot—Israel—and one place in that nation—Armageddon.

Right in the middle of telling about the drying up of the Euphrates and the frog-like spirits, and the march to Armageddon, Jesus interjects a warning to His people to watch for Him. This can have at least two interpretations: a warning to the saints of all ages to watch for His coming; or a warning and a promise to those saints living on earth at this late hour. If one will trace the previous pattern God has followed in taking care of His own in the Great Tribulation period, the evidence is overwhelming that the warning and promise are made to saints living on earth when the sixth bowl of God's wrath is poured out. By way of repetition, remember the catching away of the Bride before the Tribulation starts; the appearance of the white-robed palm-bearing multitude in chapter seven before the opening of the seventh seal and the seven trumpet judgments; the catching up to heaven of a group symbolized by the Man Child in the twelfth chapter before the revelation of the Beast as Antichrist in the thirteenth chapter; the benevolent harvest in the fourteenth chapter before pouring out the bowls of wrath in the sixteenth chapter. Here we have an intimation of another catching away. This time before the seventh and last plague with all its attendant horrors is poured out. Yes, God takes care of His own!

THE SEVENTH PLAGUE

"And the seventh angel poured out his vial into the air; and there came a great voice out of the temple in heaven, from the throne, saying, It is done. And there were voices, and thunders, and lightnings; and there was a great earthquake, such as was not since men were upon earth, so mighty an earthquake and so great. And the great city was divided into three parts, and the cities of the nations fell: and Great Babylon came in remembrance before God, to give unto her the cup of the wine of the fierceness of his wrath. And every island fled away, and the mountains were not found.... And there fell upon man a great hail out of heaven, every stone about the weight of a talent: and men blasphemed God because of the plague of hail; for the plague thereof was exceeding great" (Rev. 16:17-21).

When Jesus hung upon the cross His last words were, "It is finished." The great voice out of the temple in heaven cries, "It is done!" When this cry is made it will mean preparations have already been made for visiting the last full measure of God's wrath upon mankind.

Under this seventh plague the following things happen: an earthquake, the like of which never before had been experienced, will take place. The cities of the nations will fall. Babylon will be burned. Islands of the sea will disappear. Mountains will be levelled. Fifty pound hailstones will fall out of angry skies. The assembled armies of the world will be converging upon Israel. Total annihilation will face that tiny nation. God's miraculous deliverance will be shown in later chapters.

The Dragon, the Beast, the False Prophet and the armies of the kings of the earth will be trapped in the valley of Jehoshaphat. The Beast and False Prophet will be cast alive into the Lake of Fire. The flesh of the armies of the Beast will furnish a banquet for the vultures of the air. Satan will be bound in the bottomless pit. The Tribulation martyrs will take their places along with other resurrected saints. Details of all this will be shown later.

Chapter Seventeen

JUDGMENT AND FALL OF MYSTIC BABYLON

"And there came out one of the seven angels which had the seven vials, and *talked with me, saying unto me, Come hither; I will shew unto thee the judgment of the great whore that sitteth upon many waters: With whom the kings of the earth have committed fornication, and the inhabitants of the earth have been made drunk with the wine of her fornication. So he carried me away in the spirit into the wilderness: and I saw a woman sit upon a scarlet-colored beast, full of names of blasphemy, having seven heads and ten horns. And the woman was arrayed in purple and scarlet color, and decked with gold and precious stones, and pearls, having a golden cup in her hand full of the abominations and filthiness of her fornication: And upon her forehead was a name written, MYSTERY, BABYLON, THE GREAT, THE MOTHER OF HARLOTS AND THE ABOMINATIONS OF THE EARTH.... The seven heads* (of the Beast) *are seven mountains on which the woman sitteth.... The waters which thou sawest, where the whore sitteth, are people, and multitudes, and nations and tongues.... And the ten horns* (kings) *... shall hate the whore, and shall make her desolate and naked, and shall eat her flesh, and burn her with fire"* (Revelation 17:1-5, 9b, 15b, 16).

The seventh plague was given in bare outline in the previous chapter. A great many more details will be needed to make this section of the book more understandable. After recounting the things which will happen under the seventh or last plague, John returns to the particulars of the account. He first tells about Babylon.

A careful study of chapters seventeen and eighteen will make plain that there are two Babylons in view—Babylon in mystery and a literal city of the last days called Babylon. This is the only conclusion to be reached if one is to explain the seemingly contradictory statements made about the subject. In chapter seventeen the ten kings hate the whore, eat her flesh and burn her with fire. It can easily be seen that this is figurative language, and applies to mystical Babylon. In chapter eighteen the account of the destruction describes the burning of a literal city, at which time the kings of the earth mourn.

* * * * * * *

Sitting astride the great river Euphrates, some two hundred miles above the head of the Persian Gulf, historical Babylon sat as a queen for many centuries. Old in adulteries, her attire in this seventeenth chapter fits her admirably. According to the Bible record she was the first city built after the flood. She will be the last one destroyed before Christ sets up His Millennial kingdom.

In Genesis ten we are told she was built by Nimrod as the beginning of his kingdom. This kingdom was established in the land of Shinar, and included not only Babylon, but Ereck, Accad and Calneh. Nimrod is known in mythology as Merodach, Marduk, Nimus, Jupiter-Belus, Bel-Merekac, or simply as BEL. He was the son of Cush, grandson of Ham and a great grandson of Noah. Therefore his was the fourth generation after the deluge.

It was in old Babylon that active, organized opposition to God started after the flood. And, according to the record, its founder was the leader in building the tower of Babel, and the first man to be worshipped as a god. There were three reasons why these people wanted to construct the tower of Babel—its great height would keep them from being destroyed by some future flood (so they thought); they wanted to make a name (memorial) to themselves; they wanted this to be a beacon to keep man from being scattered over the face of the earth. All three reasons were in direct conflict with God's plan for man. No tower could be built high enough to rise above a God-sent flood. God did not want man to glorify himself. God's plan for man was for him to subdue the *entire* earth.

When the confusion of tongues took place during the building of this tower, and the people were scattered over the face of the earth, they took with them the seeds of idolatrous worship and planted them throughout the world. This partially accounts for the similarity of the mythology and idol worship of much of mankind.

Babylon is called the mother of harlots because she is the mother of nearly all false religions. In ancient Egypt her children were found in the mythological kingdoms of Orsis, Isis, Horus, Nabay and Set. She was the mother of the sun god Ra, who transported the dead in the boat of the sun, sweeping through the sky daily, and plunging into the underworld of terror each night. One of her sons was Halthor who carried off the dead to await an uncertain resurrection. Her spirit is found in the cemeteries where the dead were said to wander about looking for food and other comforts they had in their lifetimes. Carved images of animals, family members, slaves and other creatures to keep them company remind one of the Babylonians and their determination to preserve for themselves a name.

She is the mother of the Assyrian Asshur who went out of the land of Shinar and built Nineveh and was later worshipped as their supreme god. The goddess Istar who appears to have been Asshur's consort, was her child. Her sons and daughters worshipped by the Assyrians included such mythological characters as Nippur, Bel, Marduk, Arbella and Nergal.

The Greek gods Zeus, Hermes, Dionysus, Athena, Helios, Hephraestus, Hera, Apollo, Artemis and Aphrodite were her sons and daughters.

In Rome she could claim Jupiter, Minerva, Diana, Hercules, Ceres, Liber, Juno, Liba, Apollo, Mercury and many others as her offsprings.

In order to counteract all this mass of false religion God began a program of His own. He "went down" into the ancient land of Shinar and called out Abraham. Somewhat less than two hundred miles south and east of Old Babylon was located the city of Ur of the Chaldees. Historians tell us Ur was first peopled by Sumerians, a race of people of Hamatic origin. This agrees with the Genesis account of Nimrod as the founder of Babylon and the surrounding cities. Later a branch of the Semitic race migrated from the west and settled in this region. This was Abraham's people. For all practical purposes whatever knowledge these Semites may have had of Noah's religion must have been lost. For by the time of the fusion of the two cultures all had become idol worshippers.

But God's ways are past finding out. To the human mind Abraham may have appeared to be a most unlikely subject with whom to start a move back to God, establish the religion of Noah and counteract the apostasy of Nimrod and the Babylonians. Nevertheless, this is what happened. We are not told just how God did this, but in some real way He communicated the message to the patriarch to move out from his country and his father's house to a land which was later to be designated.

This was the beginning in earnest of the age-old conflict between the true God and the harlot Babylon. Since heathen worship had its roots in this old city, it is not surprising that the followers of Jehovah encountered opposition wherever they met the children of the harlot. For instance, when Jacob's family went down into Egypt to dwell, a conflict between the religion of that country and Israel seemed certain. A compromise was reached by allowing Joseph's brethren to settle in Goshen, a district in the eastern part of Egypt and somewhat removed from the more densely populated delta of the Nile.

The long years of sojourning in that Hamitic land, no doubt, influenced the Hebrews toward the worship of the heathen deities of their neighbors. This is evident from the incident of the worship of the golden calf while Moses was on Mount Sinai receiving the tables of the law from Jehovah.

The conflict continued even after Israel was firmly established in Canaan. One of the most effective influences to weaken God's people was the false worship indulged in by the inhabitants of the country who were not driven out by Joshua. Baal, Tammuz, Dagon and a number of other gods bid for the allegiance of the Israelites. Women of Israel wept for Tammuz. Their men bowed down to the sun, Ezekiel tells us.

This is the story of Babylon down through the ages. She has always been in opposition to the true worship of God. Where she could not destroy this worship she sought to join and corrupt it. How well she has succeeded is a matter of history. She was not able to destroy the early church, so she joined it under Constantine. She brought heathenism right to God's altar with her pagan practices. She attached herself to the primitive church, and only the success of the Reformation of the sixteenth century kept her from completely destroying its real spiritual life.

Nor has she been idle since. In the Christian realm her

infectious virus has entered the blood-streams of nearly every religious movement since Luther. False doctrines and evil practices even crept into some groups who opposed Rome most strenuously. The basic tenets of a certain segment of the Reformation included the doctrine that the more a person sinned the greater was God's grace. So the adherents sinned greatly that they might experience God's unmerited favor more fully.

To a certain extent the leaven of evil has always been in the visible church. The parable of Matthew thirteen where the woman hid leaven in the three measures of meal illustrates this. The meal became completely leavened. So, unless the leaven in the body politic of Christianity had been occasionally removed or drastically reduced, it would have been wholly corrupted by now. This is why many times God has had to step outside the bounds of organized Christianity and start new movements to keep the body cleansed.

The old Babylonian gods are dead. No more are God's women tempted to weep for Tammuz, nor do God's men feel the compulsion to face the rising sun and worship that heavenly body as lord of the day. But what about modern times? Did the hereditary line stop with pagan Rome? Has she been barren since then? No! Her children are still around.

The name Babylon has two meanings—depending upon who is describing her. One is "The gate of God." This was how Nimrod's people saw her. The other is "Confusion." This is how sacred writers saw her. These two names are quite expressive. Combined they spell out, "Confusion at the Gate of God." This is certainly descriptive of the religion of the Tribulation, and even of much of it in the world at the present time.

First, there are the heathen religions, many of which are loosely bound together by ties going back to Babylon. Then there is another group of false religions which had their origin a few centuries before and after Christ. Mohammedism, Buddhism and others belong to this group. A third group is made up of so-called Christian organizations. Of these latter ones we have the paganism of the Roman and Orthodox churches. Then there is that portion of Protestantism which denies the very fundamentals of the faith. Their voice is heard in the World Council of Churches. Put all these together in one organization and you certainly have "Confusion at the Gate of God."

Right before our very eyes is a movement now which could (but not necessarily would) help bring about the conditions described by John. It is the effort of what is now called the National Council of Churches in the United States to form a new organization whose rules would be so elastic that all religions could feel welcome under its "Umbrella." The present council was first called the Federal Council of Churches. Then the name was changed to National Council. What the new organization will be called is anyone's guess. If all the groups which call themselves Christian were to merge into one corporate body, with each group doing what it felt was "Right in its own eyes," this certainly would be Babylon. All her sons and daughters would feel right at home here.

In such an organization would be found those who doubt the veracity of the Scriptures, those who preach the "Social gospel" to the extent of failing to preach "You must be born again" and those who give lip-service to God while giving allegiance to the god mammon. Add to this all those hordes who have never had any connection with historic Christianity, and you get an idea of what a conglomeration of spiritual fornication will be present when the great whore sits as a queen over the minds of men in the Tribulation.

On the world scene a one-world church organization appears in the making. In its beginning the World Council of Churches was made up of Protestant denominations. It kept aloof from Rome and other non-protestant groups. Now Roman and Orthodox (Greek and Russian) Catholic Churches are sending "Observers" to its meetings. Some are openly wooing these "Separated Brethren"—meaning Protestants. All this adds up to but one thing—the coming together of almost the entire religious community in a unified body.

The religion of the Tribulation days will be that of Old Babylon. Here Bel and Baal, Semiramis and Aphrodite, Zeus and Horus, Ishtar and Minerva, and hundreds of other mythological gods and goddesses will find lodging. Here Romanism and effete Protestantism can find shelter. Here every shade of diabolical thought can be harbored. In fact, when all this is blended into one colossal organization of world religion it will be the great whore.

Now it is time for the judgment of Babylon. She is designated as the Great Whore or harlot. This suggests marital impurity on the part of a married woman. The woman has always stood for the church or organized religion—the pure woman for the true church; the impure woman for the false church. There is a true church and there is a false church. Likewise, there is a true city (Jerusalem) and a false city (Babylon). These two cities are in eternal conflict. They will have a great part in the final struggle of this age. It will be the spirit of Babylon versus the spirit of Jerusalem at the battle of Armageddon. Although she will have been destroyed by the time of this final battle, Babylon's children will be there to represent her. She is brought into view here that a glimpse may be had of her judgment.

This unchaste woman has had as her consorts the kings of the earth. By the time of the Tribulation she has become a great burden and fastened herself upon the peoples of the world. She is found sitting upon "Peoples, and multitudes, and tongues." She is seen riding the Beast himself in this chapter. Thus, we see the power of the false church. Her apparel becomes the gaudier the lower she sinks in immorality. She is adorned with purple, and scarlet, gold, and precious stones and pearls. She bears in her hand the golden goblet of abominations.

As stated before, Babylon is the mother of harlots. She is the mother of nearly every false religion. She is the mother of mythology and mystery, and evil practices. She is the abomination of the earth. Nearly every wicked, bizarre devilish and heathenish rite or practice—whether it be religious or not—has had its inception in the heart of old Babylon. Strains of her corrupting influence can be seen in all mythology. They can be found in the heathen fetishes. They can be located in every godless lodge and so-called sacred order—whether among civilized man or rankest heathen.

She was a bad mother, and has begotten bad children. She was full of bad deeds and her posterity has reflected her vileness in their own wickedness. God scattered her inhabitants in the early days, but the fire of her false worship was not entirely quenched. It was only scattered and made to spread to the different nations which her children founded. Egypt, Assyria, Persia, Greece and Rome have all drunk deeply at her polluted fountain. They have all been made drunk with the wine of her fornication.

The inhabitants of the earth also have been made drunk on the wine of her fornication or uncleanness. The woman herself is drunk on the blood of the saints and martyrs of Jesus, as well as multitudes of saints in Old Testament times. The horror of such a vile creature and the exalted place she has held in the hearts of men causes John to "Wonder with great admiration."

In the thirteenth chapter the Beast "Out of the earth" makes an image of the Beast "Out of the sea" and demands that all mankind worship this creation. One might ask, if there is a mystical or spiritual Babylon, how could she have existed under the Beast with the decree for his universal worship. Although the Antichrist is worshipped it does not proclude the possibility of additional methods of worship, at least until the Antichrist gets everything under complete control.

Since the worship under the "Great Whore" and the image of the Beast are both Satan-inspired they will go hand in hand until Babylon comes in conflict with the ten kings. So in this seventeenth chapter is found where these kings shall hate the "Whore" (Babylon), and make her desolate and naked and shall eat her flesh and burn her with fire.

Here is where mystical Babylon comes in. It would be an utter impossibility to stamp out all forms of religious worship at once. Think of all the superstitious worship, and heathen gods whose spirits are so deeply imbedded in the heart of the human race. As a matter of expediency the Antichrist kingdom will have to adjust to the situation temporarily. Here is where the ten kings come in.

These ten kings will hate religious Babylon. Her conflicting forms of worship will seriously disrupt the Christless peace they are trying to inaugurate. As long as religious Babylon exists the super-government then functioning will have to take into account the whims of all the various sects and parties into which she is divided. Do not get the idea that because Babylon is represented as unified by the figure of one woman there is anything like unity among her children. Although joined together in a loose alliance, debased Protestantism and Pagan Roman Catholicism still will be in conflict to a certain extent. Mohammedism still will be opposed to Brahamism. Their unholy coalition will find unity only in their opposition to the true way of salvation.

Therefore, as these clashing forces become disturbers of the peace, they will be hated by the ten kings. The record says "They will hate the woman; they will make her desolate and naked, and eat her flesh and burn her with fire." This is just another instance of where God makes the instruments of wrath to praise Him, and cause Satan to work God's will. God puts this thought into these kings hearts to hate this woman and destroy her.

Chapter Eighteen

JUDGMENT AND FALL OF LITERAL BABYLON

"And after these things I saw another angel come down from heaven, having great power; and the earth was lighted with his glory. And he cried mightily with a strong voice, saying, Babylon the great is fallen, is fallen, and is become the habitation of devils, and the hold of every foul spirit and a cage of every unclean and hateful bird. And the kings of the earth, who have committed fornication and lived deliciously with her, shall bewail her, and lament for her, when they see the smoke of her burning, standing afar off for fear of her torment, saying, Alas, Alas that great city Babylon, that mighty city! for in one hour is thy judgment come. Rejoice over her, thou heaven, and ye holy apostles and prophets; for God hath avenged you on her. And a mighty angel took up a stone like a great millstone, and cast it into the sea, saying, Thus with violence shall that great city Babylon be thrown down, and shall be found no more at all" (Revelation 18:1, 2, 9, 10, 20, 21).

It was brought out in the previous chapter that Babylon is both a religious system and a literal city. A parallel is found in Revelation 21:9 where the angel says, *"Come . . . I will shew thee the Lamb's wife."* Then John was carried to a great and high mountain, where he was shown not what he thought he would see, but the New Jerusalem descending from God out of heaven. Thus the Lamb's wife and the New Jerusalem merge into one figure. It is in this light that much of what is said about Babylon is to be understood. Spiritual Babylon is so identified with literal Babylon that many times they appear in Scripture to merge into one. However, there will be a literal city of Babylon during the reign of the Antichrist.

In this chapter the actual fall of literal Babylon is reached. In studying this evil city we must differentiate between mystical and literal Babylon. Mystical Babylon will have spread over all seven of the empires of world-wide scope. Literal Babylon is to be a literal city of the last days.

Where will literal Babylon be located? After examining a number of different theories concerning the city of Babylon of the end time, and comparing them with the text of Revelation itself, good evidence is found that points toward the rebuilding of literal Babylon on the banks of the Euphrates River. Some have advanced the idea of the revival of the old Roman empire and have made Rome herself stand for Babylon, the capital city, and the religion of Rome (Roman Catholicism) for spiritual Babylon. This is inconsistent because Rome never did hold sway over all the five empires preceding her. Nor was Roman Catholicism the exclusive religion of these earlier empires. On the other hand, some have sought to make Babylon a mythical thing, without substance or reality, but with this the record does not agree.

At the present time the ancient city of Babylon is only ruins. Back about 700 B.C. Isaiah described her total destruction in chapter thirteen, verses nineteen through twenty-one: *"And Babylon, the glory of kingdoms, the beauty of the Chaldees' excellency, shall be as when God overthrew Sodom and Gomorrah. It shall never be inhabited, neither shall the Arabian pitch tent there; neither shall the shepherds make their fold there. But wild beasts of the desert shall lie there; and their houses shall be full of doleful creatures; and the owl shall dwell there, and the satyr shall dance there. And the wild beasts of the islands shall cry in their desolate houses, and the dragons in their pleasant palaces; and her time is near to come, and her days shall not be prolonged."*

How then, do we reconcile these seemingly contradictory statements with the idea of a rebuilt city? The answer hinges on one thing: When was this total destruction to take place? If the destruction and lying in waste meant the condition of Babylon soon after Isaiah's prophecy, then there are difficulties with the New Testament statements. Peter says (1 Peter 5:13) *"The church that is at Babylon elected together with you."* And of course, John in Revelation has a lot to say about Babylon.

Some have contended that Peter and John really meant Rome, and used Babylon in a symbolical sense to picture Rome's corruption. But why did they not just say Rome? If we accept the Bible record, the only way to harmonize the writing of Isaiah and Peter and John is to give room for the rebuilding of Babylon. This is the only condition under which literal Babylon can be totally and finally destroyed. History records that Babylon has been destroyed at least three times. However, in none of these destructions can be found a full, complete fulfillment of Isaiah's prophecy. Sodom and Gomorrah were destroyed by fire. Babylon has never experienced such a destruction. But Babylon will be destroyed just as these plains cities were—by fire—we are told in this chapter.

At the present time the United Nations headquarters are in New York State, and may never be moved from their present location. But all necessary ingredients are found in the Middle East for someone with a great dream to build a city in this region. According to satistics in the 1971 edition of the World Almanac, the countries of the Middle East produced twenty-eight percent of the world's supply of petroleum in 1967. Add to this the almost unlimited value of the chemicals of the nearby Dead Sea. The territory of old Babylon can be made into a veritable Garden of Eden by merely re-establishing the ancient canal irrigation systems. It is not near any great city of the world. It is not within the borders of any great world power. In fact it is the ideal location for such a world center.

With these things in mind, it is not hard to envision an enterprising group of billionaires establishing such a city. We feel that the UN or some future successor to that body, will cause to be brought into being a sovereign territory upon which to build this capital city of the world. From a world-wide standpoint the Middle East would be an ideal place for such a venture. The Euphrates is the traditional boundary between east and west. What could be more logical than that locale would be decided upon in future years for this?

BABYLON OF THE LAST DAYS

Let us use our imagination and talk about this capital a little. Imagine what such a capital would cost! Think of the number of workmen it would take to construct such a city! Try to follow the streams of men and materials from their fountain heads. Think of the manufacture of all the materials going into this city! It will be modern in every respect. There will be nothing to mar the skyline; no dirty smoke, no slums, no filth (except moral filth), no dilapidated buildings, no glaring signs. Imagine everything wonderful about a city and you have the new Babylon. Men will pour into the city in streams. Unless a company has at least a branch office in New Babylon it will be out of the international picture. Billions of dollars will be invested in the new city. Every ruler and sub-ruler in the world will want at least a part-time residence there. It will be a Washington, London, Moscow, Paris and Rome all rolled into one magnificent metropolis. Let us try to get a picture in the mind's eye of this city.

What kind of a city will New Babylon of the last days be? It will be a new city! Some would see Rome as this city, but Rome is an old city. It is in decay. Other great cities of the world reflect the errors of architects and planners. Streets are narrow. Congested traffic crawls at a snail pace. Water supply, sewer, systems and lighting arrangements reflect a hodge-podge of old and new. Inadequate heating and cooling arrangements make life unpleasant for most of the world's city dwellers.

But suppose the best brains occupied in city planning were combined with those of the great financial wizards, the most efficient manufacturers of building materials, the outstanding architects, the top political strategists, and every other group who was first in its field decided to build a *New City?*

What kind of a city would this be? Search the world over for the most outstanding building, street, water, heating, cooling and sewer systems and every other feature which go to make up a modern city. Bring all this together in one place. Now you are getting a fair idea of what the New Babylon will be like. Even with the very best knowhow of the present day, there is hardly a building, street or any part of a modern city but would be built better now than when it was constructed. All such mistakes will be corrected in the New Babylon.

Now suppose the city has been constructed. Come and take a leisurely journey through this New Babylon. Standing on the alluvial plains of the lower Euphrates valley, it appears from a distance as a scintillating diamond on a setting of pure verdent emerald. As you come near this magnificent metropolis, you sense that it is not made up of garish buildings, thrown together without plan or purpose. Neither is it all metal and stone. Nearing the outskirts, you are struck with the beauty of its well-planned gardens. You know instinctively that a master gardener has made the layout. Every type of shrub and plant seem to find a place in these spacious acres. Perfect geometrical patterns are outlined by a riot of color. A fine mist is made to come from the ground itself, spraying over all this rich plant life. Rainbow hues are everywhere as the rays of the sun shine through the rising vapor.

Entering the city proper, you find yourself in the residential section. The wide, tree-lined thoroughfares are flanked on either side by majestic mansions, set in ample, beautifully landscaped grounds. Lovely fountains spray cool, clear water over graceful statuary.

With all the most modern plans for present day cities grouped together there will be some things about this city different from any city in the world. It will be a city with very little or no pollution or noise. By the time this city is constructed man will have pretty well solved these two major problems. There are two keys to this solution: Electric and nuclear power. These two sources of energy will be created far from the city, and will cause no pollution or noise in it. All means of transportation will have as their source of power either electricity or nuclear power. The larger units will be powered with nuclear force and the smaller ones by electricity.

The problem of heating and cooling in a modern city have occupied the best minds of planners for a long time. These problems will be solved in the new city. As you begin to enter the commercial section you are greeted by a sight that is awe-inspiring indeed. Where you expect to find giant skyscrapers, fingering toward the heavens, and making Nimrod's tower of Babel look like a puny mound, you find gigantic crystal-like domes reaching to great heights and spread over large segments of the city. In our day they would be called malls. In these domes the temperature is kept at a constant degree the year around. This is done two ways: first, of course, is the heating and cooling done by nuclear energy. Added to this is the built-in plan for using the sun's rays. These crystal domes look solid, but they are not. They are so constructed that they allow only a proper portion of the sun's rays to penetrate. When the surface of the dome reaches a certain temperature skillfully constructed louvers open or close, according to the need for more or less heat.

Giant gates, electrically operated, open when a light beam is broken by a moving vehicle, allowing it to pass into or out of the city. These gates close when traffic quits moving through. This conserves the heat on cold days and makes it easier to cool on hot days.

Along with many other activities, inside these domes, a world's fair goes on twelve months of the year. Here every product known to civilized man is displayed. This is the center of world trade. Let us go into one of these domes and see for ourselves what we can find. Just as an example here is gold, ivory and precious stones from Africa. In one place they are seen in the raw. Then there are finished materials ready for the manufacturer to turn them into usable items. Yet another display shows how these materials can be turned into exquisite creations to tantalize the most fastidous. Whatever the need, the supply is here. If you are in the jewelry trade you are given literature explaining just how and when you can be supplied. If you want to make your own creations, materials in quantity can be had. If you are a manufacturer, the raw materials are available.

Marble from Italy is likewise available. Fragrant spices and exotic perfumes from the mysterious East are on display. Pearls from many seas; fine linen, purple, scarlet and silk, woven by the looms of many lands; mahogony, cedar, cherry and walnut from the North American continent; rosewood from South America; other furniture woods from every corner of the globe; wines and liquors; petroleum and its products from the Middle East, the United States and Venezuela; grain, cotton, natural and synthetic fibers—all will be on display.

But the world's fair is not for the individual. This mart operates to supply whole nations with certain products. For instance, Germany needs raw cotton. Does she go to Egypt or the United States? She does not! She goes to Babylon. For it is here that the whole world supply is controlled. The German buyers see what they want and put in their order. The department controlling the cotton supply tells these buyers where and in what quantity the product can be secured. They are allowed to get it there and nowhere else, and only of a pre-determined quota. This keeps the supply and demand perfectly balanced.

Leaving the commercial district we soon come to the precincts of government. Overshadowing and out-ranking every structure in this section is a building grander than has ever been seen before. For size, beauty and symmetry it has no equal. Naturally, it is the headquarters of the world's government. The supreme ruler sits as a god and from this palace rules the world's millions down to the humblest worker. This is the home of the Antichrist. Here the ten sub-rulers (ten kings) come to get their orders and report on conditions in their respective realms of occupancy.

Another extremely important phase of operation from this headquarters is the military establishment. Here is located the supreme world command. Nothing of a military nature goes on in the entire world but is known by the men who operate from this establishment.

* * * * * * *

This is the imaginary outward view of the city of Babylon. Inwardly this is a troubled city. She is plagued with every form of sin and degradation. These cry to high heaven for chastisement. Moral filth can almost be felt. Oppression by the Antichrist government is brutal. Natural calamities have taken their toll. The great "Whore" of commercial Babylon has about reached a climax of uncleanness.

In chapter fourteen is found the announcement by an angel of the fall of Babylon. However, the final fall of this literal city is portrayed in the present chapter. In chapter fourteen there is no description of this angel, only his announcement. Here this angel is pictured as *"Having great power; and the earth was lighted with his glory. . . . He cried mightily with a strong voice."* He elaborates on the announcement of the first angel saying, *"She is become the habitation of devils, and the hold of every foul spirit and a cage of every unclean and hateful bird."* Also, that *"The kings of the earth have committed fornication with her, and the merchants of the earth are waxed rich through the abundance of her delicacies."* From the account given of this angel it is evident He is Jesus Christ Himself.

The sins of the city will cry out for punishment. Sodom

was a Ladies Aid Society compared to the New Babylon. All moral restraints will be gone. Most of the saints of God will either be gone to heaven, or martyred. Superstition and fear of a hereafter will have mostly disappeared. Man has been trying to do what God alone can do—bring a millennium of peace.

Note carefully the instructions this "Voice from heaven" gives: *"Come out of her my people . . . reward her as she rewarded you; double unto her double according to her works; in the cup which she hath filled fill to her double."* Here is a point which escapes many commentators, but which, if it be the right interpretation, clears up several things in this scene. The point is, that this voice from heaven is talking to "My people" and instructs them to do these things themselves.

Get the setting perfectly in mind. This destruction of Babylon takes place under the last, or seventh plague. The Beast has already made and broken his covenant with the nation of Israel. His animosity toward her is just as great as toward any group not completely under the dominance of the Antichrist government. He has desecrated the holy temple by causing his image to be set up therein.

In spite of all this, some Jews are scattered over the earth who have not taken the mark of the Beast nor worshipped his image. A group of these may be living at Babylon. How they have escaped punishment, right under the nose of the Antichrist is a mystery; but here they are. The angel calls to them out of heaven, *"Come out of her my people,"* says the angel. This is the only place in Revelation where *"My People"* is used of any group; therefore we conclude they are Jews or Israelites.

God puts it into the hearts of the defiant Jews to BURN THE CITY WITH FIRE! If this is the correct explanation then one major reason for the Antichrist and his armies to be gathered at Armageddon can easily be seen. They have come there in retaliation because the Jews have burned Babylon.

As has been stated before, there is a judgment of both literal and spiritual Babylon. The ten kings destroy spiritual Babylon in order that the Beast alone may be worshipped. The Jews, as instruments of God's wrath, destroy literal Babylon. Also, as has been noted in the seventeenth chapter, the ten kings were happy over the destruction of spiritual Babylyon with all her superstitions and heathenism. It is a different story with the fall of commercial Babylon. Kings bewail and lament for her. The reason for this is that they have *"Committed fornication and lived deliciously with her,"* and now this is all over. These kings committed fornication with Babylon by worshipping at her throne of Commerce. Any idol worship, whether it be a heathen image or an inordinate love of earth or love of earthly things calls for God's wrath. Thus, commerce had become the god of these kings and Babylon his shrine.

Not only were the kings sorrowful, but also the business men. The merchants weep and mourn because this great seat of commerce is destroyed. Notice here that almost every item mentioned speaks of luxury. The finest metals, the most precious stones, the best clothing, the most valuable building materials, the most expensive perfumes, the most pleasing drinks and the most satisfying of foods are brought to Babylon. This is the greatest market in the world. Now it has come to nought.

This is the upper, outward side. Underneath are the *"Bodies and souls of men,"* which are purchased. With all her vaunted wealth and prestige Babylon is still the great slave-holder. Thousands of men and women work in her as virtual slaves, while the rich live deliciously. But at heart the kings and merchants of the earth are just as much slaves to Babylon as those underneath their feet. They worship her gods, they bow down at her shrines and give unquestioned allegiance to her way of life. Now everything that made Babylon great has gone up in smoke and fire. No more will people of the earth find the things in her which they so greatly desired.

There are three classes of people who are saddened by the fall of Babylon: the kings of the earth, the merchants of the earth and the shipmasters of the sea. These classes are made rich by her, so naturally they hate to see her destroyed. These three classes utter about the same cry. The kings of the earth, *"Alas, alas, that great city ... in one hour is thy judgment come."* The merchants, *"Alas, alas, that great city ... in one hour is so great riches come to nought."* The shipmasters, *"Alas, alas, that great city ... in one hour she is made desolate."* The kings see her judgment, the merchants see her material ruin and the shipmasters see her desolation.

The thought is that it will be the Israelites who will destroy Babylon. If that is the case, then how are they to do it? They are few and weak and how can they successfully defy the Antichrist and destroy his city? Modern methods of warfare supply the answer—nuclear weapons. The Jews have been right in the forefront in developing atomic energy. In fact a German Jewish woman scientist is said to have furnished the missing data which enabled America to develop this power for a weapon of war.

These Jews will need only one small bomb to wreak such havoc as will be visited upon Babylon. That some such weapon will be used is evident from the statement that the kings, merchants and shipmasters *"Stood afar off to watch her burning."* These groups stood afar off *"For fear of her torment,"* we are told. We know that the release of atomic energy in explosions brings with it a deadly fallout.

For every wail of sadness upon the earth at the fall of Babylon there is a great cry of joy in heaven. The divine drama is about to come to a close. The vile city of the Antichrist has been destroyed. Satan has been cast out into the earth and his power limited to it and the underworld. The glad announcement is made that the earth and all its kingdoms belong to Christ. In fact, it only remains for the battle of Armageddon to be fought for Christ to take over all earthly kingdoms.

In this chapter is a resume of the final, utter fall of Babylon—both spiritual and literal. Like a millstone cast into the sea, this great city will come no more into remembrance. The Scriptures which tell of the fall of Babylon will have their complete fulfillment then.

The sound of musicians, the sound of workmen's hammers, the sound of factories will be silenced. There will be no more light in Babylon, neither will there be the sound of merrymaking such as characterizes the wedding feast. Babylon is fallen! fallen! fallen!

Just as the blood shed from Abel to Zacharias was required at the hands of the generation of Christ's day, so will the blood of prophets, saints and martyrs be required at the hands of Babylon. Babylon, whether spiritual or commercial has been and always will be the enemy of Christ and His people. NOW SHE IS NO MORE!

Chapter Nineteen

VICTORY CELEBRATION

"And after these things I heard a great voice of much people in heaven, saying, Alleluia: Salvation, and glory and honour, and power, unto the Lord our God: For true and righteous are his judgments: for he hath judged the great whore, which did corrupt the earth with her fornication, and hath avenged the blood of his servants at her hand, And again they said, Alleluia. And her smoke rose up for ever and ever. And the four and twenty Elders and the four beasts fell down and worshipped God that sat on the throne, Saying, Amen; Alleluia. And a voice came out of the throne saying, Praise our God, all ye his servants, and ye that fear him, both small and great. And I heard as it were the voice of a great multitude, and as the voice of many waters, and as the voice of mighty thunderings, saying, Alleluia; for the Lord God omnipotent reigneth" (Revelation 19:1-6).

Although we are late in the Tribulation period, the battle of Armageddon still has to be fought, the Beast and the False Prophet have yet to be cast alive into the Lake of Fire, Satan is not yet bound in the bottomless pit. However, in spite of all this, heaven is indulging in a gigantic victory celebration in this chapter.

In the previous chapter beginning with the twentieth verse there is a view of the destruction of Babylon from the vantage point of heaven. *"Rejoice over her, thou heaven, and ye holy apostles and prophets, for God hath avenged you on her,"* the voice proclaims. This is the signal for the beginning of the last great worship service recorded in Revelation.

There are seven of these worship services. The first is in the fourth chapter, and is participated in by the Living Creatures and the Elders. The occasion is the setting of the Judgment Court in preparation for the coming Great Tribulation. The second takes place in the fifth chapter when the Lion of the Tribe of Judah takes the Little Book from the hand of God on the throne, and prepares to reveal its contents. All creation gets in on this. The Living Creatures, the Elders, the angels and every creature—in heaven, on earth, under the earth and in the sea—all ascribe blessings and honor and glory to God and the Lamb. The third service had its origin in the feeling of exuberant victory of the white robed palm-bearers in the seventh chapter. These have just come up out of Great Tribulation. This mulitude was joined by the Elders, Living Creatures and the angels. The fifth was a special exclusive service. Only one hundred and forty-four thousand of all God's creation were permitted to take part in it. They were the Israelites sealed in the seventh chapter, and seen here in heaven. Their silent audience was the Living Creatures and Elders. The sixth service was by redeemed ones on the Sea of Glass before the heavenly throne. They had gotten the victory over the Beast, his image, mark and name. They are celebrating their triumph.

This scene of the seventh worship service is beyond human description and imagination. Multiplied millions of redeemed ones in heaven with one mighty voice shout *"Hallelujah,"* again and again and again. This cry rings out over the universe. *"Praise ye the Lord,"* is the meaning of this word. This is a word of universal praise, and just alike in all languages. It is said this is the one universal word, linking together Christians of every age and land. If you are in a strange country, do not know the language, do not know if any around you are Christian, if you will just say *"Hallelujah,"* and a Christian is anywhere around he will respond in kind. He may not know another word of your tongue, and you may not know a word of his. Yet, your communication is that of one Christian to another.

Perfect praise belongs to God. Such praise reaches a climax in the Psalms. A paraphrase of the one hundred and fiftieth Psalm will give just a faint idea of the Hallelujahs rising from the throats of saints in this celestial realm. *"Hallelujah, Hallelujah in the church, Hallelujah in his firmament. Hallelujah for his mighty acts. Hallelujah for his excellent greatness. Hallelujah with trumpet, and stringed instruments, and tambourines, and organs, and loud cymbals, and high sounding cymbals. Let everything that hath breath say, Hallelujah, Hallelujah!"*

One of the most arousing and inspiring songs ever sung is the famous earthly *"Hallelujah Chorus."* Imagine a congregation made up of millions singing the heavenly Hallelujah Chorus. Add to these voices the heavenly trumpets, harps, tambourines and cymbals, with the mighty celestial organs furnishing the background.

This innumerable multitude sing of God's salvation, and glory and honor, and power. The Elders and Living Creatures are simply overcome by such a demonstration of praise to God. They fall on their faces and worship God on His throne. *"Let it be so! Let it be so! Hallelujah!"* they chant

A voice from the throne urges the worshippers on. *"Everyone praise God"* it says—*"All who fear God, small and great."* Higher and higher the Hallelujahs rise. The voice of the great multitude swells in volume until the prophet can only liken it to the sound of many waters, and the roar of awesome thunder. "Hallelujah" is the title of the song, but the substance of this song itself is *"The Lord God reigneth."* These glad sounds echo and re-echo and bounce back from limitless space until earth and hell are made to realize that indeed, *"The Lord God omnipotent reigneth."*

This great victory celebration is because God has judged the great fornicating whore—Babylon. Finally, her time has come. For long, weary millenniums she had debased mankind. From the days of Nimrod to those of the scarlet colored Beast, she had held unquestioned sway over the minds and hearts of unregenerate men. Whether it was the mysticism of false religions, the arrogance of political despots, or the lure of ill gotten gains, her vile spirit pervaded every nook and corner of the world controlled by Satan. At last victory had come for the Lion of the Tribe of Judah and His people.

Now Babylon is a continual burning. No doubt the sulphureous gases underneath the earth, combining with the combustible material of the city itself, cause the great conflagration to continue to burn indefinitely. As Sodom and Gomorrah became part of the Dead Sea and sank from human sight, never to be identified again, just so Babylon as a great millstone will sink, never to rise again. Then shall Isaiah's prophecy be fulfilled: *"And Babylon . . . shall be as when God overthrew Sodom and Gomorrah."*

THE MARRIAGE AND MARRIAGE SUPPER OF THE LAMB

"Let us be glad and rejoice, and give honour to him; for the marriage of the Lamb is come, and his wife hath made herself ready. And to her was granted that she should be arrayed in fine linen, clean and white; for the fine linen is the righteousness of the saints. And he saith unto me, Write, Blessed are they which are called unto the marriage supper of the Lamb" (Revelation 19:7-9a).

Earlier in these studies we saw the Bride of Christ herself. We saw the requirements necessary to be in this company. We saw her as she was raptured between the third and fourth chapters. In the fourth chapter we saw her and her attendants portrayed by the four Living Creatures. At the marriage and marriage supper, others beside the Bridal company will be guests of honor. They will be such companies as the twenty-four Elders, the innumerable company of white-robed palmbearers, the one hundred and forty-four thousand Israelites, the company of redeemed John saw on the Sea of Glass, and the benevolent harvest of chapter fourteen, verses fourteen through sixteen.

Just who make up this Bride? A sketch of this was given in the third chapter. Also, in the comments on the fifth chapter she and her attendants are shown to be the highest type of New Testament saints. They will be the elite of the Gospel dispensation. Her guest list will be made up of the redeemed *"Out of every kindred, and tongue, and people and nation."* So they will not be Gentiles only, nor exclusively Jews.

Just where do those come from who make up this select company? There will be those of the Apostolic Age, such as Peter and Paul. Many will be of that select company of devout souls who were undaunted by Nero's chop block. Those from the dark corridors of the catacombs of Rome will be there. Victims of the terrible inquisitions of the Middle Ages will be there. The John Husses will be there, as will be the Luthers and Wesleys. In this choice company also will be those of this modern age who refuse to bow to the popular demand to dilute and compromise God's message to man.

Some will join this company through the door of martyrdom; some through natural death; some will be living when the glad resurrection day dawns and will be united to it by way of rapture. No matter the time nor place, nor the method, when the proper moment arrives the dead shall hear His (Christ's) voice, and shall rise, and with the living ones, be caught up to meet the Lord in the air all in their proper order.

All these have been workers. In their lifetime they carried the message of salvation to their age and race, whether as ministers or laymen. They have now reached the place where sin cannot invade. No more will they have to face the tempter. *"They hunger no more, neither thirst any more; neither shall the sun light on them any more, nor any heat. The Lamb shall lead them and feed them. God shall have wiped all tears from their eyes."*

Although they have come to this blessed estate, it does not mean they have been or will be idle. Heaven is a place of great activity. All these companies will be occupied in service to the Triune God. At times, some of them will be singing songs, and playing on harps, casting golden crowns before the throne, or in prostrate worship. Some will be wearing white robes and holding palms in their hands, and ascribing worthiness to God and the Lamb. Still others will be on the Sea of Glass, singing the song of Moses and of the Lamb.

All through the judgment scenes we view the work of the Bride. She appears in the picture when these four Living Creatures enter into the great worship service in the fifth chapter where Christ is declared worthy to take the Little Book, open the seals and look thereon. Under the figure of the four Living Creatures, she calls forth the action in the sixth chapter at the opening of the first four seals. She is in the worship service in the seventh chapter in connection with the white robed multitude that has come up out of Great Tribulation. She helps make up the audience for the one hundred and forty-four thousand redeemed Israelites in the fourteenth chapter. She is active in administering the seven last plagues in the fifteenth chapter.

In this nineteenth chapter we come to the marriage and the marriage supper of the Lamb. This is the grand climactic moment when anticipation will merge with reality. *"The marriage of the Lamb is come, and his wife hath made her-*

self ready." Some two thousand years have been spent in getting this company together. Of course, the twenty-four Elders were selected ages before this, but the Bride and her attendants and other guests have been under close scrutiny ever since Pentecost. The process of selection and rejection has been carried on by Jesus all these years. *"One shall be taken and another left,"* He tells us in Matthew twenty.

This taking and leaving is not only for the Bride, but for all these different companies. When we think of these companies who did not make up the Bride, we ask, as did Abraham before the destruction of Sodom, *"Shall not the judge of all the earth do right?"* Yes, the Judge of all the earth will do right. He knows just what company to place each one in. Perhaps, a particular saint will not be qualified to be a member of the Bride, but will fit in with her attendants. Or, perhaps, justice places one among the guests. But just to be there will be heaven itself! As the poet sings, *"Let us then be true and faithful, trusting, serving every day; just one glimpse of Him in glory will all the toils of life repay."*

What about these who will be among the living ones when the glorious rapture and resurrection take place? The method of selection and rejection will be about the same. There will be this difference: Those living ones who aspire to a higher rank have a chance to reach it before the rapture. But at the rapture their position is forever settled.

John's teaching is clear concerning the resurrection and rapture. There will be several companies raptured out; one at the beginning, others during the Tribulation. Those making up the Bridal company will be both the living and the dead. Likewise, those other companies will be made up of both raptured and living and resurrected dead, excluding the Tribulation martyrs, who will compose a special company of their own. *"Each man in his own order"* (rank).

When the first company—Bride and her attendants—is taken, only those who have attained to this high estate will be included—both living and dead. Those who miss the first company will have a chance (saints only) to come up later and will include both dead and living. An illustration of the different ranks is seen in David's selecting and ranking his "Mighty Men." Each man of this group of thirty-nine brave warriors was ranked according to his courage and faithfulness.

Let us get a picture of what is happening and what will happen. God the Father sent the Holy Spirit into the world to prepare a Bride for His Son. At Pentecost He began assembling this company. He began betrothing the worthy ones then. He has been adding to this company for nearly two thousand years. He will continue to do so until the rapture.

This earth is to be the scene of the honeymoon of Christ and His Bride. Now it is filled with trespassers. It must be cleared of these usurpers. This is one of the objectives of the Tribulation. Christ and His Bride will be occupied in this endeavor until the armies of the Beast are defeated and destroyed at Armageddon.

Jude gives a glimpse of this invasion of the earth when he quotes Enoch as saying he, *"Saw Christ coming to earth with ten thousand of his saints to execute judgment on all the ungodly."* After the mopping up operations at Armageddon, Christ and His Bride will begin the thousand year honeymoon here on earth. Their associates will be Christ's *"Brethren according to the flesh"*—the Israelites.

At the close of the thousand year honeymoon, there will be a renovation of the earth by fire. The great White Throne Judgment will see all sin dealt with and judged forever. Then Christ and His Bride will take up residence in their permanent new home—the New Jerusalem—there to live forever in holy bliss.

From the time of the rapture of the Bride of Christ until the battle of Armageddon is a period of Great Tribulation for those on earth. On the one hand the Bride is actively employed in helping dispense the awful judgments; on the other hand she is experiencing a period of unparalleled joy and festivities.

In this nineteenth chapter the Bride and Bridal company appear for the last time as the four Living Creatures. From henceforth they shall be seen under the symbol of the Lamb's Wife. Announcement is made in the seventh verse of this chapter of the marriage of the Lamb. Everything is in readiness. She is arrayed in *"Fine linen, clean and white,"* symbolizing her righteousness and purity.

Hardly has the Lamb's wife been introduced when the scene passes on to the supper, which follows the marriage. An invitation to this supper is one of the highest honors which can be bestowed upon any of God's creatures.

As to the available details of the marriage and marriage supper they are very meager. About the best place to look for them is in the parallels to be drawn between the marriage customs and wedding feasts of New Testament times and what little we know of these events as John records them.

Jesus had quite a bit to say about weddings and wedding feasts. You remember the first miracle He performed was at a wedding in Cana. One of the more important parables had to do with marriage and wedding feasts. In the twenty-second chapter of Matthew and the fourteenth chapter of Luke He uses these parables as typifying the King (God the Father), Who made a marriage for His Son (Christ). He goes on through the parable and brings out the prophets, apostles, the primitive martyrs, the destruction of Jerusalem, the universal call to salvation, those in the visible church—prepared and unprepared—the robe of righteousness and hell.

In all this we are not told the details of the wedding ceremony and the feast which followed. The nearest He comes to describing what will happen at the marriage of the Lamb is given in Matthew twenty-five. In this chapter, which certainly is a Tribulation scene, we have the bridegroom, the bride, the wise virgins who went into the marriage which took place at midnight, and the foolish virgins who were excluded from the marriage festivities. This pictures Jesus as the Bridegroom; the worthy saints as the Bride, the wise virgins as those whose supply of oil allowed them to light up the way for the coming Bridegroom. The left ones as the foolish virgins who, through carelessness, failed to have a sufficient supply of oil.

The *International Standard Bible Encyclopedia* has this to say concerning the marriage customs of the time of Christ:

"The first company, the wedding procession, apparently a relic of marriage by capture, was the first part of the proceedings. The bridegroom's friends went . . . to fetch the bride and her attendants to the home of the groom. The joyousness of it all witnessed by the proverbial 'voice of the bridegroom' and the cry, 'Behold the bridegroom cometh.'

"The marriage supper then followed, generally in the

home of the groom.... It is the bringing home of an already accredited bride to her covenanted husband. She is escorted by a company of attendants of her own sex, and by male relatives and friends conveying on mules or by porters, articles of furniture.... As the marriage usually takes place in the evening, the house is given up for the day to the women who are busy robing the bride and making ready for the coming hospitalities. The bridegroom is absent at the house of a relative or friend, where men congregate in the evening for the purpose of escorting him home. When he indicates that it is time to go, all rise up, and candles and torches are supplied to those who are to form the procession, and they move off. It is a very picturesque sight to see such a procession moving along the unlighted way in the stillness of the starry night, while, if it be in town or city, on each side of the narrow street . . . women take up the peculiar cry of wedding joy that tells those farther on that the pageant has started. This cry is taken up all along the route, and gives warning to those who are waiting with the bride that it is time to arise and light up the approach, and welcome the bridegroom with honor. As at the house where the bridegroom receives his friends before starting, some come late . . . it is often near midnight when the procession begins. Meanwhile . . . a period of relaxing and drowsy waiting sets in, as when in the N. T. parable, both the wise and foolish virgins were overcome with sleep. In their case the distant cry on the street brought the warning to prepare for the reception, and then came the discovery of the exhausted oil.

"After the relatives and attendants of the bride and groom have entered the house," this authority tells us, "The rest of the company leave, and so when the foolish virgins return with their oil they find the etiquette of the occasion shuts them out."

There is in this a beautiful picture of the events *after* the rapture. In the subsequent marriage of the Lamb the Groom (Jesus) is at His Father's (God's) house, the Bride is in her chamber. Bridegroom and Bride meet at the "Marriage supper of the Lamb." There is a company which turns back at the door of the marriage chamber because it is not supposed to enter. Another company fails to enter because of unpreparedness (the foolish virgins), while a third company enters because it has made proper preparations. Of course the Bride and special friends and relatives are already inside.

Jesus speaks of the exclusion and the inclusion in the seventeenth chapter of Luke when He says, *"I tell you in that night there shall be two men in one bed; the one shall be taken and the other left. Two women shall be grinding together; and the one shall be taken and the other left. Two men shall be in the field; the one shall be taken and the other left." "Taken where,"* asks the disciples. *"Wheresoever the body is, thither shall the eagles be gathered together,"* answers Jesus. Meaning: Wheresoever the Heavenly Groom is there shall the Bride be taken.

If the oriental wedding is typical of the heavenly wedding then the Living Creatures represent the Bride and the Bridal company, and the twenty-four Elders and other companies the guests. The foolish virgins picture those unprepared Christians, who, when Jesus comes, are without trimmed and burning lamps and a sufficient supply of oil. The company that did not expect to get in may represent those lax Christians who make no pretense of being prepared.

One important thing to remember about the parable of the ten virgins is that it is not a picture of the rapture. Many have interpreted it as such in seeking to stress the importance of being prepared and watching for the Lord's return. It can be used in teaching preparedness and watchfulness only in a general way. When one tries to fit the details into the picture of the rapture the parable loses its effective message.

Notice some salient facts shown: The ten virgins went out to meet the Bridegroom. Jesus as the heavenly Bridegroom does not come into the picture until the nineteenth chapter of the Revelation. It is midnight—the midnight of the Tribulation. The ten virgins picture those on earth. In the darkness no work can be done; they are just waiting. Despite the fact they *"all slumbered and slept,"* they are not criticized for it, although the five foolish virgins are criticized for having an insufficient supply of oil. Certainly this does not picture present day Christians working, watching and waiting for the Lord to come. Let it be repeated that it would be just as applicable to the apostolic age or even the tribulation days, or, for that matter, any other day.

ARMAGEDDON

"And another angel came out of the temple which is in heaven, he also having a sharp sickle, And another angel came out from the altar, which had power over fire; and cried with a loud cry to him that had the sharp sickle, saying, Thrust in thy sharp sickle, and gather the clusters of the vine of the earth: for her grapes are fully ripe. And the angel thrust in his sickle into the earth, and cast it into the great winepress of the wrath of God. And the winepress was trodden without the city, and blood came out of the winepress, even unto the horses' bridles, by the space of a thousand and six hundred furlongs" (Revelation 14:17-20).

"And I saw heaven opened, and behold a white horse; and he that sat upon him was called Faithful and True, and in righteousness he doth judge and make war. His eyes were as a flame of fire, and on his head were many crowns; and he had a name written that no man knew, but he himself. And he was clothed with a vesture dipped in blood: and his name is called the Word of God. And the armies which were in heaven followed him upon white horses, clothed in fine linen, white and clean. And out of his mouth goeth a sharp sword, that with it he should smite the nations: and he shall rule them with a rod of iron: and he treadeth the winepress of the wrath of almighty God. And he hath on his vesture and on his thigh a name written, KING OF KINGS AND LORD OF LORDS" (Revelation 19:11-16).

In the fourteenth chapter is found a symbolical view of the battle of Armageddon; in chapter nineteen is recorded the battle itself. Clusters of fully ripe grapes, waiting to be put in the winepress, are used to typify the armies of the Antichrist. The figure of the winepress is used to show the results of this great battle. Just as the blood of the grapes runs out of the winepress when the squeezing and pressing take place, just so shall the blood of the soldiers of these mighty armies be released in a great red, sullen stream when this slaughter is being accomplished.

Isaiah speaks of this battle in the sixty-third chapter of his prophecy, and uses the question and answer method to bring out the message. This is an imaginary conversation between himself and the Lord, and goes something like this:

CHRIST: *I that speak in righteousness, mighty to save.*

ISAIAH: *Wherefore art thou red in thy apparel, and thy garments like him that treadeth the winefat?*

CHRIST: *I have trodden the winepress alone; and of the people there was none with me; for I will tread them in mine anger, and trample them in my fury; and their blood shall be sprinkled upon my garments, and I will stain all my raiment. I will tread down the people in mine anger, and make them drunk in my fury. And I will bring down their strength to the earth* (Isaiah 63:3, 6).

These words are singularly like those of the fourteenth chapter of Revelation. These grapes are fully ripe—ready for the winepress of the wrath of God. Both speak of Jesus as the One treading out the grapes. In the fourteenth chapter the treading and pressing bring forth a river of blood, almost one hundred and eighty miles long.

In the beginning of the discussion of the book of Revelation, it was stated that the book was to reveal Jesus as its central figure. This is shown when He takes the Little Book out of the Father's hand in the fifth chapter; breaks the seals in the sixth and seventh chapters and the first verse of the eighth chapter; acts as High Priest at the beginning of the seven trumpet judgments; appears in the tenth chapter, standing with one foot on the sea and the other on the land, and, with the Little Book open, takes formal possession of the earth.

Here in the nineteenth chapter He shines out in all His splendor. Here He comes riding out of the clouds of heaven as a conquering Hero. God has allowed Satan long ages to prove his claims, and has permitted the Beast and False Prophet to tread the earth for their allotted time. Now everything is ready for the great climax—the overthrow of the Dragon, the Beast and the False Prophet. Christ is seen here riding a white horse. Unless otherwise intimated a white horse represents righteous warfare. The fact of Jesus as the rider make it unquestionably so. His eyes are as a flame of fire, and on his head are many crowns. He has a name written that no man knows but Himself. He is clothed with a vesture dipped in blood.

He is called Faithful and True—the very antithesis of hell's trinity, who have been running wild during their ungodly rule. He is coming to judge and make war upon His enemies. John uses the description *"His eyes were as a flame of fire,"* which he used in the first chapter of Revelation in describing Jesus. This is also the description given to Him when the message to Thyatira was given. And, incidentally, Jesus calls Himself the *"Faithful and True Witness"* in the message to Laodicea.

The Royal Prince of heaven comes down to earth, having the crowns of all earthly kingdoms. He is King of kings and Lord of lords. John says His name is called the *"Word of God."* This, and many other expressions peculiar to John's Gospel and the epistles which bear his name further prove him to be the author of the Revelation.

Christ's right is to judge and make war. He is followed by heaven's armies. He is to smite the nations with the sword of His mouth and destroy them with the brightness of His coming. A rod of iron and a winepress will be used to bring them into complete subjection. Notice the three figures used here: the sword speaks of warfare, the rod of absolute rule, and the winepress of great slaughter.

In the sixteenth chapter of Revelation and under the sixth of the seven last plagues, we find mention of the battle of Armageddon. In this sixteenth chapter three unclean, frog-like spirits come from the mouths of the Dragon, the Beast and the False Prophet in a call for the armies of the earth to assemble in Palestine. This is a program which has for its ultimate purpose the annihilation of Israel. The plan is laid under the sixth plague, but in the seventh it materializes instantly when Israel destroys Babylon.

Most of the foregoing language is figurative, but what about the actual physical battle? First, the location. It is called Armageddon in the Hebrew. From all indications it will cover a strip running diagonally across Palestine, beginning at Esdraelon in Galilee, and running in a southwesterly direction to Bozrah in Edom. It takes in the River Kishon where Deborah and Barak won the victory over Sisera by the aid of the *"Stars of heaven in their courses"* fighting against him. Here Gideon and his three hundred men won the great battle with the Midianites, the Amalekites and assorted armies of the East, with only trumpets, pitchers and lamps. Here the mighty Samson slew a thousand Philistines with the famous jawbone. David slew his giant here. Saul met his death on Mount Gilboa in this general vicinity. The infamous Ahab and Jezebel had a palace in Jezreel, one of the towns of the area.

Although the battle seems to start in the region of Mount Megiddo, the action moves swiftly to the Jordan valley, the valley of Jehoshaphat and ends far to the south in ancient Edom.

In the Hebrew the word Armageddon means *"Mount of slaughter."* This is a place where God met, judged and conquered many of His enemies (partly through human instrumentality, of course) since time immemorial. And it is quite fitting that this last great battle be fought here.

Who composes the armies? Since at this point in the Tribulation the Antichrist is ruling as god of the world and no organized opposition to his regime exists, it goes without saying that all the armies of the earth are at his side. On the other side are the armies of heaven. John tells us that these heavenly warriors are clothed in fine, white, clean linen, and are riding white horses. They are led by Jesus Christ, Who is also riding a white horse. Jude identifies this army when he says, *"Behold the Lord cometh with ten thousand of his saints to execute judgment upon all and to convince all that are ungodly among them of all their ungodly deeds which they have ungodly committed, and of all their ungodly speeches which ungodly sinners have spoken against him"* (Jude 14-15).

In his caution, the Antichrist gathers the combined armies of the world and they compass Jerusalem about just as they did under Titus in A.D. 70. They swoop down from the northwest in unrestrained fury. The Antichrist does not know just how effective are the weapons of Israel. Therefore he is taking no chances. He determines to make a last clean sweep and do what all the Hamans, the Hitlers and the Nassers for centuries have been trying to do—wipe Israel off the face of the earth, and drive her into the sea. But just as Haman, Hitler and Nasser failed in their evil designs, just so will this last mad attempt fail.

It is never safe to persecute the Jew. With all his shortcomings he still is God's chosen, and woe be unto the man or nation who would harm him. He is as eternal as the everlasting hills. He has been beaten, cuffed, spit upon, derided and persecuted, but always he has survived. He rejected his Messiah, and has been out of favor with God for ages, but God says, *"Don't you touch him; he is mine."*

About the time for the great battle to begin, the Son of God comes riding down out of heaven on a white horse. Heaven's armies follow right behind Him. They, too, are on white horses. The generals of the armies of the Beast believe they can win the victory. They set weapons of war against this King of saints, But to no avail. The swords of His armies are made bare and they fulfill the command of the angel in the fourteenth chapter when he cried, *"Thrust in thy sharp sickle, and gather the clusters of the vine of the earth, for her grapes are fully ripe."* Even before this battle starts God knows the outcome. He calls all the fowls of the air to come and be ready to feast upon the flesh of Antichrist's armies.

Here the issues are joined. It is Christ and His armies on one side and Antichrist and his armies on the other side. The slaughter starts. But, unlike most battles, the slaying is all on one side. Christ does not lose a soldier. Apparently Antichrist loses most if not all of his. The birds hover near. Blood runs to the horses' bridles for about one hundred and eighty miles. How wide this stream is we are not told. If the main force of the battle is concentrated in Israel's historic battleground, then blood flows all the way down to the Dead Sea, and beyond to Edom. The length of this blood stream would lead us to believe that it compasses the entire land of Palestine, with the main points of concentration in the valley of Jezreel and the valley of Jehoshaphat.

Preceding the slaying of the remnant of soldiers, *"With the sword of him that sat on the horse,"* the Beast and False Prophet are taken and cast alive into the Lake of Fire. This leaves only the Great Red Dragon to be cast into the bottomless pit, and then all opposition to Christ and His reign will have been put down. In the following chapter this will be shown.

THE WOMAN IN THE WILDERNESS

But before leaving this nineteenth chapter, there is a group of people who should come into the picture. They were last seen in the twelfth chapter under the figure of the Woman in the Wilderness. You remember that when the Great Red Dragon was defeated and cast into the earth, *"He persecuted the woman,"* and would have destroyed her. This was not to be because she was allowed to flee into the wilderness. *"Unto her place, where she is nourished for a time, and times, and a half time from the face of the serpent."* This allotted time is the last three and a half years of the Tribulation. The following scene is purely imaginative, but shows forth in a dim way what could well take place when she comes forth.

Storm clouds shroud the battered city of Jerusalem. A deathlike stillness has followed the turmoil and din of the last great battle. From Megiddo to the valley of Jehoshaphat, corpses are strewn. The stench of rotting flesh pervades the air. Wrecked engines of war dot the countryside.

In the distance to the west, had there been a watcher, he would have seen a dark splotch. It seemed to be moving. Yes, it is moving—coming closer all the time. It is a group of people. They are a motly crew. Burned by sun and wind they are almost black in appearance. Blowing sands of the desert have roughened their skins. All ages are here—from the very small children to the very aged. Who are they? Where did they come from?

"Who is this that cometh up from the wilderness," Solomon cries in the song. Primarily he is speaking of the Bride, but this just as faithfully pictures this group. Isaiah speaks of the road they were traveling: *"An highway shall be there and a way. . . . The redeemed shall walk there; and the ransomed of the Lord shall return and come to Zion with songs and everlasting joy upon their heads: And they shall obtain joy and gladness, and sorrow and sighing shall flee away."*

Yes, they ARE singing! For three and a half years they have been in the wilderness. But here they come! Some are riding camels, some on donkeys, some on foot, some being carried, some leaning on others for support. They are moving slowly. Their pace is set by those who can barely creep along.

All at once the western sky clears and the sun shines through. To the east a glorious scene is revealed. Arching over the ruins of Jerusalem the rainbow appears. The pilgrims hasten their steps. Even the most feeble seem to be possessed with a superhuman strength. The stronger ones begin picking up the weaker ones, and carrying them along. Even the animals seem possessed with a sense of urgency. Faster and faster they come! By the time they reach the outskirts of the city even the weak ones are running.

Although they expect to find only a mass of ruins, they are totally unprepared for the sight that meets their eyes. Thousands of white horses with heavenly riders are seen everywhere. Myriads of angels hover over the city. Seen from a distance the rainbow appeared to be east of the city. When this group composing the Woman in the Wilderness once get well inside the city, they find they are right in the midst of the rainbow itself.

One particular figure stands out; far outshining all the others. While they are gazing in wonder upon Him He seems to change forms. From the ineffable brightness of heavenly glory He changes to an ordinary looking man. He is dressed in the attire of a bygone age—coarse robe, open sandals, barehead, long hair. Scenes from the Bible would appear with Him holding the spotlight. Sitting by the seaside; trudging up a dusty road with His followers; sitting in a little boat; on a flower filled plain surrounded by little children; in a garden among the ancient olives; before an angry mob; in a judgment hall; carrying a heavy cross; hanging suspended between heaven and earth; in the throes of death agony On and on the tableau plays—alternating the earthly scenes with the Son of God on the white horse. The entire scene closes with the travellers prostrated on the ground in humble obeisance, the heads of the glorified saints bowed in holy reverence, while overhead the angels keep celestial vigil.

CHAPTER TWENTY

THE JUDGMENT OF SATAN, THE MILLENNIAL KINGDOM AND THE GREAT WHITE THRONE JUDGMENT

"And I saw an angel come down from heaven, having the key of the bottomless pit and a great chain in his hand. And he laid hold on the dragon, that old serpent, which is the devil and Satan, and bound him a thousand years. And cast him into the bottomless pit, and shut him up, and set a seal upon him, that he should deceive the nations no more till the thousand years should be fulfilled" (Revelation 20:1-3).

Here Satan comes to his third fall. Previously it was noted that he had suffered two falls—from the heaven of God's throne before Adam; and from his position as prince of the powers of the air, as recorded in the twelfth chapter. Now he is coming one step nearer his final abode, which will be the Lake of Fire.

There are a number of questions which need to be answered to make this performance clearer. Who is this angel from heaven? Who is Satan? What is this key? What is this chain? What is this seal?

The Angel From Heaven. In its general sense the word angel simply means a messenger. It is used of men in the beginning of the Revelation to designate the pastors of the seven churches. It is used of celestial creatures throughout Scripture. It is used also of Christ. As an example God told Moses He would send His angel with the Children of Israel in the wilderness after they had sinned so grievously in worshipping the golden calf. Paul speaks of the Rock that followed Israel, and said that Rock was Christ; therefore, giving a common identity to the Angel of God's presence and Christ the Rock.

In Revelation ten, the mighty angel with the opened Little Book who places His feet on sea and land, and takes possession of the earth can be no other than Christ. The angel with the sharp sickle in the fourteenth chapter is

Christ, the picture of whose actions is given in Isaiah sixty-three, where he is treading the winepress. The glory, light and power of the angel who announces the fall of Babylon in the eighteenth chapter can describe no one but Christ. With all this evidence, coupled with the actions of this angel of the twentieth chapter, one would be forced to say this was Christ.

Who Is Satan? He is given four names here: the Dragon, the Old Serpent, the Devil and Satan. As the Great Red Dragon he has been the unseen mover of the wicked forces seeking to possess the earth. He has been in the background manipulating the Beast and False Prophet. At Armageddon he was defeated and lost this power.

He is the Old Serpent. He is old in that he has been around tempting and deceiving man ever since Eden. He personifies everything evil and disgusting, and in this sense merits the name *Old* Serpent.

He is the Devil. As the Devil he is the incarnate slanderer, defamer, libeler, and malignant liar. He sought to slander, defame and libel God in his conversations with Eve in the Garden of Eden. John 8:44 says, *"When he speaketh a lie, he speaketh of his own; for he is a liar and the father of it."*

He is Satan. As Lucifer he became the great adversary in heaven, was cast out, and became Satan. As Satan he is still the great adversary, not only to God, but also the great adversary to man. He is the great accuser. After his defeat in chapter twelve in the battle between Michael and the Great Red Dragon (who also was called that old serpent the devil and Satan) the voice from heaven proclaimed, *"The accuser of our brethren is cast down, which accused them before God day and night."*

What is the Key? What is the Chain? What is the Seal? In Revelation one and eighteen Christ proclaims that He *"Has the keys of hell and death."* It is not known just what the identity of this key is, but there can be no question as to Who holds it. It is now on His royal person, and when the proper time comes He will use it to open the abyss to receive its celebrated prisoner. The key, chain and seal are not of earth's material, but their purposes are served just as though they were. The key will unlock the door; the chain will bind the prisoner and the seal will keep him until his Celestial Jailor sees fit to free him a thousand years later.

Already the battle of Armageddon has been fought and the earth has been seriously depopulated. Earthquakes, hail and fire have scarred this planet as never before. Earth's cities have fallen; its islands and mountains have disappeared in mighty convulsions. Defeat and despair could well be reflected upon the face of every person who is still alive.

The Antichrist and the False Prophet are in the Lake of Fire. Although he has lost his two chief lieutenants, the spirit of the Great Red Dragon is still infecting unregenerate mankind. The present action is somewhat like a work of modern fiction. The time has been reached where all the lesser villians have been caught and given their sentences. There remains only the arch-criminal—Mister X. In fiction this is usually the last character to be brought to justice. Sometimes he is killed; sometimes he is severely beaten physically and sometimes he is caught and reserved for punishment by a court of justice.

Now it only remains for Satan to be removed from the scene so the work of restoration in preparation for the glorious Millennium can begin. Only the mighty Hero would be the proper Person to apprehend and incarcerate this arch-criminal of God's universe. The key, the chain and the seal are here brought into play and his one thousand year sentence begins.

THE MILLENNIUM

"And I saw thrones, and they that sat upon them, and judgment was given unto them; and I saw the souls of them that were beheaded for the witness of Jesus, and the Word of God, and which had not worshipped the Beast, neither his image, neither had received his mark upon their foreheads, or in their hands; And they lived and reigned with Christ a thousand years.... But the rest of the dead lived not again until the thousand years were finished. This is the first resurrection. Blessed and holy is he that hath part in the first resurrection; on such the second death hath no power, but they shall be priests of God and of Christ, and shall reign with him a thousand years" (Revelation 20:4-6).

Immediately after Satan is cast into the abyss the Millennium of righteousness begins. Notice the wording of the fifteenth verse of chapter nineteen. First, Christ smites the nations with the sword of His mouth. After this He rules them with a rod of iron. The smiting of course, is done in the Tribulation period, climaxing with Armageddon. The ruling with a rod of iron is done in the Millennium.

The first order of business in the Millennium is to bring the nations together in a righteous government. A special company now comes into view. They are the Tribulation martyrs. Christ first began assembling this company in the sixth chapter under the fifth seal. This first contingent was *"Slain for the word of God, and for the testimony which they held."* Those who were responsible for their deaths were still on earth for these cried, *"How long, O Lord ... dost thou not judge and avenge our blood on them that dwell on earth?"*

In this twentieth chapter this company had been swelled by a great multitude *"Beheaded for the witness of Jesus, and for the word of God, and which had not worshipped the beast, neither his image, neither received his mark...."* These are to reign with Christ a thousand years. Besides this special company, all of the righteous dead and resurrected saints will have a part in the Millennium kingdom.

Before getting into a fuller discussion of the Millennium it would be well to examine Jesus' teaching concerning this wonderful period. His discourses are couched in parables in many instances. In Matthew 13:24-30, He speaks of the wheat and tares. This parable has at least a two-fold application. The first is the kingdom as seen in the church age. As the second parable of the series of seven, it represents the period of Smyrna (100-313 A.D.) in which great persecutions take place. Tares which were never uprooted are sown by heathen and false Jews. The second application is to the end-time. Jesus clearly identified this period when He says, *"The Son of man sows the seed. The field is the world* (or age). *The reapers are the angels. The tares are gathered and burned.* Only after this is done *"Shall the righteous shine forth as the sun in the kingdom of their Father."*

While Jesus speaks more of the preparation for the Millennium than of the period itself, it still gives us a picture of that marvelous day. The parable of the pounds

(Luke 19:11-27) is another instance of Jesus' teaching concerning the coming kingdom. The multitudes were expecting the kingdom to appear immediately. Jesus desired to correct this idea. He speaks of a nobleman (Christ) who goes into a far country (heaven) to receive a kingdom for himself (His Millennial kingdom) and returns (back to earth). He calls his ten servants (those of the Gospel age) and tells them to *"Occupy till I come."*

His citizens (the world in general, and the unbelieving Jews in particular) refused to allow Him to rule over them. Upon his return (to take possession of the earth at the beginning of the Millennium) he calls his servants and gives them authority to rule over certain portions of the kingdom. One man is placed over ten cities; another over five. One man would have been placed over one city, but he is unfaithful in his duties, so is counted unworthy to have a place of authority in the kingdom.

The final verse (27) gives a view of the last enemies of Christ. This refers to Gog and Magog, who, at the expiration of the thousand years, are destroyed by fire from God out of heaven.

In speaking to His disciples concerning the reward for having *"Forsaken all and following him,"* He tells them *"When you which have followed me in the regeneration, when the Son of man shall sit in the throne of his glory, ye also shall sit upon twelve thrones, judging the twelve tribes of Israel"* (Matthew 19-28b).

A close study of the prophecies in the Old Testament concerning the coming of a future kingdom in which Israel *"Shall be the head and not the tail,"* will help us understand why the Jews were so disappointed in Jesus as their Messiah.

The age-old hope of Israel was the establishing of an earthly kingdom, along the lines laid out by the prophets, especially of Isaiah. Every time a Jewish hero would come to the front this hope would be revived. During the time of the Maccabees it shone with a great brilliance. At last, the Jews felt, the time had come for them to throw off the yoke of foreign usurpers and establish again their national independence. But their expectations were short-lived—dashed to pieces against the rocks of stubborn reality.

When Christ came this dream was revived in the hearts

of multitudes. It was the basis of Christ's temptations in the wilderness. Satan tried to induce Jesus to follow the route others had tried and failed—arouse the people to throw off Roman rule and establish a free kingdom.

Since Christ was the Son of God, this could be brought about. He could turn stones into bread and prove His power. He could cast Himself down from the pinnacle of the Temple and prove Himself indestructible. He could use Satan's methods and bring about the kingdom and all men would follow Him. When Christ refused every one of Satan's propositions, He was rejected by the nation and crucified by the Romans.

The blindness of the Jews in Christ's day hid from them a great hiatus—the church age. In fact, this was not revealed to the Old Testament prophets themselves. They could see clearly the Millennium kingdom, but the Gospel dispensation was to them a mystery. To them a Messiah—a Maccabee or a Christ—would arise and establish a kingdom of righteousness. They failed to see that Israel was in no way ready to enter such a kingdom. A great inner change would have to take place in the hearts of the people. Also, they failed to see that in this kingdom the citizens would enter it one by one—in a spiritual rebirth.

The nation could not be blamed altogether for this concept. To the disciples and even the apostles themselves, this was a stumbling block. Until the very end some of Jesus' followers were looking for Him to set up this kingdom at His first advent.

Let us look at this Millennial kingdom through the eyes of the Old Testament prophets. Going back to the book of Revelation and the chapter which deals with this golden age, we find the marriage of the Lamb has taken place. The battle of Armageddon has been fought and won by Christ. The bones of the men of the Antichrist army have been picked clean by the vultures of the air. The Beast and the False Prophet have been cast alive into the Lake of Fire. And the last act of the Tribulation is performed when an angel from heaven (Christ) comes down with the key to the bottomless pit. He binds Satan with a great chain and casts him into the abyss.

All this is in preparation for that wonderful period known as "The Thousand Years," or "The Millennium."

Descriptions of this glorious time of peace and righteousness fill much of the prophecies of the Old Testament. Since these prophecies were written with Israel primarily in mind, we may expect their messages to deal mostly with the Jews in the Millennium.

Gleanings from their writing are given here. They are placed together in an effort to give a fuller picture of what it will be like in the Millennium. Some of those gleanings will be direct quotations, some will be paraphrases, and some will be explanations of the prophecies.

ESTABLISHMENT OF THE MILLENNIUM KINGDOM

The Prophet Isaiah has a lot to say about the Millennium. This age is referred to in no less than twenty-five chapters of his prophecies. As with the other prophets, his predictions deal mainly with Israel; only indirectly does he bring into view other nations. In the first chapter of Isaiah God promises, through the prophet to *"Purge away* (her) *dross and take away all her tin."* This can only refer to a future time, and the only future time consistent with the rest of the Scripture is the Millennium.

He speaks of a time when *"The mountain of the Lord's house shall be established in the top of the mountains, and shall be exalted above the hills; and all nations shall flow unto it. And many people shall go and say, Come ye, let us go up to the mountain of the Lord, to the house of the God of Jacob; and we will walk in his paths; for out of Zion shall go forth the law, and the word of the Lord from Jerusalem. And he shall judge among the nations, and shall rebuke many people; and they shall not lift up sword against nation, neither shall they learn war any more."* This certainly refers to the Millennium.

"Comfort ye, comfort ye my people, saith your God, Speak comfortably to Jerusalem and cry unto her, that her warfare is accomplished, that her iniquity is pardoned; for she hath received of the Lord's hand double for all her sins."

"Israel shall be in her own land; strangers shall be joined to her. She shall have rest from sorrow, from fear and from hard bondage."

"In that day I will raise up the tabernacle of David, close up the breaches, raise up the ruins and build it as in the days of old."

"Zion (Jerusalem) *shall be called a righteous, faithful city, and she shall be redeemed with judgment, and her converts with righteousness."*

"A king shall reign in righteousness, and princes shall rule in judgment. There shall be no dim eyes, no dull ears and no stammering tongues."

In speaking of the Millennium as it affects Israel, Jeremiah tells us: *"And I will give you pastors according to mine heart, which shall feed you with knowledge and understanding.... At that time shall they call Jerusalem the throne of the Lord* (cf. Jesus sitting on David's throne in Jerusalem in the Millennium); *and all nations shall be gathered unto thee."*

"In the days of these kings (represented by the ten toes of Nebuchadnezzar's image) *shall the God of heaven set up a kingdom which shall never be destroyed."*

THERE WILL BE A WONDERFUL TIME OF WORSHIP IN THAT DAY. *"In that day shall ye say, Praise the Lord, Call upon his name, declare his doings among the people. Make mention that his name is exalted. Sing unto the Lord; for he hath done excellent things.... Cry out and shout.... For great is the holy one of Israel in the midst of thee."*

THERE WILL BE GREAT JOY IN THE MILLENNIUM. The prophet cries out (Isa. 14:7, 8). *"The whole earth is at rest, and is quiet; they break forth into singing, yea, the fir trees rejoice at thee, and the cedars of Lebanon, saying, Since thou art laid down* (speaking of Satan in the bottomless pit), *no feller is come up against us."*

"With joy shall ye draw waters out of the wells of salvation," sings the prophet.

THIS WILL BE A DAY OF WONDERFUL BLESSINGS FROM THE LORD. *"Their peace shall be like a river and their glory like a flowing stream." "In that day shall the deaf hear the words of the books, and the eyes of the blind shall see. The meek and poor shall possess the joy of the Lord." "In Jerusalem there shall be no more weeping nor crying. They shall build houses and plant vineyards and their labor shall not be in vain." "Mourners shall have beauty for ashes; oil of joy for their mourning; praise for heaviness."*

ANIMAL NATURE WILL BE CHANGED. The wolf and

the lamb, the leopard and the kid, the cow and the bear, the lion and the ox, the child and the serpent all with dwell, feed and lie down together.

VEGETATION WILL BE CHANGED. The thorn and the briar shall be changed to the fir tree and the myrtle tree. The mountains and hills shall sing, and the trees shall clap their hands.

ENEMIES WILL BECOME FRIENDS IN THAT DAY. Listen to this: *"In that day shall Israel be the third with Egypt and Assyria, even a blessing in the midst of the land; whom the Lord of hosts shall bless, saying, Blessed be Egypt my people, and Assyria the work of my hands, and Israel mine inheritance."*

God promises to have mercy on Jacob ... and choose Israel.... Set them in their own land (where) strangers shall be joined with them.

THE EARTH ITSELF WILL BE CHANGED. We hear the prophet telling us: *"Streams shall be in the desert; dry ground shall become pools of water. Old wastes shall be built; desolate places shall be raised up, and the waste cities shall be repaired."*

"The wilderness, the solitary place and the desert shall rejoice. Lebanon, Carmel and Sharon shall see the excellency of the Lord. Blind eyes shall see, deaf ears shall hear, lame men shall leap, muted voices shall break forth in song."

"The ransomed of the Lord shall obtain joy and gladness, and sorrow and sadness shall flee away."

"FOR THE EARTH SHALL BE FILLED WITH THE KNOWLEDGE OF THE GLORY OF THE LORD, AS THE WATERS THAT COVER THE SEA."

WHO IS TO RULE IN THE MILLENNIUM?

Who is to rule during the thousand years and who are to be ruled? Upon the answers to these questions hinges the whole doctrine of the Millennium. In three places in Revelation the statement is made that there is to be a rule with a rod of iron. This suggests inflexible discipline. The first place noticed is in the second chapter, in the message to Thyatira where those who overcome are to be given power over the nations. These nations are to be ruled with a rod of iron, and as the vessels of a potter they are to be broken in shivers. The Man Child in the twelfth chapter is to rule all nations with a rod of iron. At the Revelation of Christ in the nineteenth chapter it is stated that He shall rule the nations with a rod of iron. Then back to the Messianic second Psalm we turn to find that Christ is to break the heathen and the uttermost part of the earth with a rod of iron and dash them in pieces like a potter's vessel.

While this ruling with a rod of iron always includes Christ, yet it does not speak of Him exclusively. The second Psalm speaks of Christ and the nineteenth chapter of Revelation refers to Him, but by no stretch of the imagination could one say that the heavenly messenger was speaking of Christ when He promised those in Thyatira that they could rule the nations with a rod of iron. Nor does the twelfth chapter speak of Christ, but of the one hundred and forty-four thousand Israelites who were translated during the Tribulation period. Thus, we conclude that preeminently Christ is to rule the nations with a rod of iron, but He is to be aided by His Bride, by Israel, by the martyrs of the Tribulation and by the saints in general.

If Christ and His people (Jew and Gentile) are to rule over the nations of the earth, who will compose the nations then living on earth? Some hold that at the end of the Tribulation period there will be no living people on earth—all the righteous are in heaven and all the wicked are in hell. But a careful analysis of Revelation fails to show where all mankind will be killed. True, a great portion of mankind will be destroyed, the Beast's army included, but nowhere can be found a total destruction. Do not make the mistake of believing that those killed at Armageddon will include every living person at this time. These are the armies of the world and do not include all living civilians. We are persuaded to believe that the proportion of civilian to military strength will be maintained under the reign of the Beast somewhat as it is at present, and at the most will not be over one military to ten civilians. Thus it is seen that there will be millions of civilians left after this great battle.

It is this civilian population over which Christ and His servants are to rule. There will be a systematic destruction of all that pertains to the Beast and the False Prophet. Christ will reign as King of the world, and His servants will rule under Him. One may be given authority over a continent, one over a nation on that continent, one over a state and one over a city. Thus Christ's servants will rule according to their faithfulness and ability. All political and commercial life will be controlled by righteous people. There will be those who will not accept Christ and His rule in their hearts. They will be kept in subjection. It will be the kind of a world that the present day rulers are trying to bring in. If they only knew the day of their visitation, and would turn to God, they could inaugurate a rule of righteousness. But they are trying to bring Christ-like results with Satan-like devices. Greed, avarice, treachery, lies and falsehoods will never bring in the Millennium; only Christ's coming will do it.

THE CLOSE OF THE MILLENNIUM

For a thousand years there has been a reign of universal righteousness and peace. Satan has been in the bottomless pit and the Beast and False Prophet in the Lake of Fire. Christ has used the compulsion of love in efforts to get the nations to accept Him in their hearts. But these nations have not been forced to accept Christ as their Savior. There have been great revivals, especially among the heathen. But in the Millennium man is still the free moral agent he has always been when it comes to spiritual things.

The thousand years close with many men unsaved. Rebellion against Christ is in their hearts. The only reason they have not been able to practice evil openly is because the tempter has been bound and the force of public opinion has restrained them. All they can do is to be neutral. God does not compel men to obey Him against their wills. Those who have not been made willing will be permitted to resist and go to hell in the end. Such will be the conditions at the close of this age of righteousness.

Therefore, Satan will be loosed a *"little season."* When this loosing takes place he comes back to earth to gather the insurgents. Gog and Magog form a great portion of this horde. Many modern Bible expositors of the pre-millennial school say Gog and Magog describe modern Russia. This may be the case. Her present atheism and opposition to God cause her to fit the picture well. In the Millennium Russia and China probably will be the great strongholds against

Christ and His reign. Of course, they will not be able to effectively oppose Him, and no doubt many will be converted during this time. These two atheistic nations are contaminated with godlessness, and as soon as Satan is loosed he may head for them to stir up opposition to Christ.

Puny Satan and pitiful man, to think they can successfully fight with the Christ of glory! Christ does not even deign to muster an army. He just lets fire come down from heaven and devour this great mass of rebellious mankind. This is the fire which renovates the earth and prepares it for the eternal ages.

In verse ten of this twentieth chapter Satan comes to his last, final fall. He has been a long time reaching the Lake of Fire, but when he led the rebellion in heaven, long before man was created, he started toward this place. Only two creatures will be there when he arrives—the Beast and the False Prophet. However, all the present hell will eventually be turned into the Lake of Fire and then Satan will have abundant company of his own breed.

THE GREAT WHITE THRONE JUDGMENT

"And I saw a great white throne, and him that sat on it, from whose face the earth and the heavens fled away; and there was found no place for them. And I saw the dead, small and great, stand before God; and the books were opened: and another book was opened, which is the book of life: and the dead were judged out of those things which were written in the books, according to their works. And the sea gave up the dead which were in it; and death and hell delivered up the dead which were in them: and they were judged every man according to their works. And Death and hell were cast alive into the lake of fire. This is the second death. And whosoever was not found in the book of life was cast into the lake of fire" (Revelation 20:11-15).

In verses eleven to fifteen John is shown the last judgment. He sees a great white throne. On it sits One of terrible majesty. Heaven and earth cannot face Him. They seek to hide from His countenance. This is God Himself, manifested in all His divine attributes—knowing everything, being everywhere and having all power.

It is this face that Moses could not look upon at Sinai. This is the face man in his mortal body is not able or allowed to look upon and live. Now every unregenerate person from the very beginning down to the last rebel of Gog and Magog must stand in His presence. Each must give an account for himself. He will have no advocate to plead his case. He will be judged according to what is found in these books. However, the final determining factor in each case is to be found in another book—the Book of Life. Regardless of all the good deeds one may plead, unless his name is found in this Book of Life his good deeds will avail nothing.

The accumulated results of each wicked deed have been added to the account of the one committing it. This could not have been done before, because the results of a wicked deed will accumulate until that great and dreadful day.

Many think there will be a general judgment where all people will stand to be judged for the deeds of this life. If the good outweighs the bad then a person will go to heaven, and vice-versa. This is not true. The Christian sends his sins on ahead to be judged. So he will never have to face a sin which has been forgiven him in this life. All whose names are not written in the Book of Life will be cast into the Lake of Fire. Their punishment or degree of torment will be determined by those things found in the other books.

Although the account of the Great White Throne Judgment is mentioned first and the coming forth of the wicked dead is mentioned after, in reality, the action will be just the reverse. The sea will give up its dead. Death and hell will deliver up their dead, then they will be judged. This is the second resurrection. Not a godly person will be in it. The resurrection of the righteous dead will have been completed a thousand years previously—or at the beginning of the Millennium. Also, this is the second death. Not a godly person will die this death. For the saint of God there is just one death, then eternal life forevermore. For the lost person there are two deaths—that of the physical body and the eternal death of the soul. These lost ones will be forever dying, but never experiencing the rest or cessation which comes with physical death.

Here the wicked man will reach his final abode. Here a lake of eternal fire awaits. Its sulphurous flames belch out gases that choke and stiffle, but do not terminate man's existence. Here will be Satan and Antichrist and the False

Prophet. Here all the arch criminals of earth's long troubled history will find beds. Here gay youth who did not have time for God will be troubled with an eternal restlessness, and, forever will be seeking to satisfy unfulfilled longings. Here the moral man and the moral woman will forever curse their own morality which gave them a false sense of security in life. Here everyone whose name is not found in the Book of Life will find a bed in a literal burning Lake of Fire.

CHAPTER TWENTY-ONE

THE NEW HEAVEN AND THE NEW EARTH

"And I saw a new heaven and a new earth: for the first heaven and the first earth were passed away; and there was no more sea" (Revelation 21:1).

A new heaven and a new earth! What does this mean? There is a hint of the passing away of the earth and the heavens in the eleventh verse of the twentieth chapter of Revelation where it says of God, *"From whose face the heavens fled away; and there was no place found for them."* Malachi hints at the method of this destruction, and especially of the wicked inhabitants of the earth when he says, *"The wicked ... shall be ashes under the soles of your feet."* Peter goes a step further by stating, *"Wherein the heavens being on fire shall be dissolved and the elements shall melt with fervent heat."* He goes on to say, *"We ... look for a new heaven and a new eatrh."*

"Behold I make all things new," the Occupant of the throne tells John. He starts out by making a new heaven and a new earth. Hebrews 1:10-11 says, *"Thou, Lord, in the beginning hast laid the foundations of the earth; and the heavens are the works of thy hands: they shall perish; but thou remainest; and they shall wax old as doth a garment; and as a vesture shalt thou fold them up."*

This sounds like the heavens and the earth shall be "Folded and put away," not to be used any longer. In other words they shall perish. And in the sense that the world perished in the flood as stated by Peter (2:3-6) the world will again perish after the Millennium. But, just as this planet itself did not cease to exist when the flood covered it, just so this planet will still be in existence after the renovating time is over. There will be a baptism of fire which will destroy every mark man has made on this globe. The fire coming down out of heaven destroying the hordes of Gog and Magog will be the same fire which will purge the earth. Someone may say, "What about the people living on earth who were not involved in the rebellion at the end of the Millennium? What will happen to them during this baptism of fire?" God will take care of them just as effectively as He did the three Hebrew children in the fiery furnace of Nebuchadnezzar. He can either preserve them in the fire, or transport them elsewhere until the earth becomes habitable again.

How long it will be from the time this purging fire starts until man begins rebuilding is not known. However, the time element is not important, because time will have merged into eternity. A hundred, a thousand, a million years as we count time will make no difference.

"No more sea." Some take this to mean that there will be no more sea in the new earth. A careful examination of the text will show the disappearance of the sea will take place in the same manner and at the same time of the passing away of the first heaven and earth. So, since there will be a new heaven and a new earth it follows there will be a new sea.

After this John sees the *"New Jerusalem coming down from God out of heaven, prepared as a bride adorned for her husband."* Details of its light, its walls, its gates, its foundations and its streets were given one of the seven plague-angels. This glorious city will be discussed later.

A great voice out of heaven announces that *"The tabernacle of God is with men; he will dwell with them, and they shall be his people."* In the garden of Eden one of the great blessings coming to that first pair was God's coming down in the cool of the day and communing with them. Sin broke the connection, and the voice of God has been mostly stilled since. No more does God talk face to face with man. No more can man behold the divine presence. Yes, God, through His Spirit, talks with man in our day, but we do not hear His audible voice. In the dim ages of long ago Job was made to cry *"...I know that my redeemer liveth, and that he shall stand at the latter day upon the earth ... in my flesh shall I see God: whom I shall see for myself, and mine eyes shall behold, and not another"* (Job 19:25-27). There is only one place and time consistent with Scripture where and when this can take place, and it is right here in this twenty-first chapter. God will not just make occasional visits as He did in Eden, but He shall *dwell* with His people.

What will be the results of this *dwelling?* Can you

imagine any tears being shed in the presence of God? No; He shall have wiped all tears from their eyes. Can you imagine anyone dying in the presence of God? No; death shall have been swallowed up in victory. Can you imagine any sorrow when God is present? No; joy will be in every heart and a smile of happiness on every face. Can you feature anyone suffering any pain in the presence of God? No; pain will all be gone!

When this glad age arrives it will be the fulfillment of 1 Cor. 15, where Christ delivers up *"The kingdom to God, even His Father; when he shall have put down all rule and authority and power. For he must reign till he hath put all enemies under his feet."* Only then will Jesus' redemptive work have been finished. On the cross He cried, *"It is finished!* But it was only the plan for redemption of which Christ spoke. Here complete redemption is an accomplished fact.

This turning the kingdom over to the Father does not mean Christ will have no part in earthly affairs. The Holy Trinity is involved in everything affecting the universe. And Christ is to reign from the earthly Jerusalem, even after the Millennium. In telling of the coming birth of Jesus the angel Gabriel tells Mary, *"The Lord God shall give unto him the throne of his father David; and he shall reign over the house of Jacob forever; and of his kingdom there shall be no end."* Thus, Jesus Christ will rule from earthly Jerusalem forever.

However, Christ had a special work to do in the scheme of divine things. This was the redemption of man back to the Edenic state. In accomplishing this He purchased for Himself a particular people—the redeemed. With His glorified saints He will live eternally in the New Jerusalem. This will be His palace, His residence. With His bride He will have a special relationship. But He will also continue as ruler from earthly Jerusalem. He will be assisted by the glorified saints of both Old and New Testaments. Then will come to pass what Isaiah prophesied in the fifty-third chapter: *"He shall see the travail of his soul, and shall be satisfied."* So, the Father's special sphere of operation will be the nations walking in the light of the Holy City. God will start again where He left off in Eden when man sinned. A further discussion of this will be found under the heading: "Perpetual Generations" at the close of this chapter.

THE NEW JERUSALEM

"And there came unto me one of the seven angels which had the seven vials full of the seven last plagues, and talked with me, saying, Come hither, I will shew thee the bride, the Lamb's wife. And he carried me away in the spirit to a great and high mountain, and showed me that great city, the holy Jerusalem, descending out of heaven from God" (Revelation 21:9, 10).

In order to view the destruction of wicked Babylon, one of these seven angels having the vial containing the seven last plagues, carried John away in the spirit into the wilderness. What a contrast here! One of these same angels carries him away in the spirit to a *great and high mountain,* where he sees the holy Jerusalem, descending from God out of heaven.

The New Jerusalem! Who shall describe it? Who *can* describe it? What adjectives can do justice to its walls, its gates, its foundations? What superlatives are great enough to show forth its light, its honor, its glory? What words can give even a little inkling of the happiness of its inhabitants? What sacred terms can be employed to reveal the majesty of its Ruler?

When an all-knowing, all-powerful and everywhere-present Creator prepares the very best possible home for some of His creatures, no words of human tongue are equal to the task of showing it forth. And when that same Creator, Himself as the Lamb of God, desires to tabernacle with these creatures Himself, then the ultimate is reached in all the vastness of the universe. Nothing else can be added.

The Antichrist will prepare for himself a city—Babylon—and will use every resource and ingenuity of man and Satan to do so. As an earthly city it will be the most magnificent city ever constructed on earth. In comparison with the New Jerusalem it will be nothing but a pile of rubbish.

ITS LIGHTS

"... having the glory of God: and her light was like unto a stone most precious, even like a jasper stone, clear as crystal.... And the city had no need of the sun, neither the moon, to shine in it: for the glory of God did lighten it, and the Lamb is the light thereof" (Revelation 21:11, 23).

The New Jerusalem's crystal clear light "like a jasper stone" will not be from the sun or the moon or the stars: the glory of God and the Lamb will lighten it as no mere physical orb can do. When Moses came down from Mount Sinai the lingering light of glory on his face was so intense that he had to wear a veil; otherwise the children of Israel in the wilderness could not look upon him. On the Mount of Transfiguration the ineffable light of heaven was reflected only dimly, yet the faces of Jesus, Moses and Elijah outshone the sun, and their garments were white as the light. The fierce sunlight at midday near Damascus seemed to Paul not equal to the light from heaven which shone about him when he met the Master on the road outside the city.

These are just a few of the instances where man came in contact with the light of God. In this Holy City its inhabitants will bask in this glorious light forever, and never feel any shrinking or drawing back from these beneficent rays.

John gives a picture of this city. He sees the glory of God shining out from it. A careful reading will reveal just how skilfully the apostle does this. It is first seen from a distance and appears as an object of indescribable beauty. As he comes closer he sees its light, then its wall, its twelve gates, its twelve foundations, its immense size, the materials from which it is made. Inside the city he sees its streets, its rivers and its trees. The closer he comes to it the more glorious it appears.

These particulars point up the great contrast between the ark of God and that of man. The closer you get to man's work the more imperfect it will appear. If you want to admire a famous painting you are told not to get too near it; otherwise its imperfections will become evident. In other words, it looks better from a distance. In contrast to this, the closer you observe God's work the more you realize its perfection. Note the snowflake. To the naked eye it might appear to be just a splotch of frozen mist. Put it under a powerful microscope and the more it is magnified the more beautiful it becomes. Each flake is of a perfect geometric pattern. Just so is all of God's handiwork. The closer you get to it the more beautiful it becomes.

ITS WALL

"...And had a wall great and high, and had twelve gates, and at the gates twelve angels, and names written thereon, which are the names of the twelve tribes of the children of Israel; on the east three gates; on the north three gates; on the south three gates; on the west three gates. And he measured the wall thereof, an hundred and forty and four cubits, according to the measure of a man, that is, of the angel. And the building of it was of jasper" (Revelation 21:12, 13, 17, 18a).

The New Jerusalem will have a wall. It is great and high. This wall is of jasper. Whether the jasper here is the same as the jasper of verse eleven is uncertain. If, as modern authorities say, it is our modern quartz, then the wall could be opaque, and of a red, brown or yellow hue. This substance polishes to a high degree of brilliancy, and would indeed, make a beautiful wall. The twelfth stone on the breastplate of ancient Israel's high priest was jasper. Also, the Occupant on the heavenly throne of the fourth chapter *"Was to look upon like a jasper ... stone."* Whether as a crystalline purveyor and reflector of light or as having the opacity and high polish property of the modern red, brown or yellow quartz, the beauty of this wall is inexpressible as the light from the city shines through it.

ITS GATES

Set in this wall are twelve gates. In the arrangement of them we see the same order as that of the camp of Israel in the wilderness. There the tabernacle was in the center. Immediately at the front were camped Moses and Aaron and their families. Next to the tabernacle on the other three sides were camped the three families of Levites. Then the arrangement of the tribes follows: East—Judah, Issachar, and Zebulun; North—Dan, Asher and Naphtali; South—Reuben, Simeon and Gad; West—Ephraim, Manasseh and Benjamin. The arrangement of the tribal names for these gates will be somewhat changed if the arrangement found in the seventh chapter is observed.

These gates are of pearl. They are not made up of the tiny spheres created by the oyster, either. Each gate is one single pearl. Nothing is said as to the size and shape of these gates, but if their proportions are in keeping with the wall itself they must be enormous.

Every color, every measurement, every precious stone in this city has a meaning all its own. So the twelve gates of pearl reflect the attributes, personalities, and strong and weak points of everyone who ever passes through them.

The pearl is created by the oyster. We are told the oyster is a *"Bivalve mollusk found in salt or brackish water, and moored by the shell to stones and other shells,* etc." The pearl it creates is a smooth, rounded, variously tinted nacreous concretion, formed as a deposit around a foreign body in the shell of the oyster.

What happens in the formation of the pearl is that when a foreign body, such as a grain of sand, gets inside the hard shell which surrounds the oyster, the creature secretes a whitish substance which surrounds the object and neutralizes it as far as its irritating nature is concerned. Layer after layer of this secretion wraps the object and it becomes rounded to a perfect orb. Thus the very thing which would injure the live oyster is changed into a thing of rare beauty, and is highly prized by man as an ornament.

Thus the twelve gates of pearl take on a rare and wonderful meaning. The twelve sons of Jacob were once as annoying grains of sand inside the universal oyster. The secretion of layer after layer of the white substance of God's mercy and grace hid the grating grains so they could form the nucleus around which an object of beauty could be formed, fit to embellish the walls of the New Jerusalem in the form of these twelve gates.

So everyone who ever passes through these gates was one time as valueless as the troublesome grains of sand in the oyster. Now they are pearls of great price, created layer by layer out of the love and grace of the Heavenly Bridegroom.

Look at these twelve sons of Jacob. On the whole they were a worthless band. Only Joseph received special praise, and he alone received no word of condemnation by the sacred writers.

For instance, there was Reuben, the oldest son—*"Weak as water,"* sensual, cowardly, vascillating, without the courage of his convictions. He never could excel. True he intervened in behalf of Joseph when his brethren wanted to kill the boy, but he went ahead and allowed them to sell him into slavery. He offered to allow his father to slay his two sons if he did not deliver Benjamin back to him, when the brethren wanted to take him to Egypt in proof of their good faith to the "Man" Joseph. But he was safe; Jacob would not slay his own grandsons.

Of all the sons, you Reuben would be among those least worthy to have one of these gates named in your honor. Your father's lament over you when giving his dying blessing to his sons sums up your life. *"Reuben, you are my firstborn. I had great hopes for you. In you would be my might and the beg,nning of my strength. But Reuben, you never could excel; you are weak as water."*

Also, your tribe did not have too good a record. Your Dathan and Abiriam conspired with Korah the Levite to challenge Moses' leadership. For this great sin, God allowed the earth to open up and swallow these two families of yours. Your tribe led the first division of Israel. It wanted its inheritance *"On this side of Jordan."* Also, their erection of the altar which was called "Ed" almost caused civil war among the tribes.

Reuben, your tribe was a sorry lot. In spite of this, one of these wonderful gates will be named for you. Not only for you, but for all the redeemed Reubenites of the world. Just as Abram's name was changed to Abraham, and Jacob became Israel, just so will all the Reubenites' names be changed as their natures are changed by the power of God. No longer will they be weak as water, sensual, cowardly, without the courage of their convictions, but ransomed saints of God. The memory of their "former selves" will bring joy only because of the great change which has taken place. To think, they, who were once so debased, could rise to such heights as to have a beautiful pearly gate in the New Jerusalem named for them!

Then there was Simeon. Yes, Simeon, God heard your mother Leah's cry of anguish because she was hated and gave you as her son. But you failed to honor her and your father Jacob. Your actions in slaying all the men of a city because of the defilement of your Sister Dinah by just one man, earned you the eternal stigma of "cruel." Your extreme cruelty and fierce anger caused your descendants to be *"divided in Jacob and scattered in Israel."* And as a tribe you were swallowed up by your betters.

Simeon the murderer? Yes! But one of those magnificent gates named in your honor? Yes! Your gate symbolizes every redeemed murderer of all ages. Your cruelty and anger thus shows to every rehabilitated manslayer whose terrible traits brought him so low, that he, too, can pass through your gate and thank God that he was brought out of such a horrible pit.

Levi—priest of God—your tribe, like Simeon's was scattered throughout Israel. Because you were with Simeon in murdering the men of Shechem, you were denied an inheritance among the sons of Jacob. As a punishment you were scattered, but as a blessing you were given the high honor of an earthly priesthood. Your gate is an emblem to every priest and minister of succeeding ages who had no certain dwelling place, but had to travel from place to place, living in houses provided by others. When such a one passes through that gate he will realize it is not just for Levi, but for him also, that the gate has been prepared.

Judah—Lionlike, noble, courageous, fearless; progenitor of kings and nobles, warriors and poets, humble carpenters and guileless maidens. Also schemer, mercenary, crafty; perpetrator of dark deeds and shady deals; subject to shameful chapters, you too, have a gate here.

These Judahs of the long ages who have arrived in this Holy City *"When they from yon portals look backward, across the long path they have trod* (they will find) *they have been true to the journey* (so) *will rest forever with God."* Their supreme joy will be in realizing their natures had been so changed that they could pass through this gate of pearl and walk those streets of gold. They will know the memory of their former traits which were so repulsive, will be retained only to show the full measure of their redemption.

Dan — judge, umpire, executor and administrator of judgment: a lion's whelp, a serpent, an adder; dangerous foe; selfish, as proved by your failure to help your brethren in the battle with Jabin the Canaanite. Your ships were more important to you than the well-being of the rest of the tribes. You went on with your shipping because the war was not in your part of the land. Dan the idolater, your name is not once mentioned by Jesus nor the New Testament writers. But, Dan, one of those pearly gates *may* be named for you. Then all the redeemed Danites of the world will rejoice because of the great transformation God's love brings about.

Naphtali—your father Jacob said you were a good talker; you were like a female deer let loose. Moses said you and your tribe were satisfied with favor and were full with the blessings of the Lord. No expressed evil has been charged against you. You and your tribe seem to be among those who were willing to accept things as they found them. Perhaps your gate of pearl will represent all those who had to accept situations they did not like, but could not change. In doing this, you avoided many things which would have caused you to become involved in controversies detrimental to your welfare. You will have a gate here.

Gad—you were the overcomer. When you were overcome by a troop, you lived to fight another day and win the final victory. Then you dwelt as a lion and as a lion defended that which was yours. You set with the people of the lawgiver and yourself dispensed judgment. Overcomers will love your gate. Looking at it they will in a measure, be rewarded for the fierce battles they fought to be themselves overcomers.

Asher—yours was the riches of the world. Your bread was fat and your land yielded royal dainties. You were blessed with children. You were acceptable to your brethren. Your shoes were as iron and brass, and as your days were so was your strength. The rich men of the earth who finally make it to the Holy City will especially like your gate. They will realize how easily they could have let their riches keep them tied to earth's treasures. The family ties and earthly power made their dedication to God and His cause harder, but like Asher, they have made the journey successfully.

Issachar—you were somewhat like Asher; industrious, contented, getter of wealth. Standing on the Mount of Blessing when Moses divided the tribes to show forth the blessings and the curses conditioned upon the future activities of Israel, you represented much of the good in Israel. You came to the aid of Deborah and Barak in the war with Canaan under Jabin. Always on the proper side of things, you were contented to be a burden-bearer. You were greatly increased in numbers as generations succeeded each other. You have a gate in that Holy City. Your numbers will be greatly swelled by godly ones who were contented to form the foundation upon which the kingdom of God on earth is built.

Zebulun—tenth son of Jacob and youngest son of Leah, your tribe was industrious and became very rich through trade with sea-farers. Rich caravans traversed your territory and you profited greatly thereby. You and your neighbor Naphtali furnished ten thousand soldiers to fight the host's of Sisera's army when King Jabin came against Israel. Our Saviour grew up in Nazareth within your borders. Your gate in the New Jerusalem will bring great joy to all the Zebulunites of the world who make it to that blessed place —whether they have blood ties with you or only spiritual ones.

Joseph—you were the long-hoped for son of Rachel. Many long weary years of family bickering and strife preceded your birth. Jealousy and hatred awaited you. Four mothers, one father, one sister and ten brothers—all divided into rival factions—made up the family into which you entered. The inordinate love of a doting father only aggravated your situation. Years of frustration made your father unreasonable in dealing with his family. Making a spy out of you to report the evil deeds of the sons of his concubines fed the fires of hatred and malice. But that was Jacob's doing; not yours.

The blessing your father gave in his last hours of life in a small measure made up for your adversities. Remember when he said, *"The God of thy fathers ... shall help thee; and the Almighty, who shall bless thee with blessings of heaven above, blessings of the deep that lieth under; blessings of the breasts and the womb. The blessings of thy father have prevailed above the blessings of my progenitors unto the utmost bounds of the everlasting hills; they shall be on the head of Joseph, and on the crown of the head of him that was separate from his brethren."*

In you is seen all those who have suffered for righteousness sake. Every tear shed, every grief felt, every false accusation faced; all envy, hatred, malice and strife which swirled about your head—all this will be reflected in the beautiful pearly gate opening into that Eternal City of the Bride. Not as sorrows will this be so, but as a happy reminder to all those who have likewise suffered, that final, eternal victory has at last been realized.

Benjamin—last of your father's sons, the protecting hand of God seemed to have been always about you. As a wolf, said your father, you couched and devoured the prey in the morning, and divided the spoil at night. Of your tribe Moses said, *"The beloved of the Lord shall dwell safely by him, and the Lord shall cover him all the day long, and he shall dwell between his shoulders."* In spite of some unhappy chapters in the history of your tribe, it survived. It attached itself to its big brother Judah and thereby shared in his blessings of earthly glory and heavenly bliss. Your gate of pearl stands as a reminder to all ransomed Benjaminites that there is a place for them in this city.

ITS FOUNDATIONS

"And the wall of that city had twelve foundations and in them the names of the twelve apostles of the Lamb. And the foundations of the wall of the city were garnished with all manner of precious stones. The first foundation was jasper; the second, sapphire; the third, chalcedony; the fourth an emerald; the fifth, sardonyx; the sixth, sardius; the seventh, chrysolyte; the eighth, beryl; the ninth, a topaz; the tenth, a chrysoprasus; the eleventh, a jacinth; the twelfth, an amethyst" (Revelation 21: 14, 19, 20).

The walls of this city has foundations—twelve of them. Each foundation is garnished with a different type of precious stone. The first foundation is of jasper. Since the wall itself is of jasper, there must be a variety of shades of this stone. Red, brown and yellow are doubtless used in contrasting forms to bring out the most beautiful combinations. The combination of red and yellow speaks of Christ—the red of His shed blood and the yellow (gold) of His divinity.

The second foundation was sprinkled with sapphires. This is a deep blue stone, and was the second stone of the second row found in the breastplate of the Jewish high priest. Blue, purple and scarlet (red) were the principal colors used in the curtains and hangings of the tabernacle in the wilderness. Blue is the heavenly color and was almost always mentioned first of these three colors in describing the ancient tabernacle. This stone speaks of heaven itself.

The stone used for garnishing the third foundation is a chalcedony. Perhaps this too was one of the stones of the high priest's vesture, but through the centuries a change in name could have taken place and the original name lost. The best evidence to be found suggests this stone was a pale blue color, speaking once more of the heavenly.

The emerald comes fourth in these foundations. It also was number four in the high priest's garment. The green of the emerald speaks of God's mercy. The emerald-like rainbow of the fourth chapter seems to bear this out.

The fifth one is the sardonyx. Some modern writers identify the sardonyx with the diamond. Since the diamond is not mentioned as such as one of the stones garnishing one of these foundations, this is quite likely so. The diamond is considered the most valuable of stones. A diamond-studded crown of gold, sitting upon the head of a reigning monarch suggests the ultimate in power and authority. So this fifth foundation sprinkled with diamonds shows forth the reign of the saints of God.

Certain colors keep appearing in these foundation gems. Red, yellow, blue and green are the most predominant. The sixth foundation stones will be of the sardius variety. This jewel is described as of a red or "honey" yellow. Both colors speak of Christ just as they do in the foundation with the jasper stones.

The gilding of the seventh foundation will be with the chrysolyte. The gold color of this decoration speaks of divinity in general.

The beryl of the eighth foundation comes in a variety of colors—light blue, yellow, pink and white. They all are significant and give a message to the dwellers of the Holy City.

The topaz comes in varying shades of green—everyone of them speaking eloquently of God's everlasting mercy. Thus the ninth foundation also gives its message to redeemed mankind and all creation that God's mercy is from everlasting to everlasting.

The apple-green of the chrysoprasus only repeats what other stones have indicated—God's message of mercy. The tenth foundation will be garnished with this gem.

The eleventh foundation will be decorated with the jacinth. This ancient stone was of a blue or purple hue. The blue speaks again of heavenly things. Being a blend of red and blue, the purple tells of Christ and heaven.

The amethyst will enhance the beauty of the twelfth foundation. This stone has been identified with the carbuncle. In fact, the English Version of the Bible translates the word carbuncle in preference to the amethyst of the Authorized Version. The definition of the carbuncle as a precious stone is given as a *"Red garnet, cut without facets, and concave below, to show the color."* Some authorities would class this stone as a ruby. The modern definition of the ruby is that it is a *"Translucent, deep purplish red variety of corundum, highly valued as a gem stone."* Whatever the real appearance will be, all authorities agree as to the red and purplish colors. These significant colors close the picture, emphasizing over and over and over the mercy of God, the love of God and the power of the blood of Christ to redeem mankind.

These foundations are named for the "Twelve Apostles of the Lamb." Just where these foundations fit into the structure of the City is not certain. But since the city "Lieth foursquare"—twelve thousand furlongs in length, breadth and heighth—it may be these twelve foundations support twelve street levels.

The first foundation is named for the Apostle Peter. How such a person as this high-strung,, impeteous man called Peter could rate such an exalted place in God's scheme of things is a great mystery. But here it is! This man who was always talking when he should have been listening; listening when he should have been speaking; bragging when he should have been effacing himself; fighting when he should have been submitting; denying his Lord when he should have been standing by His side—this man of all men getting the highest honor among his fellow apostles? Only an all-wise Heavenly Father knows the why.

But beneath all this rough exterior was a heart of love and courage. Man is not to be judged when he puts his armour on, the Bible tells us, but when he takes it off. And when Peter took his off on that far off day in that far off place he completed a victorious life. As he was nailed to an inverted cross, feet in the air, head downward and arms extended at a grotesque angle, his life ebbing away, he could say with Paul, *"I have fought a good fight . . . there is a crown laid up for me."* He will indeed be worthy of this jasper-studded foundation.

James comes next in the list of the apostles (according to Mark). Right in the inner circle with Peter and John, this man completed the trio whom Jesus selected as His closest confidants. He must have been a man with a great voice. Jesus called him a son of thunder. He was with Jesus, Peter and John on the Mount of Transfiguration, at the raising of Jairus' daughter, on the Mount of Olives when Jesus gave that great discourse recorded in Matthew twenty-four and twenty-five. He was at the gate while Jesus was in the Garden of Gethsemane, praying and agonizing over certain aspects of His coming crucifixion.

With all his greatness James had a streak of selfishness and personal ambition—at least before Pentecost. He once requested (with John) that they two be given places above the other apostles—one on the right hand and the other on the left hand of Jesus in His coming kingdom. Little did he ralize what he was asking. Jesus told him and John they would indeed drink of His (bitter) cup and be baptized with His baptism (of suffering), but that would not make them worthy. Such places were reserved for those for whom they were prepared.

Also, he slept at the garden gate when he should have been watching. According to good authority, he only lived nine years after Pentecost, and was killed in the great persecution under King Herod Agrippa the first, about 42 A. D. In spite of all this the second foundation—sapphire-encrusted—will bear his name.

John is the third apostle, so the third foundation is named in his honor. This man was the closest of the apostles to Jesus. While Peter was the unquestioned leader of the group, it was left to John to be more of a companion to our Lord. This is abundantly shown throughout the Gospels. He is said to have been the youngest of the twelve and nearest to Jesus' own age. He is also said to have suffered every known indignity at the hands of his Roman persecutors. Tradition says he was once put in a barrel of boiling oil, but survived. For a time he was banished to Patmos, but later allowed to return to the mainland. Tradition has it that he was the only apostle who died a natural death.

Then the honor of having the third foundation named for him memorializes his life and the lives of those who have suffered in like manner for the *"Word of God, and the testimony of Jesus Christ."*

Then there is Andrew, the fourth apostle. His greatest claim to fame was being the brother of Peter. But do not dismiss this man as of no importance too quickly. Although seldom in the limelight, he had a very successful ministry. He was present at the healing of Peter's wife's mother. He was present with Peter, James and John at Jesus' great Olivet discourse. He passed the information on to Jesus that *"There is a lad here which hath a few barley loaves and two small fishes."* This is what Jesus used to feed the five thousand. Finally, he was the messenger who told Jesus that *"Certain Greeks desired to see* (him) *Jesus."*

Here was a man who could easily be lost in a crowd. He never projected himself into a situation for personal recognition. He did not appear to have too much faith—*"But what are they* (loaves and fishes) *among so many?"* Yet he kept his eyes open for any opportunity to further the ministry of Jesus.

It has been such men as Andrew who have kept the church functioning. Without such the great leaders down through the ages would have had no foundation upon which to build the kingdom of God. For many others like him, who go through life without any special fanfare, but who are ready at all times to seize the opportunity to serve, this foundation is named. These represent the "Little People" of the church who quietly carry the burdens while others are out in the forefront.

Next in the list of the apostles is Philip. Although not outstanding in any special way, yet he is remembered for a *few things. One of them is that Jesus Himself sought out* Philip and gave him a personal invitation to become one of his followers. Philip then went after Nathanael. Being of a somewhat inquiring mind, Nathanael needed some convincing that Jesus was indeed the one about whom Moses wrote. To his objections that Nazareth was a place out of which nothing good could come, Philip used the direct approach and simply invited Nathanael to *"Come and see"* for himself. To the Phillips of all the ages who seek to convince doubters that Jesus is the Christ, is this fifth foundation named.

"Bartholomew was there." That is about all you can say of this apostle. Not one word is given about anything he did or said. Also, he is always mentioned as being with Philip. But he will forever be identified with those people who *"also stand and serve."* No trumpet blast announces their presence or anything they do. They only form the background for their more illustrious fellows. In fact, Bartholomew really represents the majority of God's people. They are just doing their duty. So, they too will have a foundation in their honor.

In almost every society there is a group ostracized by their fellow men. Sometimes it is caused by race, color, religion or occupation. Among Jews of Christ's time it was the publicans. They were tax collectors for the hated Roman government. The feeling was that no loyal, self-respecting Jew would take money from his brethren and turn it over to their conquerors. Yet many Jews did just this. They endured the animosity of their community because tax collecting was a very profitable business.

Perhaps this explains why Jesus had to give Matthew the publican a personal invitation to become a disciple—there was no one else to do it. Evidently he did not have a brother Andrew or a friend Philip to introduce him to Jesus. All the friends he had were fellow publicans. How many people are left out of so many things because some condition has forced them beyond the pale of acceptable society?

Matthew did not argue with Jesus. He did not ask for proof. He just left his money counting and followed the Master. He immediately became a missionary and a personal worker. He made a great feast in his own house and entertained a great host of his fellow tax collectors. We may well assume that here he announced his decision to follow Jesus. No doubt this action had a great bearing on these friends. How many publicans became followers of Jesus because of Matthew we do not know, but the number must have been considerable.

There seems to be no record of anything else the man did during Christ's ministry. He is mentioned five times as Matthew and twice as Levi. His decision to follow Jesus and his great feast are the only instances in which he figures. The other times mentioned are found in the list of the apostles.

His bid for fame came at a later date. He wrote one of the most important books of the entire Bible. Having been in government service it was only natural that he should view Christ's work from that standpoint. While Mark saw Jesus as a man, Luke saw Him as a servant and John as the Son of God, it was left to Matthew to show Him as King of the Jews.

From a tax collector to an apostle, to a recorder of divine things, to a place and a foundation in the Holy City marks the route of this man. Those who have been cast out from the society of their fellowmen for whatever reason will find a haven on this foundation. Also, those who have gained very little prominence on earth for their deeds, but who faithfully rfecorded the triumphs of others, will find this foundation and what it stands for as a reward and recognition enough.

"Thomas the doubter!" How easy it is to gain an undesirable reputation in a moment of doubt or indecision! The fact that Thomas was willing to risk his life to go back with Jesus at the death of Lazarus is all but forgotten. His sincere inquiry as to where Jesus was going when He spoke of leaving to prepare a place for the disciples is scarcely ever mentioned. This is characteristic of humanity today. Let a person who is supposed to be filled with wisdom do something foolish and it is hardly ever forgotten. Many of his good traits will be forgotten, but not his foolish acts. So for all those who for all their lifetime were hounded with honest doubts, will this foundation be made.

Although overshadowed by James the Brother of John and James the brother of our Lord, James the son of Alphaeus had his place among the twelve. Nothing is recorded of his activities, only that he was usually present to help make up Jesus' retinue. In all the lists he always is ranked ninth of the apostles. The ninth foundation in the Holy City was embellished with the greenish hued topaz. Thus James typifies those who occupy important positions in God's church, but whose labors go mostly unnoticed. What a host this beautiful foundation will picture!

Then there was Thaddaeus, sometimes called Judas (not Iscariot). His is the tenth foundation. Like most of the other apostles, he is not known for anything outstanding. His foundation will be ornamented with the lovely yellowish-green chrysoprasus. One could wish to know more about these *"Silent Apostles,"* but the sacred record is silent much of the time. So we must assume that there will be a lot of Thaddaeus' represented in this tenth foundation. And when that time comes we will know more about them.

Simon the zealot! Fiercely loyal to everything Jewish, he and kindred spirits many times took the law into their own hands in their efforts to uphold the traditions of their fathers. Only the taming by the Spirit of the gentle Jesus could win such a man from violence to a turn-the-cheek attitude. What he did as an apostle we are not told. No doubt many times his zealous spirit would have to be curbed by the Master lest he use carnal means to promote the cause of God. It may have been at Thaddaeus' instigation that James and John suggested to Jesus that maybe they should call fire down from heaven and consume those of a certain village of Samaria who refused to render the proper hospitality to Jesus and his disciples on one occasion.

The eleventh foundation of the New Jerusalem will be ornamented with the reddish-orange jacinth. Referring to the significance of the different colors of the rainbow, it is found that the red stands for blood, and the orange for the dual nature of Christ—God and man. This foundation may show forth the marvelous work wrought in the hearts of those violent people who only can be gentled by the transforming power of Christ.

Judas! Poor Judas! There will be no foundation memorializing your life and work. The twelfth one might have been yours, but you failed. You failed Jesus, yourself and all humanity. You had such a great opportunity, but fell so low. Had you not allowed the devil to enter into you, no doubt this great honor would have been waiting you.

This last foundation will be sprinkled with the amethyst stone. We are told this jewel is of a violet-purple shade. How fitting! Violet speaks of God's love as illustrated by the rainbow. So the love of God will be forever shining out from this foundation.

But for whom will this foundation be named? Matthias? Hardly! Although he was elected at Pentecost to fill the vacancy created when Judas proved himself unworthy, nothing else is known of him. Paul is the logical one. He called himself an apostle born out of season. Coupled with this is the violet of the amethyst. Only God could forgive Paul the crimes he committed against the young church. Only an all-embracing divine love could include such a murderer.

When the time comes for the saints of God to occupy the celestial city, the Pauls of all the ages who have persecuted and killed God's people in ignorance will find this foundation a wonderful place in which to bask in that supreme love.

* * * * * * *

Try to imagine the light of this city, shining through the jasper wall with its gem-studded foundations. This light will bring out all the luster and beauty of the jasper, the sapphire, the chalcedony, the emerald, the sardonyx, the sardius, the chrysolyte, the beryl, the topaz, the chrysopraus, the jacinth and the amethyst.

The fiery flashing of these precious stones will make all modern earthly lighting displays sink into insignificance. The red, the blue, the yellow, the purple, the green and the pink will be sending forth these special colors to mix and harmonize with all the others.

This will not be just a magnificent display of color and light. Every color and shade will have a meaning, and a message. The red will remind of the blood of Christ which makes all this possible. The orange will show Him as the God-man. The yellow (gold) will speak of divinity. The green will show forth God's mercy. The blue will tell of heaven itself, the final abode of the redeemed.

Inhabitants of the nations of the earth, walking in the light of this city will receive this message every time they look upward. It will speak anew the message of redemption. It will tell them how the many generations fought Satan and won the victory, thereby giving them this wonderful privilege of not having to deal with sin or Satan in the least degree.

Beyond all this, they will see the great sacrifice of Christ on Calvary as the one overshadowing event in all earth's long and weary history. Every ray will have its message. Every hue will show a different facet of that message.

ITS DIMENSIONS

After telling something of its wall, its gates, and its foundation the seer gives some of its dimensions. He says the wall is one hundred and forty-four cubits high (approximately 216 feet, according to modern measurements). There is some question here as to what this measurement means. John sees the wall "Great and high" in relation to other measurements. But this heighth would be insignificant when compared with the height of the city itself. So, if the city is a perfect cube, then this figure must refer to its thickness. Either that or we just do not have enough information to understand what the meaning is.

John saw that the city "Lieth foursquare," and is twelve thousand furlongs in length, width and height. Changed to modern day measurement it would be some 1,379 miles cubed. Since all measurement used here have a distinct meaning, it is evident that the ancient furlong and not the modern foot will be the standard of measurement.

ROOM FOR EVERYBODY?

Some have wondered about the adequacy of this city to house all the redeemed. In order to try to find just how many people it will accommodate, let us begin by reserving one-half of the area of the city for streets, parks, rivers, etc. Divided up into the average modern city block the remainder would have 270,000,000 such squares. Allowing forty persons to the block there would be room for 11,040,000,000 (eleven billion and forty million) people on one street level. Suppose there were twelve such levels, then there would be room for 132,480,000,000 (one hundred thirty-two billion, four hundred and eighty million) people. Or suppose there were twelve hundred street levels, one on top of the others, with one thousand furlong between each level (somewhat over a mile). There would be room for 158,976,000,000,000 (one hundred fifty-eight trillion, nine hundred and seventy-six billion) people. This number is greater than the total number of people born on earth since Adam. Yes, there will be room for all the redeemed, as well as for a few billion angels.

These calculations are based on the assumption that each individual inhabitant would desire to stake off a little tract of the Holy City for himself. However, it is very doubtful that this will be the case. Dwellers in that city will be as one great company. The thought of private property and privacy as we know them now will be unknown and undesirable.

This New Jerusalem is to be the Bride's home. She personifies the city itself. This may seem strange, but when we speak of a modern city we do not necessarily mean just the steel and brick and mortar which go into it to make it up. Neither do we think just of its buildings, its streets and its parks. We think mostly of the people who dwell in it. A city without inhabitants would be only a ghost town. The dwellers give life to it just as the blood flowing through the veins of the body gives life. So the Holy City and the Lamb's Wife are so closely associated that thought of one brings thoughts of the other.

In the final chapter will be found a quick look inside the city itself. But before leaving the present chapter a few words about perpetual generations of people living on earth after the Millennium are given.

PERPETUAL GENERATIONS

Unending generations will inhabit the earth. When it again becomes suitable for human occupancy after God's renovating fire has swept over it, men in the flesh will live here as God intended Adam and Eve to have done in the Garden of Eden. Man's long test will be over, and those who do not fall for Satan's snares, and who are still here in the flesh at the close of the Millennium, will re-populate the earth. Man will no more be subject to a test of loyalty to his Creator. Those who come to this glad time will have already passed it. He will forever be free from any taint of sin and evil, and will live as God planned from the beginning.

At the beginning of the eternal ages the New Jerusalem will come down and be suspended in the heavens. The nations of the earth will walk in the light of it. The beauty of the city is beyond description. This is the place Jesus went away to prepare as recorded in the fourteenth chapter of Saint John's Gospel. Here Jesus said, "I go to prepare a PLACE for you." This place is the Holy City. Some say the mansions in the Father's house are planets and stars; some say they are mansions in this city. I do not profess to know, but I do know the PLACE Jesus went away to prepare for His people is the New Jerusalem. There will be free passage between earth and the New Jerusalem. It will be headquarters and anyone having business there can enter it.

The results of this will be that tears, death, sorrow, crying and pain will be taken away. Take these five things out of the world today and we would have a heaven here on earth. Sin made a hell of the earth, but when sin and its consequences are done away, then it will be heaven—whether it be the Holy City, the earth, Jupiter, Mars, Saturn or the North Star.

The divine drama is rapidly coming to a close. The Occupant of the throne reminds John that He is the same Alpha and Omega He was in the first chapter of the Revelation. He still has the water of life for the thirsty. He still holds out the promise that the overcomer of every age will inherit all things and be a son to God. He still is warning the fearful, the unbelieving, the abominable, the murderer, the whoremonger, the sorcerer, the idolaters and all liars that they have their part in the Lake of Fire—unless they repent before it is too late.

Chapter Twenty-two

INSIDE THE NEW JERUSALEM

"And he shewed me a pure river of water of life, clear as crystal proceeding out of the throne of God and of the Lamb. In the midst of the street of it and on either side of the river, was there the tree of life, which bare twelve manner of fruit, and yielded her fruit every month: and the leaves of the tree were for the healing of the nations. And there shall be no more curse: but the throne of God and of the Lamb shall be in it; and his servants shall serve him; And they shall see his face; and his name shall be in their foreheads. And there shall be no night there; and they need no candle, neither light of the sun; for the Lord God giveth them light; and they shall reign for ever and ever" (Revelation 22:1-5).

These first five verses of this chapter really belong to the twenty-first chapter. Beginning with the ninth verse of the previous chapter is a description of the Holy City. And in the twenty-second chapter the city is still being described.

The Garden of Eden is a dim replica of this heavenly scene. Two important things found in Eden were the river with four heads and the Tree of Life. The river watered the garden and the Tree of Life was to give the human race eternal existence. Man disobeyed God by partaking of the forbidden fruit, and access to the Tree of Life was denied him. The river thus lost its importance. This is all restored in this twenty-second chapter.

John is given a list of things which will not be found in this city and another list of things which will be found. He is told there will be no more curse. This again refers back to Eden and man's expulsion from the garden. No more will Satan bruise the heel of man. No more will woman be troubled with the sorrows of conception. No more will the woman be subservient to the man. No more will the ground be cursed for man's sake. No more will man eat in sorrow its fruit. No more will thorns and thistles spring forth. No more will man have to earn his bread in the sweat of his face. Finally, no more will man return to dust.

There will be no night in that city. Night is both a blessing and a curse to man and the earth. The earth needs the night to allow a cooling off and a relaxing of the processes of nature. Man needs the night to sleep and rest. But night can also be a time of terror. *"Men love darkness rather than light because their deeds are evil,"* the Bible tells us. Men creep in the darkness of night to do their vile deeds, which would not be done in the light of day.

The Holy City will have no need of night. Since man neither needs rest or sleep night will be unnecessary. Artificial light from the candle and natural light from the sun will be replaced by the light of God and the Lamb.

There will be no criminals in the city—no dogs, whoremongers or murderers. There will be no idolaters there; these will all have been cast into the Lake of Fire. No liars or lovers of lies will ever enter that city; its gates are forever barred to such.

There will be no temple in the Holy City. When one considers the purpose of a temple, cathedral or church building it becomes clear why there will be no need of such. The purpose of an earthly sanctuary is for the worship of an absent entity. Although God is everywhere, His presence cannot be seen. So inside some physical structure God wills that man shut himself away from the outside world and commune with Him. But if God's presence could be seen there would be no need of a special place to meet Him. He would be just like a friend; you could meet and commune with Him anywhere. This is why John saw no temple, because *"They shall see his face; and his name shall be in their foreheads."* God and the Lamb will take the place of a temple.

The foregoing is the negative side of the picture. What about the other side? First, the river of life will be there. John sees this river as flanked on either side of the street of the city. Imagine a wide boulevard, and in the middle of it is a flowing river. From a casual reading of this one could get the idea this is just one street of the city, but this is not the case. This river will be in the midst of every street in the city. Although it starts at the throne of God and the Lamb, it goes everywhere.

This river is flowing bank full with the *water of life.* But what is this *water of life?* Jesus answers this question clearly in the seventh chapter of Saint John in verse thirty-seven to thirty-nine. *"In the last day* (of the feast of tabernacles) *Jesus stood and cried, saying, If any man thirst let him come unto me and drink. He that believeth on me ... out of his belly shall flow rivers of living water."* John adds the explanation in the thirty-ninth verse, *"But thus spake he of the Spirit."*

In his Gospel John records Jesus' dealing with the subject of *living water* in other places. In the third chapter Christ tells Nicodemus, *"Except a man be born of water* (and of the Spirit) *he cannot enter the kingdom of God."* In the fourth chapter He tells the Samaritan woman, *"If thou knewest the gift of God, and who it is that saith unto thee, Give me to drink; thou wouldst have asked of him and he wouldest have given thee living water."* The woman asks, *"From whence then hast thou that living water?"* Jesus closes the subject by saying, *"The water that I shall give* (thee) *him shall be in him a well of water springing up into everlasting life."*

Notice the progress of the teaching about water in its symbolical application. Isaiah fifty-five introduces the subject by crying out, *"Ho, everyone that thirsteth, come to the waters,"* Jesus speaks first of the spiritual birth to Nicodemus. Next is the well; then it becomes an individual river. John sees that great numberless multitude in Revelation seven being led by the Lamb to living fountains of water. And finally, here is the mighty river of life flowing out from the throne of God and the Lamb.

Now back to the river. It proceeds out of the throne of God and the Lamb. This recalls Ezekiel's waters of the forty-seventh chapter of his prophecy. His is an earthly scene; John's is of the heavenly. Ezekiel's waters issued out from the threshold of this earthly temple, and went into the desert and on to the sea. They gave life to everything they touched. On either side of Ezekiel's waters are to be found "Many trees." These trees are for "Meat." *"Their leaf shall not fade, neither shall the fruit thereof be consumed." "It* (they) *shall bring forth new fruit according to his months ... the fruit thereof shall be for meat, and the leaves thereof medicine."* Just where these waters and this temple fit into God's plan for man on earth in the eternal ages is not clear, but that there will be such waters and such a temple the Bible makes abundantly clear.

Between each of the segments of the street and the bank of the river is the Tree of Life. Like the trees of Ezekiel, this Tree of Life (not just one tree, but one species) will bear fruit every month, and like the leaves of Ezekiel's trees those here will be for the healing of the nations. Since it does not say who will consume the fruit, it is safe to assume it will be for the inhabitants of the Holy City as well as for the nations of the earth. These leaves will be for the healing of the *nations.* The nations are not the inhabitants of the city. Neither are the inhabitants of the city the nations. These nations are made up of people living on earth in their fleshly bodies. They are the everlasting generations pictured in different places in the Revelation.

"And he said unto me, These sayings are faithful and true: and the Lord God of the holy prophets sent his angel to show unto his servants the things which must shortly come to pass" (Revelation 22:6).

* * * * * * *

From the time John was in the Spirit on the Lord's Day and heard the great trumpet-like voice in the first chapter until the last details of the description of the New Jerusalem were given him, the prophet had been held in a vice-like grip of enrapturement.

The scene of the glorified Christ, the rainbow encircled throne and the heavenly court with the four Living Creatures, the twenty-four elders, the Lamb with the Little Book, the victory of Michael over the Great Red Dragon, the marriage supper, the descent of the Holy City and a view of the everlasting generations walking in its light—all held him spellbound. Although he realized all this must take place before the earth could be cleansed, he felt the sorrows of humanity when he saw the results of the riding of the four horsemen with their wars, bloodshed, famine and death; the convulsions of the universe; the infernal locust, horsemen and beasts; the fall of Babylon and the battle of Armageddon.

Quite abruptly he finds himself back at Patmos. The familiar scenes are still there. The slap of the waves as they beat on the shore and the cries of the birds overhead tell him the vision is about over. The divine drama is rapidly coming to a close. The Occupant of the throne reminds John that He is the same Alpha and Omega He was in the first chapter of the Revelation. He still has the water of life for the thirsty. He still holds out the promise that the overcomer of every age will inherit all things and be a son to Him.

Thus the vision does close and John takes up some few last remarks before he gives the final words which close the canon of Holy Scripture. In these concluding words, he re-emphasizes the faithfulness and truthfulness of the things of the vision, and again tells how it came to be written. He gives Jesus' warning that He is coming quickly, and pronounces blessings upon those who keep the sayings of the book.

Daniel was told to seal up the prophecy of his book for the time was long. But John is cautioned not to seal up his vision for the time was at hand. This no doubt caused many people to think this prophecy had its fulfillment in the time just following the Apostolic Age, when the Roman emperors so persecuted the Christians. This "Time is at hand" does not necessarily mean that it is to happen in the next few days, but that it is to happen soon enough for it to be profitable to study about it.

This angel says, through John, that if a person will be unjust and filthy, then let him be so; if he will be righteous and holy let him be that way. This simply means there is no compulsion to be either good or bad. Each of us has the right of free choice. We can be sinful or holy, just as we choose.

The message throughout the ages of the soon coming of Jesus has been calculated to stir the hearts of mankind. Conversely, the idea that Jesus will not come back for at least a thousand years tends to cause His servants to become careless. The coming of Jesus was the burden of the preaching of the primitive church. These people expected Him to come in their lifetime. Indeed He could have come for His Bride and no prophecy would have been left unfulfilled by the event. He could have come in the dark ages and not violated Scripture. He could have come back at any time after His ascension and not contradicted any prophecy.

He could not have come back to fight the battle of Armageddon until the close of this age. Keep in mind the rapture can happen at any time. But the revelation must come at the close of this dispensation. The longer the rapture is delayed the shorter will be the Tribulation period. The quicker He comes after His Bride the longer will be the time of the Tribulation. The time of the rapture is indefinite. The time of the revelation is definite. Only the Father in heaven knows the exact time of the rapture. But a careful study of prophecy will show approximately when this age will close and Jesus will come at the revelation.

The chronologies from the time of Adam until now are in such a state of uncertainty that it is impossible to accurately forecast the revelation of Jesus Christ. But if we had positive proof as the just how many years have gone by since the creation of man we could come close to telling the time of the revelation of Christ at Armageddon.

We can take the natural week and find that God gave the seventh day for rest. Likewise, every seventh year was to be a Sabbath for the Israelites. It is believed that this dispensation will close approximately six thousand years of human history. This being the case, we see further that the seventh thousand years of man's history will be a Sabbath. This is what the Millennium is to be—the thousand year Sabbath of God. But how many years have actually elapsed no one knows. It may be 5946, 5,972 or even more. There are a number of recognized authorities on chronology and most of them disagree on vital dates of the Bible. No doubt, it is in God's plan that mankind not be able to determine the exact time of the revelation of Jesus Christ.

Revelation ends with man being cautioned as to how he is to handle this prophecy. If anyone adds to the words of the prophecy of this book, God shall add unto him the plagues contained therein, John warns. Likewise, if anyone takes from the words of the prophecy of this book then God will take away his part out of the Book of Life, the holy city and the promises written in the Book also, says John.

The soon coming of Jesus is the great hope with which this prophecy closes. *"Even so, come, Lord Jesus,"* should be our deepest heartfelt response to this promise. Pray that all who read this shall be ready and waiting when Jesus comes for His Bride. Amen.

Epilogue

GOD'S ULTIMATE PLAN FOR MANKIND

Much has already been said about Perpetual Generations and God's ultimate Plan for Mankind in these studies. By way of resume a few more words are appropriate at the close.

Many aeons ago, long before man was created, a glimpse into God's heavenly abode would have shown it to be one of peace and tranquility. There was nothing to mar the bliss and happiness of its inhabitants. Angels in serried ranks sang beautiful doxologies to the Triune God. Archangels' orders to their hosts were obeyed with prompt dispatch. Everything was calm and serene.

All of this was disrupted though, when one of the archangels, Lucifer, rose up in pride and sought to overthrow the existing order of the celestial realm. Indications are that he made an effort to dethrone the Son of God, and himself take the place left vacant.

Details of this rebellion are meager indeed. Isaiah Fourteen gives a few details. This prophet speaks of *Lucifer, son of the morning,*" and his fall. The list of "*I wills*" recorded tells of these ambitions, and the fall. Ezekiel twenty-eight gives a little more information. In his writings are some details of his description: "*Thou hast been in Eden the garden of God; every precious stone was thy covering, the sardius, topaz and the diamond, the beryl, the onyx and the jasper, the sapphire, the emerald and the carbuncle, and gold: The workmanship of thy taberets and thy pipes was prepared in the day thou wast created. Thou art the anointed cherub that covereth.... Thou wast upon the holy mount of God; thou hast walked up and down in the midst of the stones of fire. Thou wast perfect in all thy ways from the day thou wast created till iniquity was found in thee.*"

This beautiful creature was lifted up in pride to the extent that he determined to seek a higher place in the heavenly economy. He controlled one-third of the heavenly hosts, so used them in the rebellion. The outcome of this great upheaval was that Lucifer and his third of the celestial forces were defeated and cast out of the presence of Deity. These *"Angels which kept not their first estate, but left their own habitation, he hath reserved in everlasting chains under darkness unto the judgment of the great day,"* Jude tells us. Lucifer's name was changed to Satan. He is now the *"Prince of the powers of the air,"* Paul says.

The departure of this fallen company left a vacancy in heaven. This is where man comes into the picture. Only in eternity will all the purposes of God in the creation of man be known, but enough has been revealed in Scripture to give a dim outline. From available evidence it appears that at least one purpose in the creation of man was to fill this vacancy.

The angels served and loved God because that was all they knew until Lucifer led the rebellion. In this supreme test one-third of the angels chose not to love and serve God, while two-thirds remained loyal to Him. God does not desire forced love or obedience. When He created man and placed him in the garden of Eden He gave Satan access to him. The results of this are quite familiar. Man fell into Satan's trap and sin entered into the world.

When the angels fell God did not give them a second chance. However, a different plan was put into effect for man. He was created *"A little lower than the angels,"* so provisions were made whereby man could come back to God and be accepted of Him.

This is where Christ and the plan of redemption come in. Although God's plan for man included this return to his Creator, it did not stop there. This plan envisions the complete restoration of God's heavenly kingdom back to its original order, and more.

There is a thread-like scheme running through all redemption. It involves the first-born. In the Old Israelitish economy, should a man die childless, his brother was to marry the widow and provide an heir for the dead. The first-born from this union was considered as the dead man's heir. Other offsprings were to be the heir (or heirs) of the live brother fulfilling the obligation of the *"Near kinsman."*

The angels were here before man. One-third of them died as far as the heavenly household was concerned when they rebelled with Lucifer. It then became the plan of God to allow man to fill this vacancy. This vacancy has been filling up at least ever since righteous Abel offered his *"Acceptable sacrifice"* and was murdered by his jealous brother Cain. When this vacancy will be filled God alone knows. At any rate, when this number is reached God will be satisfied. This number will include every glorified saint from the earliest days of man's creation until the last sinner accepts salvation during the Millennial reign of Christ.

A careful study will reveal that there will be people iving on earth after the Great White Throne Judgment. John sees *"Nations"* walking in the light of the New Jerusalem. Only the *"Saved"* are seen. Therefore, there will not be a sinner left. All who will ever be saved are saved and all who will not be saved have already reached the Lake of Fire.

Now back to the thought of the near kinsman and the duty to raise up seed for the dead brother. By the time of he Great White Throne Judgment man will have fulfilled his obligation. The vacancies of heaven's ranks will have been filled. Glorified saints have replaced fallen angels.

Even so, what about the rest of humanity? Using the igure of the near kinsman and his duty to provide an heir or his dead brother, it is found that after this heir was orn the rest of the children would belong to the *"near kinsnan"* himself. This is what happens with mankind. Not nly did God plan to use man to fill up the vacant ranks n the celestial realm, but He also planned that there would e other men born who would go on living on earth in heir natural bodies, multiplying all down through the easeless ages of eternity.

When one begins to contemplate the grand plan of God or the propagation of perpetual generations, the horizons re raised to infinity. God did not create the universe, the eavenly kingdom and this planet for just a few billion ouls to get to heaven, and then everything stop. Men will e born throughout eternity. Some may wonder where all ese multitudes of billions will live. Do not worry about at. God has plenty of room. He has billions of stars and lanets larger than our earth. If these are not already inabitable He knows just how to make them so. Jesus said,

"In my father's house are many mansions. . . . I go to prepare a place for you." These mansions are probably not mansions in the New Jerusalem, about which so many songs have been sung and sermons preached. Whatever the mansions may be in the Holy City when it comes down from God out of heaven, they will have been prepared by Christ. The mansions He speaks about in the fourteenth chapter of John were *already in existence* when Jesus spoke these words. No doubt these mansions in the *"Father's House"* are the heavenly bodies we see as the stars.

There will be plenty of room in the Father's house. Should the present earth become too crowded with these *"Everlasting generations"* there will be other *"mansions"* ready and waiting. And there are billions of them.

Our universe is so vast that astronomers do not measure the distance from one star to another in miles; they measure it in "Light years." One light year is said to be the time it takes for light to travel six trillion miles. They tell us there are stars so distant from the earth that light which started from them the night Jesus was born has not yet reached our planet. If all this is true, it will be no problam for God to find a place for every man, woman and child who will be born in the eternal dispensations. It should thrill our hearts with joy when we realize the magnitude of God's grand designs for His creatures.

Although man in the flesh will go on multiplying throughout eternity, glorified man will not do so. He wil be as the angels in this respect. However, he will have a great place in God's overall plan for humanity. Jesus wil sit upon the throne of His father David and rule from Je-rusalem forever. His saints will rule and reign with Him. Some will have charge of ten cities, some five. Some wil rule over a nation and some over a continent. And whe the time comes to move some of the population from thi earth to some other planet, no doubt many of the redeeme will have places of authority assigned them in the ne *"Mansion."*

On and on the subject could be expanded, but this enough to give a little inkling of God's Ultimate Purpose i creating man.

BIBLIOGRAPHY

THE APOCALYPSE, by Joseph A. Seiss (Marshall, Morgan & Scott, London)

JESUS IS COMING, by W. E. Blackstone, 1908 (Fleming H. Revel Co.)

THE SECOND COMING OF JESUS, by G. F. Taylor, 1950 Edition (Advocate Press, Franklin Springs, Ga.)

QUESTIONS & ANSWERS, by Dr. Paul F. Beacham, 1950 Edition (Advocate Press, Franklin Springs, Ga.)

THE REVELATION MESSAGE, by Rev. Dan W. Evans, 1951 (Advocate Press, Franklin Springs, Ga.)

THE RAINBOW, by Rev. G. F. Taylor, 1924 (Advocate Press, Franklin Springs, Ga.)

NTERNATIONAL STANDARD BIBLE ENCYCLOPEDIA, by James Orr, General Editor, 1949 (Wm. B. Eerdsman, Grand Rapids, Mich.)

COFIELD BIBLE, 1917 Edition (Oxford University Press, New York)

HE BOOK OF THE REVELATION, by Lehman Strass, 1964 (Loizeaux Brothers, Neptune, New Jersey)

HE SECOND COMING OF JESUS, by M. R. DeHaan, 1944 (Zondervan Publishing House, Grand Rapids, Mich.)

HE REVELATION, by Arno C. Gaebelein, 1961 (Loizeaux Brothers, Neptune, New Jersey)

N EXPOSITION ON THE BOOK OF THE REVELATION, by Louis T. Talbot

LL THINGS NEW, by Arthur E. Broomfield, 1959 (Bethany Fellowship, Minneapolis, Minn.)

HE DAWN OF THE SCARLET AGE, by Edgar Ainslee, 1954 (Sunday School Times)

TORY OF THE CHRISTIAN CHURCH, by Lyman G. Hurlbut, 1933 (The John C. Winston Co., Chicago, Ill.)

IAMONDS FROM DANIEL, by W. G. Heslop (Nazarene Publishing House)

ANIEL'S PROPHECY OF THE SEVENTY WEEKS, by Alva J. McClain, 1940 (Zondervan Publishing House, Grand Rapids, Mich.)

TANDARD COLLEGE DICTIONARY (Published by **Reader's Digest**)

EW WINSTON DICTIONARY, (Published by Universal Book & Bible House)

BLE HANDBOOK, by Halley (Henry H. Halley, Chicago, Ill.)

ISPENSATIONAL TRUTH, by Clarence Larkin, 1920 (Rev. Clarence Larkin Estate, Philadelphia, Pa.)

IAT BLESSED HOPE, by M. R. DeHaan

NERAL HISTORY, by Philip Van Ness Myers, 1906 (Ginn & Company, Boston, New York, Chicago, London)

TERLINEAR GREEK NEW TESTAMENT, by George R. Berry, 1950 (Zondervan Publishing House, Grand Rapids, Mich.)

HAUSTIVE CONCORDANCE OF THE BIBLE, by James Strong, 1890 (Abingdon-Cokesbury Press, New York, Nashville)

RLD ALMANAC, 1970 Edition

ARIOUS OTHER BOOKS, PAPERS, LECTURES, SERMONS, ETC.)